The Peculiar Life of

SUNDAYS

STEPHEN MILLER

HARVARD UNIVERSITY PRESS
Cambridge, Massachusetts
London, England
2008

Library of Congress Cataloging-in-Publication Data
Miller, Stephen, 1941–
The peculiar life of Sundays / Stephen Miller.
p.   cm.
Includes bibliographical references and index.
ISBN-13: 978-0-674-03168-5 (alk. paper)
1. Sunday.   2. Sabbath.   3. Rest—Religious aspects.   I. Title.
BL595.S9M55 2008
263'.3—dc22   2008027460

To Eva, Katherine, and Elizabeth

Acknowledgments

This book benefited from discussions with many people, including Jeff Field, Claudia Anderson, Achsah Guibbory, Tony Kaufman, Barbara Wilson, Joe Shattan, and Sandy Kaiser. I am grateful to Jane Caden, Kevin Caden, Karen Seehausen, Arline Youngman, Sarah Courteau, Christine Rosen, and Walter Connor for telling me about the Sundays of their childhood.

I want to thank Barton Swaim for his careful reading of a draft of the first chapter. I am indebted to David Mikics for his many suggestions for improving the manuscript. The recommendations of my editor, John Kulka, have been invaluable. I am grateful to Maria Ascher for her excellent copy editing. This book relies on the work of many outstanding scholars. It also could not have been written without the encouragement and support of my wife, Eva Barczay.

Contents

Chapter One

Sunday Gladness,
Sunday Gloom

*I*n 1941 Billie Holiday recorded "Gloomy Sunday," a powerful song about feeling depressed on Sunday. "Sunday is gloomy," the song begins, "my hours are slumberless/Dearest the shadows I live with are numberless." In the second stanza, the speaker decides to commit suicide: "Gloomy is Sunday, with shadows I spend it all,/My heart and I have decided to end it all." Written in Hungarian in 1933 by Reszö Seress, "Gloomy Sunday" was a big hit—performed by many singers in many languages. (The English lyrics were written by Sam M. Lewis, an American songwriter.) The song reportedly inspired so many suicides that it was called the "Hungarian Suicide Song." During World War II the BBC barred it from the airwaves because the lyrics were too depressing. In 1968, shortly after his sixty-ninth birthday, Seress committed suicide by jumping from the window of his apartment. He did it on a Sunday.[1]

In Holiday's version a third stanza was added to suggest that the speaker's suicidal thoughts were only a bad dream. The lyrics do not say why Sunday is gloomy. Billie Holiday's life was a difficult one, so she might have felt gloomy on Sunday, but we cannot assume that her own feelings on Sundays were the same as those expressed by the lyrics of "Gloomy Sunday."

Are more people likely to commit suicide on Sunday than on other days of the week? Jonathan Edwards, the eighteenth-century American theologian, said that on Sunday, June 1, 1735, "Satan seemed to be more let loose, and raged in a dreadful manner." On that Sunday Joseph Hawley II, Edwards' uncle, slit his throat and died. According to one historian, in late nineteenth-century America "a disproportionate number of the desperate attempted suicide on Sundays," but the evidence is anecdotal.[2]

Data about suicides in the United States and Britain do not support the claim that more suicides occur on Sunday than on other days of the week. According to the Centers for Disease Control and Prevention, suicide rates in the United States are highest on Monday and Tuesday. According to a British study of suicides in England and Wales from 1993 to 2002, the day of the week with the highest number of suicides is Monday.[3]

Sunday is not a gloomy day for most Americans. A national poll conducted in 1998 found that 79 percent of Americans regarded Sunday as the most enjoyable day of the week. Yet many American painters and writers, including Hawthorne, Twain, and Edith Wharton, have described Sunday in gloomy terms. John Updike writes that the painter Edward Hopper "often . . . creates a Sunday mood, of vacant buildings and minimal human activity."[4]

Hopper's painting *Sunday* (1926) shows a solitary man sitting on a curb, smoking a cigar. He is sitting in front of a store, but the store seems vacant. The store's windows are blank, and so are the windows of an adjacent shop. The urban landscape is desolate; there are no signs of any kind on the buildings, and there are no scraps of litter on the ground. It is a sunny day but the sunlight is yellow and thin. Some observers say that the man in the painting looks helpless or pathetic. He seems to be looking down, thinking about something, but it's hard to read his expression.[5]

In 1947 an English movie appeared, *It Always Rains on Sunday*. Is there such a thing as a gloomy Sunday mood? In 1919 the Hungarian psychiatrist Sándor Ferenczi published a paper entitled "Sunday Neuroses," in which he argued that some people get sick or depressed on Sunday because they have difficulty coping with so much free time. A writer in the *Washington Post* speaks of the "Sunday Blues" and the "Sunday Slump." She quotes a psychologist who says: "If you think about Sunday, it's the day of the week where there's a change in direction. Every week you're starting over. . . . You're back at the bottom of the ladder."[6]

Many writers and songwriters have talked about their gloomy Sundays. In *The Life of Henry Brulard*, which is an autobiography despite its name, Stendhal says: "I still can't explain to myself today, at the age of fifty-two, why Sundays tend to make me miserable." In *Sleepless Nights* (1979) Elizabeth Hardwick speaks mysteriously of "the downtrodden Sunday air." Two popular songs describe Sunday morning as a time of despair. In "Sunday Morning Coming Down," Kris Kristofferson laments: "Well, I woke up Sunday morning,/With no way to hold my head that didn't hurt." On Sunday morning he has a hangover. He is also lonely and despondent. "'Cause there's something in a Sunday/That makes a body feel alone." The Velvet Underground, an American rock band, describes Sunday morning—the name of the song—as a time of anxiety and despair. "Sunday morning and I'm falling/I've got a feeling I don't want to know."

Emily Dickinson seems to have disliked Sundays. In the poem that begins "I never felt at Home—Below," she says that she doesn't like Paradise "Because it's Sunday—all the time—/And Recess—never comes—" Sunday, she implies, is boring. In "Sunday" Howard

Nemerov, a mid-twentieth-century American poet, offers a gloomy view of the day.

> He rested on the seventh day, and so
> The chauffeur had the morning off, the maid
> Slept late, and cook went out to morning mass.
> So by and large there was nothing to do
> Among the ashtrays in the living room
> But breathe the greyish air left over from
> Last night, and go down on your knees to read
> The horrible funnies flattened on the floor.

The poem is about a rich man—he has a chauffeur, maid, and cook—who doesn't know what to do on a Sunday morning. Seeing the "ashtrays in the living room," he may be thinking about what he did on Saturday night. Are the funnies "horrible" because he is in a gloomy mood?[7]

Two English poets have also described Sunday in a negative way. John Keats often dined with friends on Sunday, but one Sunday afternoon he was despondent. "At this moment I am in no enviable Situation. I feel that I am not in a Mood to write any [poetry] today, and it appears that the loss of it is the beginning of all sorts of irregularities. . . . You tell me never to despair. I wish it was easy for me to observe the saying. Truth is I have a horrid Morbidity of Temperament which has shown itself at intervals."[8] Was Keats more likely to suffer from "Morbidity of Temperament" on Sunday than on other days?

Keats occasionally was gloomy on Sundays for another reason: it disturbed him that people went to church on Sunday. In "Written in Disgust of Vulgar Superstition," he says:

> The church bells toll a melancholy round,
> Calling the people to some other prayers,
> Some other gloominess, more dreadful cares,
> More hearkening to the sermon's horrid sound.

Keats wonders why people go to church, where they must listen to "horrid" sermons. He blames it on a "black spell."

> Surely the mind of man is closely bound
> In some black spell; seeing that each one tears
> Himself from fireside joys, and Lydian airs,
> And converse high of those with glory crowned.

A "black spell" makes people forsake pleasurable things—"fireside joys"—for the "gloominess" of church service. "Still, still they toll," Keats says, referring to the church bells, yet he is confident that Christianity is dying. In the second stanza he says that Christian worship is so unnatural that it is bound to disappear.[9]

The twentieth-century Anglo-Irish poet Louis MacNeice also mentions church bells in his poem "Sunday Morning." The poem begins with a sense of hope. Sunday morning is "Fate's great bazaar" —a time when we can do whatever we like. "Man's heart expands to tinker with his car/For this is Sunday morning, Fate's great bazaar." Yet the exhilaration that one feels on a Sunday morning is an illusion.

> But listen, up the road, something gulps, the church spire
> Opens its eight bells out, skulls' mouths which will not tire
> To tell how there is no music or movement which secures
> Escape from the weekday time. Which deadens and endures.

Comparing church bells to skulls' mouths—a grotesque analogy—MacNeice says there is no permanent escape from weekday time.[10]

MacNeice offers a plausible reason for the fact that Sunday evening—if not Sunday morning—is gloomy for some people. We begin Sunday with great expectations, yet as Sunday afternoon fades into Sunday evening we realize that we have not done all the things we wanted to do. Or we realize that we have not enjoyed ourselves as much as we had hoped we would. We escaped from weekday time, but only briefly, and the escape was less rewarding than we expected.

Keats and MacNeice were lapsed Christians. Are unreligious people more likely to be gloomy on Sunday, especially if they spend Sunday by themselves? Perhaps, but we cannot assume that people who do not go to church on a Sunday morning spend their Sunday mornings alone. They may enjoy Sunday morning breakfasts or brunches with family or friends. The Australian writer Robert Dessaix, who is not an observant Christian, describes a Sunday morning in Baden-Baden: "There were a few young men sitting around with newspapers, drinking coffee and chatting in a Sunday morning sort of way." He also talks about a Sunday afternoon in Moscow: "The whole city seems to break out in a smile on a springlike Sunday afternoon."[11]

Sunday should not be a day of gloom for Christians. It should be a day of gladness because it is the day the Resurrection is celebrated. The seventeenth-century English poet George Herbert calls Sunday "a day of mirth" because "This day my Saviour rose."[12] "Mirth" means religious joy. Herbert, an Anglican priest, thought Christians should be joyful on this holy day, which Christians call the Lord's Day, but he also thought Sunday should be regarded as a holiday—a day for enjoying traditional sports and pastimes.

Many contemporary Americans have a similar view of Sunday.

"That's What I Love About Sunday," a song by Craig Morgan, was *Billboard* magazine's number-one country music single in 2005. The song describes a joyful Sunday that begins with churchgoing on Sunday morning. Sunday afternoon is devoted to barbecuing, cat-napping on a porch swing, playing football, and fishing.[13]

The young Wallace Stevens was a lapsed Christian, yet—unlike Keats—he enjoyed hearing church bells on Sunday. "There is a church in the neighborhood," he writes his fiancé on a Sunday morning in 1909, "that has the grace to ring its bell on Sundays. It has just stopped. It is so pleasant to hear bells on Sunday morning. By long usage, we have become accustomed to bells turning this ordinary day into a holy one." In 1942 Winston Churchill decided to reinstate the ringing of church bells on Sunday because "he missed the famil-iar sound of an English Sunday."[14]

Whether Sunday is a day of gladness or gloom, it has been tradi-tionally regarded as the first day of the week. The *Oxford English Dic-tionary* defines Sunday as "the first day of the week, observed by Christians as a day of rest and worship, in commemoration of Christ's resurrection; the Lord's Day." The New Testament says that Christ was resurrected the day after Saturday, which is the Jewish Sabbath. Matthew 28 begins: "After the Sabbath, as the first day of the week was dawning, Mary Magdalene and the other Mary went to see the tomb. And suddenly there was a great earthquake; for an angel of the Lord, descending from heaven, came and rolled back the stone and sat on it."[15]

In Genesis the seventh day is Saturday—the day God rests—but many people (Christians and non-Christians) think of Sunday as the end of the week and therefore as the seventh day. A cartoon in the *New Yorker* shows God in heaven flipping hamburgers on an out-door grill. The caption is: "On the Seventh Day."[16] The cartoonist assumes that the seventh day means Sunday. European calendars, unlike American calendars, usually show Sunday as the last day of the week. They follow the recommendations of the International Organization for Standardization (ISO), which calls Monday the first day of the week.[17]

In many Slavic languages, including Russian, the week begins on Monday. In Greek, though, Sunday is the first day of the week. In Western Christendom the notion that Monday is the first day of the week was commonplace more than a millennium ago. Around 1010 c.e. the English Abbott Aelfric complained that "Monday is not the first day of the week, but the second. Sunday is first in creation, sequence, and dignity."[18]

Whether Sunday is the first day, as in Genesis, or the seventh day, as the ISO recommends, it has been a special day for non-Christians as well as Christians because it was the only day most people were off from work. In the 1880s a boy described his father as "the man who spends Sunday here."[19] "Weekend" is a word that didn't come into general usage until the last two decades of the nineteenth century. At first it meant the period from Saturday noon to Monday, reflecting the fact that many people worked on Saturday morning.

For most Christians Sunday is the Sabbath even though the Old Testament (or Hebrew Bible) calls Saturday the Sabbath. According to the *Oxford English Dictionary*, "the notion that the Lord's day is a 'Christian Sabbath' . . . occurs in theological writings from the 4th c. onwards." In the United States when a Christian mentions the Sabbath, he or she is probably referring to Sunday, even though some Christians, such as Seventh-Day Adventists and Seventh-Day Baptists, regard Saturday as the Sabbath.

Because Western culture has been such a powerful force in the world, Sunday has now become a special day in many places that have never been part of Christendom. A writer in the *New Republic* notes that the Japanese director of the Nagoya Bridegroom School scheduled a lecture "for a Sunday afternoon, in part because that was the sole day the men had off from work."[20]

In the late nineteenth century, Reform Jews in the United States chose to worship on Sunday. This practice, which has mostly died out, suggests how powerful the notion of Sunday as the Sabbath has been in America. "Throughout North America," Alan Wolfe says, "Sunday worship has proven extremely popular." Wolfe notes that in recent years many mosques in the United States have begun to offer a Sunday service as well as the traditional Friday service.[21]

Wallace Stevens speaks of "the peculiar life of Sundays."[22] Sunday's peculiar life is reflected in many idioms that non-Christians as well as Christians use. We speak of a Sunday dinner, a Sunday painter, a Sunday outing, a Sunday driver, our Sunday best, a Sunday punch. These idioms are somewhat outdated, but they remain in use. In Claire Messud's novel *The Emperor's Children* (2006), people attend church "in their ill-fitting Sunday best." And there are many popular songs about Sunday, including Etta James's "A Sunday Kind of Love," and U2's "Sunday Bloody Sunday."

Sunday of course is charged with more meaning for Christians— even lapsed Christians. Elizabeth Bishop, who was raised a Baptist, entitles one of her poems "Sunday, 4 A.M." The gloomy poem, which is about disturbing dreams, does not specifically refer to Christianity, so she could have called it "Tuesday, 4 A.M." But Bishop may think a disturbing dream on a Sunday morning is more unsettling than a disturbing dream on a Tuesday morning.

Sabbatarian Sunday

Though Sunday is a day of gladness for Christians, until roughly a century ago it was a day many Protestant children did not look forward to. "I hate Sunday!" the young Laura Ingalls Wilder says in *Lit-*

tle House in the Big Woods (1932), an account of her childhood in Wisconsin in the 1870s. It was also a day many adult Protestants remembered with bitterness. Samuel Johnson told James Boswell that Sunday "was a heavy day to me when I was a boy. My mother confined me on that day, and made me read *The Whole Duty of Man*, from a great part of which I could derive no instruction."[23] Johnson eventually came to admire *The Whole Duty of Man*, which was a popular eighteenth-century religious guidebook, but he did not think anyone should be "confined" on Sunday.

Johnson's mother, like many English, Scottish, and American Protestants, thought Sunday should be observed in a rigorously sabbatarian fashion—that is, according to the Fourth Commandment: "Remember the sabbath day, and keep it holy. Six days you shall labor and do all your work. But the seventh day is a sabbath to the LORD your God" (Exodus 20:8). According to the *OED*, a sabbatarian is "a Christian who regards the Lord's Day as a Sabbath, deducing its obligation from the Fourth Commandment. *Also, and more commonly, one whose opinion and practice with regard to Sunday observance are unusually strict*" (emphasis added).

Sabbatarians think Sunday should be strictly observed as a holy day, whereas other Christians think Sunday should be both a holy day and a holiday. According to sabbatarians, the Lord's Day should be spent in worship, Bible reading, and visiting the poor. All travel should be avoided, as well as all recreation. "Ye shouldna sing upon the Sabbath at least," Jeanie Deans says to her companion in Walter Scott's novel *The Heart of Midlothian* (1830).

"Sabbatarian" also refers to Christians who think the Sabbath should be observed on Saturday. Referring to this kind of sabbatarian, the *OED* says: "A member of a Christian sect founded towards the close of the sixteenth century, the members of which maintained that the Sabbath should be observed on the seventh and not on the first day of the week; a Seventh-Day Baptist."

The first meaning of "sabbatarian"—someone who observes Sunday strictly—is by far the more common one. Until the last two decades of the nineteenth century sabbatarianism was a strong force in the United States. In the early years of the new American republic every state prohibited Sunday travel, though the laws were not strictly enforced. Bowdoin College, like most colleges, had strict Sunday regulations, including the warning that "they who profane the Sabbath by unnecessary business, visiting or receiving visits, or by walking abroad, or by an amusement, or in other ways, may be admonished or suspended."[24]

Benjamin Franklin disliked sabbatarians. In 1762 he wrote a Connecticut friend: "When I traveled in Flanders I thought of your excessively strict observation of Sunday; and that a man could hardly travel on that day . . . without hazard of punishment; while where I was, everyone traveled, if he pleased, or diverted himself any other way; and in the afternoon both high and low went to the play or the opera, where there was plenty of singing, fiddling, and dancing. I looked round for God's judgments but saw no signs of them."[25]

Tocqueville agreed with Franklin. In *Democracy in America* he notes that even though "the strict Puritanism that presided at the birth of the English colonies in America is already much relaxed, one does still find extraordinary traces of it in habits and in laws." He is referring to Sunday observance laws. "Sunday observance in America is even now one of the things that strike a stranger most. In one great American city in particular, the whole movement of social life is suspended from Saturday evening on. . . . It is not just that no one seems to be working; they do not even seem alive. One can hear no sound of folk at work or at play, and not even that confused noise which constantly rises from any great city." In a letter to a friend, he said that few Americans were "permitted to go on a hunt, to dance, or even to play an instrument on Sunday."[26]

Sunday observance laws would surprise a Frenchman or Italian who visited the United States because sabbatarianism was a weak force in Catholic countries. French soldiers quartered in America during the Revolutionary War were horrified by New England Sundays. "One Frenchman was arrested for having dared to play the flute on the Sabbath." A character in William Dean Howells' *Indian Summer* (1886), which is set in Italy, speaks of "these Sabbathless Italians," meaning that Italians are not sabbatarians. Sunday observance laws would not surprise a British traveler, for sabbatarianism was a strong force in nineteenth-century Britain. Lord Melbourne, the Whig prime minister in 1837, deplored "the Sabbatarian heresy which prevails in the country."[27] To annoy sabbatarians, Melbourne often traveled on Sunday.

Given the strength of sabbatarianism in nineteenth-century America and Britain, it is not surprising that the phrase "a month of Sundays," which means a long, dreary time, came into general use in the 1840s.

The Decline of Sabbatarianism

By the end of the nineteenth century sabbatarianism was waning in the United States. Writing in 1888, the British historian and jurist James Bryce says that "the strictness of Puritan practice has quite disappeared, even in New England, but there are still a few out of the way places, especially in the South, where the American part of the rural population refrains from amusement as well as from work [on Sunday]."[28]

Lutherans and Catholics preferred the so-called Continental Sabbath—one in which Sunday was both a holy day and a holiday. On Sundays, Catholics and Lutherans liked to eat, drink, and dance in restaurants, beer gardens, and dance halls. Or they liked to go to museums filled with curiosities. Unitarians also promoted the Continental Sabbath. Henry Whitney Bellows, a leading Unitarian, told his congregation that "society is the better, the safer, the more moral and religious for amusement." By "amusement," he meant mainly cultural activity—going to museums, libraries, art galleries, theaters. In the 1880s Boston, Philadelphia, and New York opened their public libraries, museums, and art galleries on Sunday. Antisabbatarians also encouraged the working man to go out with his family and explore nature: "In the fields and woods he might offer acceptable homage and worship to the Highest."[29]

The antisabbatarians pushed for a relaxation of blue laws. The origin of the term "blue law" is unknown. Some historians argue that the term refers to the color of the paper that the original blue laws were printed on in colonial Connecticut. Others say that those who advocated a rigid moral code were known in the United States as "blue noses," so the Sunday restrictions they demanded were called blue laws.

The sabbatarians continued to object to the transformation of Sunday, but they were fighting a losing battle. "The habit of playing outdoor games and that of resorting to places of public amusement on Sunday," Bryce wrote, "have much increased" in recent years.[30]

In 1893 sabbatarians opposed the opening of the Chicago World's Fair on Sunday. A National Committee on Sunday Closing of the World's Fair was formed, and it promoted a grassroots campaign to influence Congress. Congress appropriated $5 million to the fair owners, but only if the fair remained closed on Sunday. The antisabbatarians fought back. A Catholic bishop said that "while Sunday is a day of worship, it is also a day on which the whole people should be invited to cultivate and improve themselves." If the fair were closed on Sunday, it might reap "a harvest for the saloon, the brothel, and the gambling hell."[31] At first the fair remained closed on Sunday, but a few weeks later the directors changed their mind—forfeiting the $5 million congressional appropriation. Forty-six years later, when the New York City's World's Fair opened at 11 A.M. on Sunday, April 30, 1939—the same hour that services began in many churches—there were no protests.

In the 1930s Sunday still remained a day when few stores were open. A 1920s advertisement in the *Chicago Tribune* for the department store Marshall Field makes a point that most Americans would have agreed with: "The first day of the week is for the things unseen—rest, and worship, and family life, and freedom from thoughts of business."[32] In the 1920s and 1930s most Americans wanted Sunday to be a day of rest, but they also wanted it to be a holiday as well as a holy day.

In Russell Baker's *Growing Up* (1982) we can see the gradual decline of sabbatarianism in one Protestant family. Baker, a former columnist for the *New York Times*, describes his grandfather George, who began raising a family in the 1880s. "His devotion to Christian worship was remarkable. He required a minimum of two church services each Sunday to keep his soul in sound repair, and after partaking of the Gospel at morning and afternoon servings he often set out across the fields for a third helping at dusk if he heard of a church with lamps lit for nocturnal psalming."[33]

It is unlikely that Baker's grandfather would have traveled on Sunday, but roughly three decades later "on Sunday afternoons" Baker's Uncle Tom often drove up in his expensive car (an Essex). Baker doesn't say that his churchgoing family disapproved of Uncle

Tom's Sunday driving. The Sunday drive—or train trip—was becoming commonplace. In the middle of the nineteenth century, railway schedules usually had the qualifying phrase "except Sundays." By the turn of the twentieth century the phrase had become rare.

If traveling became popular on Sundays, so did newspaper-reading. (The first Sunday newspapers in America were published during the Civil War.) In the 1920s Baker takes it for granted that one reads a newspaper on Sundays. His mother buys the *New York Times* because a distant relative, Edwin James, is the managing editor as well as a columnist. Baker dislikes the Sunday *Times* because it does not have comic strips. Reading his relative's column was a tedious Sunday ritual. "On Sunday afternoons, Edwin's column was a leaden family duty that filled the parlor."³⁴

Attending a sports event was another Sunday activity that was slowly gaining acceptance. One Sunday morning in the 1930s Baker's stepfather said to him: "Let's the two of us go over to Oriole Park and see the double-header this afternoon." Sunday baseball had been legal in most cities for several decades—the first Sunday game was in 1892 between the Cincinnati Reds and the St. Louis Browns—but it still was prohibited in Boston, Philadelphia, Pittsburgh, and several Southern cities. (Sunday football began in the 1920s.) Baker's stepfather tried to listen to the Sunday baseball game while eating Sunday dinner. "Herb would sit at the other [end of the table] straining to hear the Washington Senators baseball game on the living room radio while flattering my mother on the crispness of the fried chicken."³⁵

Baker's family saw nothing wrong with amusement on Sunday afternoons, but they continued to go to church on Sunday morning. "Men who wanted to make something of themselves went to church, and they went well dressed. Each Sunday she [Baker's mother] rolled me off the couch to put on the suit [he had recently bought] and accompany her to the Wesley Methodist Church on Washington Avenue [in Newark]. Her 'Papa' had been a Methodist, and he had been a good man."[36]

Was Baker's family a typical American Methodist family? In a country where, as the English novelist Frances Trollope noted, "the whole people appear to be divided into an almost endless variety of religious factions," it is hard to make generalizations about Sunday observance. Alistair Cooke, the American correspondent for the *Guardian*, traveled around the United States during World War II, and one Sunday morning he stopped at a gas station in Wisconsin. "I was whistling, and the operator of the gas station rebuked me." The rebuke for profaning the Sabbath by whistling reminded Cooke of his sabbatarian childhood. "I thought of my mother tearing in to the drawing room on Sundays if my piano fingers wandered from 'Sweet and Low' or a Beethoven minuet and slipped into a single chord of jazz. I remembered it was Sunday. And felt oddly ashamed."[37]

Cooke says that "nowhere in America have I ever been aware of Sunday as a sacred day, except in Minnesota and Wisconsin."[38] Sabbatarianism probably was more widespread in wartime America than Cooke realized. A friend of mine grew up in a sabbatarian household in West Virginia during World War II. Her Methodist parents limited her activities on Sunday. She could read, play board games, and visit with friends and relatives—but since she had to wear her Sunday clothes all day, she could not play outdoors. One Sunday she asked her mother if she could go with some friends to see the movie *Bambi*, but her mother said no, because it was the Sabbath. Another friend, who grew up in a Catholic family in Pittsburgh, was allowed to go to the movies on Sunday afternoon, but only if she went to church on Sunday morning.

Two contemporary writers have described their sabbatarian childhoods. Craig Harline, who grew up in the 1960s in California, recalls that "Sunday was a nondescript, rather sterile day, characterized partly by long hours in church but mostly by a constant, low-grade anxiety over what should be done—or more precisely *not* done— during those precious hours outside of church." Christine Rosen, who grew up in Florida in the 1970s, says: "We were never allowed to play games on Sunday. . . . 'Remember the Sabbath and keep it holy!' Mom would cheerfully exclaim when we complained." Rosen was encouraged to see the English movie *Chariots of Fire* because it was about a Christian athlete who refused to run on Sunday.[39]

Sabbatarianism is a spent force in the United States, but it is also rapidly waning in Scotland, which was the most rigorously sabbatarian country in Europe. When Robert Louis Stevenson's nanny, on her first trip outside Scotland, saw barges on the Thames on a Sunday, she lamented: "God's Holy Day is dishonoured!" Around the turn of the twentieth century, Edith Wharton reported that the editor of a Scottish magazine objected when Thomas Hardy had the protagonists of a short story go for a walk on a Sunday. The editor "obliged him to transfer the stroll to a week-day!"[40] Even in the early 1980s a travel brochure warned tourists that in Scotland they would not be able to travel by train or ferry on Sunday.[41] But in the past two decades Sunday has become increasingly associated with secular pleasure. In contemporary Scotland "a Sunday face" now means "a sanctimonious expression." Visiting Edinburgh in June 2007, I occasionally went to a café on Edinburgh's High Street called Always Sunday. It describes itself as "a sunny refreshing experience in the heart of Edinburgh's old town."

Sabbatarianism remains strong in some of Scotland's outlying areas. In 2006 two-thirds of the residents of South Harris, a strongly Presbyterian community on the island of Harris, signed a petition opposing Sunday ferry service from the mainland to the island. The petition failed, and ferry service began in April 2006. A year later the chairman of the local branch of the Lord's Day Observance Society complained: "The spiritual heritage and values of the locals have been violated in a despicable manner. There is more to life than the convenience of travel and a 24/7 lifestyle."[42] Despite the objections of many island residents, Sunday ferry service is likely to continue.

Living in Post-Sabbatarian Times

Few Christians would welcome the return of strict sabbatarianism, but some Christians are disturbed that the gradual disappearance of blue laws in the past half-century has transformed Sunday into another shopping day. By 2006 only thirteen states continued to ban the selling of some products—usually liquor and cigarettes—on Sunday. In July 2004 a columnist for *Time* asked: "What do we lose if Sunday becomes just like any other day?"[43]

Several observers have argued that the lifting of blue laws undermines religion and increases social isolation. In a sermon entitled "Breaking the Sabbath To Honor It," Scotty McLennan, the dean of religious life at Stanford University, says: "Blue laws are gone in most states, so stores are open and commerce is in full swing seven days a week. . . . When are we all getting a festive day of rest from our labors—a day off to share with our families and our friends?"[44]

In *Dies Domini*, a lengthy apostolic letter delivered in July 1998, Pope John Paul II said that many Christians no longer understand the significance of Sunday.

> Until recently, it was easier in traditionally Christian countries to keep Sunday holy because it was an almost universal practice and because . . . Sunday rest was considered a fixed part of the work schedule. Today . . . changes in socioeconomic conditions have often led to profound modifications of social behaviour and hence

of the character of Sunday. The custom of the "weekend" has become more widespread . . . spent perhaps far from home and often involving participation in cultural, political or sporting activities.

The Pope acknowledged that "this social and cultural phenomenon is by no means without its positive aspects," yet he exhorted "the disciples of Christ . . . to avoid any confusion between the celebration of Sunday, which should truly be a way of keeping the Lord's Day holy, and the 'weekend,' understood as a time of simple rest and relaxation." Sunday, John Paul II said, "is a day which is at the very heart of Christian life."[45]

In September 2007 Pope Benedict XVI made the same point. "Give the soul its Sunday, give Sunday its soul," he said. Without an "encounter" with God, Sunday "becomes wasted time that neither strengthens nor builds us up."[46] (The Catholic church may have contributed to the decline of Sunday worship when it instituted Saturday evening Masses in some dioceses in the 1970s. Some Catholics attend Mass on Saturday evenings in order to free the entire Sunday for trips, outings, and family events. Perhaps the church offered this option because of insufficient numbers of priests to celebrate Masses only on Sunday. Or perhaps it realized that more parishioners were working on Sundays and could not attend Mass.)

It is not only Christians who worry about the transformation of Sunday. In an article entitled "Bring Back the Sabbath," Judith Shulevitz, who is Jewish, says that we no longer have a day of rest. "Americans still go to church . . . but only in between chores, sporting events and shopping expeditions." In her view, "the eclipse of the Sabbath is just one small part of the larger erosion of social time." We need to rest, Shulevitz says, "in order to honor the divine in us, to remind ourselves that there is more to us than just what we do during the week." A Sabbath is good for everyone—the irreligious as well as the religious—because it "provides two things essential to anyone who wishes to lift himself out of the banality of mercantile culture: time to contemplate and distance from everyday demands." Yet Shulevitz admits, "I have a hard time imagining a Sabbath divorced from religion: who would make the effort to honor the godly part of himself if he didn't believe in a deity, no matter how ecumenical?" Shulevitz says that she has become a moderately observant Jew—going to a synagogue occasionally on Saturday, the Jewish Sabbath.[47]

Has the commercialization of Sunday affected communal worship? The evidence is unclear. A survey conducted in January 2005 by the Barna Group suggests that a "historic shift" is occurring in the nation's spirituality; a large and growing number of Americans "are rejecting congregational life but not Christianity." Yet a survey conducted in September 2006 by the Baylor Institute for Studies of Religion found that an increasing number of Americans are not turning away from communal worship. Rather, they continue to enjoy communal worship but they are reluctant to join a particular denomination.[48]

Craig Harline argues that the commercialization of Sunday has not affected church attendance. "It is striking that even while opportunities for Sunday recreations were increasing, Americans were also going to church in steadily increasing numbers. And while at the founding of the republic, not even two in ten Americans belonged to churches, by 1950 six in ten did." In Western Europe many European countries have blue laws, yet church attendance is low in these countries. A *Wall Street Journal* editorial notes: "Though the churches are mostly empty and France is a 'secular' republic, the Sabbath is sacred."[49]

It may be that those who worry about the transformation of Sunday exaggerate its negative effects. The authors of an article "The

and the Ides fell on the thirteenth day of the month (or the fifteenth day in a thirty-one-day month).² We remember the soothsayer's warning in *Julius Caesar*: "Beware the ides of March." When Ovid was exiled to Tomis on the Black Sea, he wrote a long poem called *Fasti* that is a witty and politically subversive account of the first six months of the Roman calendar.³

By the third century the Romans had begun to favor a weekly calendar that was based on the observation—first made by Babylonian astrologers—that seven heavenly bodies moved in an unusual manner. These "wandering planets," as they were called, are the sun, the moon, Mercury, Venus, Mars, Jupiter (or Jove), and Saturn. In the so-called planetary week, the first day was Saturday—the "day of Saturn" (*dies Saturni*)—followed by Sunday (*dies Solis*); Monday, the "day of the moon" (*dies Lunae*); Tuesday the "day of Mars" (*dies Martis*); Wednesday the "day of Mercury" (*dies Mercurii*); Thursday the "day of Jove" (*dies Iovis*); and Friday the "day of Venus" (*dies Veneris*).⁴

Many pagan Romans regarded Saturday as a day of rest—but not because it was a holy day, as it was for the Jews. Saturday was an unlucky day because Saturn was considered to be an unlucky planet, so it was a day when no business should be conducted. Romans also celebrated Thursday because it was Jove's day. There were other special days as well. Different cities venerated different gods, and different emperors declared their own festival days, so there was a patchwork of continually changing festival days.

A leading historian of ancient methods of reckoning time notes that "in the ancient world each city had its own calendar and its own way of calibrating past time. . . . The distinctive power of the Roman calendar derives overwhelmingly from its specificity to the culture, since it is a religious and political instrument for shaping Roman cultural memory before it is an instrument for measuring time."[5] In certain periods there were more than two hundred festival days. Ovid's *Fasti* describes a superstitious world in which the gods play an important role and are appeased on many festival days with animal sacrifices: goats, sheep, pregnant cows, and dogs. Ovid mentions at least thirty major festivals—some of them lasting several days. Roman emperors tried to cut back on the number of festival days—with little success.[6]

Constantine's edict modified the Roman calendar. The first day of the week remained Saturday and there still were many festival days dedicated to different gods, but now every week had a holy day—Sunday.

Constantine's decree does not refer to Sunday as the Lord's Day. The decree says that Romans should make Sunday a day of rest in order to honor the sun god. "All magistrates, city-dwellers and artisans are to rest on the venerable day of the Sun, though country-dwellers may without hindrance apply themselves to agriculture." The decree repeats the point that Sunday is the day of the sun. "The day celebrated by the veneration of the Sun should not be devoted to the swearing and counter-swearing of litigants, and their ceaseless brawling."[7]

Was Constantine a worshiper of the sun god? Edward Gibbon thinks he was. "The devotion of Constantine was more peculiarly directed to the genius of the Sun, the Apollo of Greek and Roman mythology. . . . The Sun was universally celebrated as the invincible guide and protector of Constantine." Gibbon mentions Apollo because that god was often associated with the sun. In *The City of God* Augustine says: "Our adversaries [i.e., pagans] . . . say that he [Apollo] is also the sun."[8]

Gibbon also assumes that Constantine made Sunday a pagan holiday because many Romans were sun worshipers. "Constantine styles the Lord's Day *dies Solis*, a name which could not offend the ears of his Pagan subjects." Coins minted during Constantine's reign often attribute his victories to the sun god, and they also portray Constantine as an "invincible companion to the Sun." In Rome the monuments Constantine erected to celebrate his victory over his rival Maxentius were pagan in content. In Constantinople he erected a statue of himself as the sun god, and he had an image of himself "paraded about the hippodrome in the so-called Sun Chariot."⁹ Chariot races were dedicated to the sun god.

If Constantine wanted to appease sun-worshiping Romans, why did he say he was a Christian? He told the historian Eusebius that he converted to Christianity because of a vision and a dream he had in 312, on the day before a major battle, which took place outside Rome, near the Milvian Bridge. Eusebius tells us:

> Around noon-time, when the day was already beginning to decline, he saw before him in the sky the sign of a cross of light. He said it was above the sun, and it bore the inscription, "Conquer with this." . . . He said he became disturbed. What could the vision mean? He continued to ponder and to give great thought to the question, and night came on him suddenly. When he was asleep, the Christ of God appeared to him and he brought with him the sign which had appeared in the sky. He ordered Constantine to make a replica of this sign which he had witnessed in the sky, and he was to use it as a protection during his encounters with the enemy.

After the victory Constantine (Eusebius says) "resolved to worship none but the God who had been revealed to him."¹⁰

Constantine's conviction that the Christian God favored him was strengthened when—three years later—he defeated the pagan Licinius, who ruled over the eastern half of the empire. Constantine,

Gibbon says, embraced Christianity because it was "a religion so propitious to his fame and fortunes." Constantine believed he had been anointed by the Christian God to rule the Roman Empire. "Success had justified his divine title to the throne, and that title was founded on the truth of the Christian revelation."[11]

Historians have pondered the question of Constantine's religious beliefs. Most would agree with Michael Grant, who says that Constantine's beliefs "were in a bit of a muddle."[12] Perhaps Constantine did not change religions so much as add a new god, Christ, to the ones he already venerated. (He had previously regarded Mars as his protector.) He may have come to the conclusion that the sun god and Christ were one and the same.

Whatever Constantine's religious beliefs, he clearly favored the spread of Christianity. He built many churches, destroyed pagan temples, and decreed tax policies that were favorable to Christian clergy and Christian institutions. In 325 he convened the First Council of Nicaea, an assembly of clerics who, after two months of discussion, drew up the Nicene Creed, which describes the key tenets of the Christian faith. In the same year he abolished the gladiatorial contests that Christian writers had always despised. In 330, when Constantine inaugurated Constantinople, the new eastern capital of the empire, he had the dedication ceremonies conducted by Christian clergy.[13]

Constantine, Gibbon speculates, may have decided that Christians were more likely than pagans to be obedient subjects. In Constantine's time "the cause of virtue derived very feeble support from the influence of the Pagan superstition. Under these discouraging circumstances, a prudent magistrate might observe with pleasure the progress of a religion which diffused among the people a pure, benevolent, and universal system of ethics . . . enforced by the sanction of eternal rewards or punishments."[14] Ruthless and paranoid, Constantine worried about plots against his rule. He murdered his son, who he thought (probably wrongly) was a rival to the throne. And he murdered his second wife for reasons that are unclear. He may have thought she was conspiring against him. He delayed his baptism until the hour of death, apparently hoping that in doing so he would escape punishment for the evil deeds he committed.

Since Constantine favored Christianity, why didn't he curry favor with Christians as well as pagans by saying in his decree that Sunday is the Lord's Day as well as the day of the sun? The first imperial edict to mention the Lord's Day was not issued until sixty years after Constantine's decree.

Constantine may have refrained from calling Sunday the Lord's Day because he thought it was important to shore up support among his soldiers, many of whom were sun-worshiping Mithraists. Mithraism, which (according to Plutarch) arose in the first century in Asia Minor, was a mystery cult that worshiped the sun god. It flourished in the third century and faded away toward the end of the fourth century. Mithraism was especially popular with the military. The soldiers who fought with Licinius against Constantine did so under the banner of Mithras.

Though Mithras was a Persian god, Mithraism was a Roman religion. No Mithraist sacred texts have been found, so we know little about Mithraism's teachings. Many well-preserved Mithraist temples have been discovered, yet scholars continue to debate the meaning of the artwork found in them. In Mithraic temples one finds representations of a tauroctony, a bull-slaying scene in which the sun is usually depicted. Mithras is often called *Sol invictus*: the unconquered Sun. (In 274, when the emperor Aurelian dedicated a temple to *Sol*, sun worship was "a cult popular in the empire at large, and not without some roots in the archaic religion of Rome.") Mithras is sometimes depicted as the invincible sun god, but he is also shown as a separate figure.[15]

Evidence of the widespread cult of Mithras among Roman soldiers can still be found. In 1933 Patrick Leigh Fermor, the English travel writer, visited a ruined Roman amphitheater a few miles from Budapest. There he "dug for bones in the Temple of the Unconquered Sun," and in the local museum of antiquities he looked at "disturbing bas-reliefs of Mithras in a Phrygian cap, plunging a dagger into the bull's throat. . . . A favourite of the [Roman] legions, he [Mithras] was worshipped all along the frontier." Mithraism was also embraced by Roman officials. Women were not allowed to join the cult, but there may have been some female Mithraists, since a dedication to a Mithraist temple in Rome is by a woman.[16]

Mithras is also closely connected with Apollo. A leading scholar of Mithraism says "there is clearly a special reason for the worship of Apollo in the Mithras cult. The key factor here is his role as a solar deity rather than guardian of the Muses. Some inscriptions equate him with Mithras, and the figure of Helios [Greek sun god], with whom Mithras is so closely connected, is sometimes completely Apollonian in character."[17]

Mithraism was a cult religion that did not seek converts, so it was not a major rival to Christianity. Yet perhaps because Mithraism and Christianity had some practices in common—a ritual meal and associating God with light—Christian thinkers strongly attacked Mithraism as a false religion that was spawned by the devil. During the reign of Constantius II (337–361) suspicion of Mithraists was so strong that, according to one observer, people were afraid to watch the sun rise or set, for fear of being persecuted as Mithraists.[18]

Long before Mithraism became a cult religion, worship of the sun god was widespread in the ancient world. In the mid-fourteenth century B.C.E., a Pharaoh, Akhenaton, decided that the sun god, Aton, should be the only god the Egyptians worshiped. When Akhenaton died, Aton was demoted—becoming one god among many. In *Works and Days*, written in the eighth century B.C.E., Hesiod tells his readers to respect the sun: "Do not urinate standing turned towards the sun." The Stoic philosopher Cleanthes (Eusebius says) "held that the Ruling Principle of the kosmos was the sun." Plotinus, an Egyptian Greek neo-Platonist who strongly influenced Augustine, called the sun a "visible god" who revolved far above the world.[19]

Even Jews paid homage to the sun god. In the first century C.E. many Greek-speaking Jews were strongly influenced by Greek culture, and in several ancient synagogues Helios sits enthroned in floor mosaics.[20]

Perhaps the most famous sun worshiper in Roman times was the emperor Julian—often called Julian the Apostate because he tried to restore paganism. (He reigned from 361 to 363.) Julian (in Gibbon's translation) says: "The SUN, whose genial influence pervades and sustains the universe, justly claimed the adoration of mankind, as the bright representative of the LOGOS." Twice a day Julian sacrificed to the sun god. "Every morning he saluted the parent of light with a sacrifice; the blood of another victim [a sheep or goat] was shed at the moment when the Sun sunk below the horizon."[21]

The sun was important to the members of a religious movement called Manichaeism, which was named after its Persian founder, Mani, who lived in the third century. Manichaeism, which was far more popular in the fourth century than Mithraism, was a radically dualistic religion that understood the world as an endless struggle between the forces of light and darkness. Its devotees included the young Augustine, who describes his Manichaean beliefs in the *Confessions*. The Manichees saw the sun not as a god above man but, rather, as an externalization of a force within man.

It may seem strange to us that the early Christians often conflated Jesus with the sun god. Clement of Alexandria, a second-century Greek, writes of Christ driving his chariot across the heavens. Roman tomb paintings often show Jesus "in guises familiar to pagan painting and sculpture (as a shepherd, or as the sun god)," and many early statues of Jesus depict him as if he were the young Apollo. When Julian attempted to restore paganism, the Bishop of Troy apparently had no trouble switching from Christian to pagan worship, for he had never stopped praying to the sun god while serving as a Christian bishop. In a fourth-century mosaic found beneath St. Peter's in Rome, Christ is driving a chariot, as if he were Apollo the sun god.[22]

By the fifth century most Christians thought of Sunday as the Lord's Day, but some were reluctant to give up the notion that it was also the day of the sun. In Constantinople Christians sacrificed to the statue of Constantine "as if it stood for Sol." In the latter part of the fifth century Pope Leo I criticized the members of his congregation who bowed to the sun on the steps of St. Peter's before they entered the church. They were doing it, Leo said, "partly in ignorance" and "partly in a pagan spirit." In sixth-century Syria some Christians paid homage to the birthday of Helios—i.e., the winter solstice. A bishop complained that they "celebrated a great [pagan] festival."[23]

Attacking Sun Worship

In *The City of God*, which appeared in installments between 416 and 422, Augustine frequently attacks worship of the sun god. Referring to Solomon, who Augustine thinks is the author of Ecclesiastes, he says: "This wisest of men devoted the whole of his book to an adequate description of this vanity. His motive in doing so, clearly, was that we should desire not a life of vanity under the sun, but a life of verity under the sun's Creator" (969). Humankind has a choice: worship the sun and live a life of vanity or worship the Christian God and live a life of verity. The good Christian, Augustine says, will be rewarded in heaven. In heaven "the sun does not rise upon the good and evil; rather, the Sun of righteousness protects only the good" (216). Jesus Christ was often called the Sun of Righteousness (*Sol Justitiae*).[24]

To persuade his readers that the sun is not a god, Augustine also cites two pagan writers: Anaxagoras and Epicurus. Anaxagoras, who lived in Athens in the fifth century B.C.E., was charged with impiety for saying that the sun is not a god. Epicurus, an Athenian who was born roughly 150 years later, agreed with Anaxagoras but was not charged with impiety. Augustine is puzzled by their different fates, but his main point is that both writers argued that the sun is not a god.

To strengthen his argument, Augustine even cites Porphyry, the author of a well-known anti-Christian tract. "Even Porphyry says that divine oracles have declared that we are not cleansed by offering sacrifice to the sun and moon, and that this shows that a man cannot be purified by sacrificing to any gods. For what rites can cleanse us, if those of the sun and moon, which are held to be the foremost of the gods of heaven, do not cleanse?" (424). According to Augustine, sacrificing to the sun or the moon is not only blasphemous; it is also a waste of time.

Augustine often praises sunlight, but he always argues that whatever pleasure we get from sunlight is nothing compared to the joy we will derive from God's light. "For that City in which it is promised that we shall reign is as far removed from Rome as heaven is from earth, as eternal life is from temporal joy . . . and as the light of the sun and moon from the light of Him Who made the sun and moon" (218).

To stress God's power over the sun, Augustine says that God can change the sun's course. "God . . . Who made the visible heaven and earth, does not disdain to perform visible miracles in heaven or on earth" (411). There was an "unnatural" solar eclipse, he says, "when the Lord was crucified by the cruel and impious Jews" (113). This eclipse was a miracle because "this latter concealment of the sun did not come about through the natural movement of the heavenly bodies. . . . It took place during the Passover of the Jews. For this festival is held at full moon, whereas eclipses of the sun normally happen only at the last quarter of the moon" (113).

Boethius, an influential Christian writer who lived a century after Augustine, also argued that the sun is not a god. In *The Consolation of Philosophy* Boethius first quotes Homer about the power of Phoebus Apollo (i.e., the god of the sun), and then says: "But the sun's weak rays cannot pierce the bowels of the earth nor the depths of the sea. It is not so with the Creator of this great sphere. . . . He sees at once, in a single glance, all things that are, or were, or are to come. Since He is sole observer of all things, you can call Him the true Sun."[25]

The attacks on sun worship by Augustine and Boethius suggest that sun worship remained a temptation for many Christians. Yet sun worship had already declined when Boethius was composing his philosophical treatise. According to Corippus, a Christian writing in 565, chariot races in the circus were no longer regarded as a pagan spectacle dedicated to the sun god. (The circus or hippodrome was a long U-shaped structure. The Circus Maximus in Rome could seat 250,000 people.) Chariot races were now a Christian event. "When God took the shape of humankind from a virgin, then the games of the sun were abolished." Now "the pleasant amusements of the circus" are in honor of the "New Rome"—that is, Christian Rome.[26]

Defining Sunday: Augustine

In *The City of God* Augustine also wants to persuade Christians that Sunday is the new Sabbath. On this question he was preaching to the converted, since most Christians had already come to regard Sunday as the new Sabbath. Though some Christians continued to regard Saturday as the Sabbath, all Christians called Sunday the Lord's Day. In English Sunday was not called the Sabbath until the late sixteenth or early seventeenth century.

The notion of a Sabbath day—a day of rest or, more accurately, a day of ceasing from work—was unknown in the ancient world before it appeared in Genesis. James Kugel calls it "the first sabbath rest in history," and he notes that modern Bible scholars think the main point of the account of Creation is "*to stress the importance of the seventh day, the sabbath*" (emphasis Kugel's).[27] *Shabbat*, the Hebrew word for Sabbath, comes from a Babylonian word, *sabbatu* (or *shappatu*), but *sabbatu* means either the eleventh month of the year in the Babylonian calendar or the fifteenth day of the month, the day of the full moon. It was not a day of rest for Babylonians.

Many early Christians observed the Jewish Sabbath as well as the Lord's Day; and many insisted that Gentiles who converted to Christianity should be circumcised and should adhere to the law of Moses. Paul, a converted Jew, strongly disagreed with these views. "It was Pauline doctrine that the Mosaic law was not the way of salvation, that circumcision was not a condition of salvation and that Jewish 'customs' were without significance with regard to salvation."[28] Paul frequently attacked Mosaic law because Jewish Christians, as they are called by scholars, were a powerful force. "Again and again in the writings of the church fathers, we hear of Jewish-Christian groups who were incensed by Paul's strictures against circumcision and the law and who refused to acknowledge the authority of his writings."[29]

Paul's view of Jewish law and Jewish customs eventually triumphed because Christians could argue that Paul's view was supported by Jesus himself. Jesus says that his coming has abrogated Jewish law. In a dispute with the Pharisees about Sabbath observance, Jesus says:

"The sabbath was made for humankind, and not humankind for the sabbath; so the Son of Man is lord even of the sabbath" (Mark 2:28). Jesus makes the same remark in Matthew 12:18: "For the Son of Man is lord of the Sabbath." The Pharisees are so angry with Jesus that they plot to kill him. "The Pharisees went out and conspired against him, how to destroy him" (Matthew 12:14). This is the first mention of a plan to destroy Jesus.

Jesus of course said nothing about Sunday's being the new Sabbath. Sunday became the holy day for Christians because the New Testament says that Jesus was resurrected on the day after the Sabbath. Given the fundamentally different views that Jews and early Christians (many of whom had been Jews) held about Jesus, it was inevitable that there would be differences of opinion about which day of the week was holy. A leading scholar of Judaism notes that Jews observe the seventh day of the week in order "to celebrate the creation of the world and to create the seventh day all over again, the majesty of holiness in time."[30] The early Christians observed the first day of the week for a very different reason: to celebrate the resurrection of Jesus. On the first day of the week, Paul and his disciples "met to break bread" (Acts 20:7).

Annotating a passage in Acts in which Paul breaks bread with other Christians, the editor of the Oxford Bible says: "The meal in which all partake has clear eucharistic overtones." Christian worship began with the breaking of bread on Sundays and giving thanks to God for the Resurrection. According to a leading scholar of early Christianity, "the Eucharist was the central act of Christian worship, and its communal celebration each Sunday set the rhythm of Christian life."[31]

Justin Martyr, who was born in Palestine in the second century but settled in Rome after he converted to Christianity, describes what Christians did on Sunday.

On the day called Sunday all who live in the cities or in the country gather at one place and the memoirs of the apostles or the
writings of the prophets are read. . . . When the reader has finished, the one who is presiding instructs us in a brief discourse and
exhorts us to imitate these noble things. Then we all stand up together and offer prayers. . . . When we have finished the prayer,
bread is brought forth, and wine and water, and the presiding
minister offers up prayers and thanksgiving to the best of his ability, and the people assent, saying the Amen; after this the consecrated elements are distributed and received by each one.[32]

In 364 the Council of Laodicea made official what was standard
practice among Christians. It decreed that Christians should honor
the Lord on Sunday only and that Saturday should not be a day
of rest.

Though Augustine knew that most Christians regarded Sunday as
the new Sabbath, in *The City of God* he wants to settle the point
conclusively. First he cites Seneca, a playwright and philosopher
who lived in the first century c.e. Augustine admired Seneca even
though he did not agree with Seneca's negative view of the Jewish
Sabbath. Seneca, like many Romans, derided the Jews for not working on Saturday. Augustine admired Seneca because he thought
Seneca merely paid lip service to paganism. Seneca, he says, was
"made free by philosophy"—free in the sense that he understood
that Roman religion was a foolish superstition. Yet for careerist reasons Seneca conformed to traditional Roman religious practice. "Because he was a distinguished senator of the Roman people, he none-
theless worshipped what he condemned, did what he deplored, and
adored what he blamed" (264).[33]

Augustine's main reason for bringing up Seneca is not to praise
him for realizing that paganism is a foolish superstition. He brings

up Seneca because the Roman philosopher is the first writer to note
that Sabbath observance is a growing phenomenon among non-
Jews, despite the fact that many Roman writers look down on the
Jews. "It is in speaking of the Jews that he [Seneca] says: 'meanwhile,
the customs of this most accursed race have achieved such strength
that they are now received in all lands: the conquered have given
laws to the conquerors'" (264).

Why is the Sabbath becoming popular among non-Jews? Seneca
has no explanation for this turn of affairs. Augustine does. Divine
providence is responsible for the spread of Sabbath observance, yet
Augustine says that divine providence no longer regards the Jewish
Sabbath as the Sabbath. "The religious institutions of the Jews were
established by divine authority and then, in the fullness of time, and
by that same authority, taken over by the people of God to whom
the mystery of eternal life has been revealed" (264–265). In other
words, the Jewish Sabbath has been superseded by the Christian
Sabbath.

Augustine supports his argument about the new Sabbath with a
quotation from Genesis in which God says to Abraham that every
male child must be circumcised when he is eight days old (Genesis
17:10–12). Augustine sees a great deal of significance in the command that circumcision must take place on the eighth day. The Resurrection also took place on the eighth day. "For what does circumcision signify but the renewal of nature by the sloughing off of old
age? And what does the eighth day symbolize but Christ, who rose
again after the completion of seven days, that is, after the Sabbath?"
(737). For a Christian the eighth day is a special day, and therefore it
is a day that should be the Sabbath as well as the Lord's Day.

What does circumcision have to do with the Sabbath? In Augustine's tortured argument, circumcision is a form of rebirth. "Circumcision," he says, "was instituted as a sign of rebirth because, thanks to

the original sin by which God's covenant was first broken, birth itself brings a not-undeserved ruin upon the infant, unless rebirth redeems him" (739). Circumcision is a kind of ritual purification, but the Resurrection obviates the need for such a religious ceremony.

Augustine devotes so much time to interpreting the passage in Genesis because he wants to "save" the Hebrew Bible for Christians, many of whom wanted to ignore it. The Hebrew Bible, he says, is a sacred text for Christians because it is an "Old Testament" that is a hidden form of the New Testament. "For what is that which we call the Old Testament but a hidden form of the New? And what is that which we call the New Testament but the revelation of the Old?" (737). Augustine is saying that the Old Testament has to be read through the lens of the New Testament. If Jews would read the sacred text properly, they would realize that it foretells the coming of Christ. "It is so that, when the images, altars, groves and temples of false gods are everywhere overthrown and their sacrifices prohibited, it may be shown from the Jewish Scriptures how all this was prophesied long ago" (186).

According to Augustine, Judaism is a religion that has been "completed" by Christianity. In a sermon he says that Jewish rites and customs were ordained by God and therefore they should not be abhorred. But the "spirit" has passed out of them and they should be taken reverently to the grave. A leading Old Testament scholar notes: "The writings of ancient Israel, both those which were concerned with her past relationship to God and those which dealt with her future, were seen by Jesus Christ, and certainly by the Apostles and the early Church, as a collection of predictions which pointed to him, the saviour of Israel and of the world."[34]

Augustine, then, agrees with Paul that Sunday is the new Sabbath and the sacrament of baptism is the new circumcision. Paul says: "For in Christ Jesus neither circumcision nor uncircumcision counts for anything; the only thing that counts is faith working through love" (Galatians 5:6). Paul says that circumcision lacks religious meaning. "For it is we who are the circumcision, who worship in the Spirit of God and boast in Christ Jesus" (Philippians 3:3). Paul also says that the Resurrection relieves Christians of the obligation to adhere to Jewish religious practices. "Therefore do not let anyone condemn you in matters of food and drink or of observing festivals, new moons, or sabbaths. These are only a shadow of what is to come, but the substance belongs to Christ" (Colossians 2:16).

Observing Sunday: Augustine

How was Sunday—the new Sabbath—to be observed? Even though Christian thinkers said that Mosaic law had been superseded by the Resurrection, all Christian writers thought the Ten Commandments remained in force. The Fourth Commandment now applied to Sunday, the new Sabbath. Christians thought no one should work on the Lord's Day, but what constitutes work? The Hebrew Bible is unhelpful on this question. "The Pentateuch," notes Kugel, "said that a person had to refrain from working on the Sabbath, but nowhere did it say what constituted 'work.'" The Church broadly agreed with Jewish rabbinical law that work of any kind was inappropriate on Sunday, though it made an exception for harvest time. Christians also were supposed to abstain from public buying and selling, and from pleading in the law courts.[35]

In Isaiah 58:13 the Lord says that the Sabbath should be a day of delight, but what constitutes delight? Heschel says that the Sabbath is a day of joy and "it is a sin to be sad on the Sabbath day," yet he also says that "levity would certainly obliterate the spirit of the day. . . . It must always be remembered that the Sabbath is not an occasion for diversion or frivolity."[36] The church said the new Sabbath should be a day of gladness, a day when Christians celebrate the Resurrection. In an Apostolic Letter, Pope John Paul II reaffirms this view of the Lord's Day when he says: "Rightly, then, the Psalmist's cry is applied to Sunday: 'This is the day which the Lord has made: let us rejoice and be glad in it'" (Psalms 118:24).[37]

Augustine thought Sunday should a day of gladness, but it disturbed him that many Christians thought Sunday should be a day of diversion—a day spent enjoying pagan spectacles. By 400 C.E. paganism posed a greater threat to Christianity than Judaism, since most of the recent converts to Christianity were pagans. Moreover, Jewish proselytism, which was never as strong as Christian proselytism, had been proscribed. The question of Jewish proselytism is mired in scholarly controversy. Some scholars suggest that it was extensive before it was outlawed in the middle of the fourth century, whereas others argue that Jewish proselytism was a weak force even before it was proscribed. Melvin Konner notes the difficulties Jewish proselytes faced. "A Christian shows up on the pagan's doorstep with the good news of eternal love and forgiveness in exchange for a genuine declaration of faith and a promise to be good. A Jew shows up the next day talking about hundreds of commandments, including dietary restrictions, prayer schedules, and Sabbath laws. . . . And, oh, for the men in the family . . ."[38]

In his sermons Augustine criticized Christians who attended pagan spectacles on Sunday or practiced pagan rites on Sunday (or any day of the week). Christian thinkers had always condemned pagan spectacles, which included gladiatorial contests, obscene plays, and chariot races. In *On Spectacles* Tertullian, who wrote around 200 C.E., warns Christians that they should not attend them. After the Roman Empire was Christianized, gladiatorial contests were banned. (Gladiators did not usually fight to the death. "The average fight ended either with a wound to one of the contestants or when one fighter's endurance gave out.")[39] Chariot racing became the most popular spectacle. The church generally tolerated chariot racing, which continued to exist in Byzantium until medieval times. In the Catholic West it waned slowly in the sixth and seventh centuries, less because of church disapproval than because of a lack of civic funds to support the races.

The full title of *The City of God* is *The City of God against the Pagans*. A recently discovered letter from Augustine makes it clear that *The City of God* was written mainly for "waverers"—for Christians who were reluctant to give up pagan practices. Peter Brown says that "almost a century after the conversion of Constantine, a sense of the uncanny powers of the gods" was strongly felt by many Christians.[40]

On Sundays early in the second decade of the fifth century, when Augustine was preaching in Carthage, many Christians went to a nearby circus to view chariot races. The circus "drew not only 'pagans' and Jews . . . but also the very people he [Augustine] thought most ought to be in church—the baptized faithful."[41] Augustine admits that he too once enjoyed spectacles. "I myself, when a young man, used sometimes to come to their sacrilegious spectacles and games, and watch the ecstatic priests and listen to the musicians and enjoy the most disgraceful exhibitions which were enacted in honour of the gods and goddesses" (54). Now he has contempt for them, so he says sarcastically: "What wonderful spectacles are displayed in the theatres. . . . What ingenious methods do we find employed in capturing, killing or taming wild beasts!" (1162).

Augustine realized that no matter how much he and other clerics inveighed against pagan spectacles, many Christians would continue to enjoy them—especially the chariot races. Augustine wants to persuade his readers that they will derive far greater pleasure from attending the "spectacle" of divine worship. He frequently invokes the world of pagan spectacles to make a point about Christianity. A pious Christian, he says, is a great gladiator who defeats demons that try to corrupt his soul. "It is an august theatre, God is the spectator of your fight." Even when a Christian is sick, he is still fighting: "You are in the arena: lying down, you are fighting."[42]

In *The City of God* Augustine praises the Sunday churchgoer and implicitly attacks the Sunday spectacle-goer. In church "no foul or disgraceful spectacle or example is ever presented when the teachings of the true God are expounded, or His miracles told, or His gifts praised, or His blessings sought" (91). Those who do not go to church on the Lord's Day are in danger of being corrupted by "false and deceitful gods. . . . Let these spirits be excluded from your piety by Christian cleansing" (92–93).

Pagan spectacles, Augustine says, are a waste of time, but they are not as dangerous to Christians as pagan rituals, which are idolatrous. He tells Christians they cannot hedge their bets by going to church and also engaging in pagan rites. "God doesn't wish to be worshiped along with those others [pagan deities], not even if he is worshiped a great deal more and those others a great deal less."[43] According to Augustine, the Christian's journey on earth is a difficult and dangerous one. If a Christian performs pagan rites and attends pagan spectacles instead of participating in communal worship on Sunday, he is more likely to lose his way.

Augustine's concern about pagan temptations may seem excessive, since Christianity was a fast-growing religion in the fifth century. In 391 Theodosius closed down pagan temples and banned pagan worship. Works by pagan writers were burned in great bonfires, including the writings of Porphyry. Scribes who wanted to copy the work of pagan writers were threatened with having their hands cut off. Yet even though paganism was outlawed, it continued to flourish. In 400 the population of the Roman Empire was evenly divided between pagans and Christians. Moreover, many Christians took part in traditional Roman festivities. They thought "continued prosperity meant also the continuance of the façade of pagan life: they would join pagan literary circles, [and] would patronize great circus shows."[44]

Augustine was right to worry that paganism remained a strong temptation for many Christians. Many were half-persuaded by pagan arguments that the Christianization of the Roman Empire had been a military and civic disaster. Augustine points out that when paganism was the state religion, Rome had many military setbacks. He also notes that pagans tend to blame Christians for every unfortunate event. "I am still speaking against those ignorant men from whose lack of knowledge has arisen the vulgar saying, 'No rain: blame the Christians'" (53).

According to Augustine, it is foolish to assume that Rome can be protected by worshiping the pagan gods. There are so many Roman gods—which ones should be worshiped? "Who, then, can count the many gods who thus protected Rome? Native gods and alien, celestial, terrestrial, gods of the infernal regions, of the seas, of fountains, of rivers . . ." (106–107). Given the number of pagan gods, how does one choose which god or gods to blame when bad things happen? "Which god, or which gods, out of the great swarm that the Romans worshipped, did most to extend and preserve their empire?" (152). After listing many pagan gods, Augustine says: "I do not mention them all . . . [because] it bores me [to do so]" (153).

Perhaps the most effective strategy Augustine and other Christian writers employed in their attempt to shore up the beliefs of wavering Christians was to imply that paganism was a system of beliefs that only backward and rural people embraced. "Pagan" had been a neutral term, referring at first to a rural person, but gradually it also came to be a derogatory term for a nonmilitary person. Christian writers took both notions of "pagan"—a rustic and a nonmilitary person— and made it serve their purposes. To be a pagan was to be backward and cowardly. Some modern historians always put "pagan" in quotation marks because they think it is a term of abuse. They prefer to speak of "polytheists" rather than "pagans."

By the fifth century most educated urban Romans in Italy were Christian, yet Christianity was a weaker force in the cities of North Africa, where Augustine preached on Sunday for thirty-nine years—in Carthage, Hippo, and many small towns. In 401 a Council of Bishops at Carthage petitioned the state for aid against the pagans. "Christians are under pressure from pagans to join . . . [pagan] celebrations," the council maintained, so the authorities should prohibit them. The council was especially disturbed by pagan practices on the Lord's Day and Easter. "Furthermore, this too is to be requested: that theatrical shows and those of the games be removed from the Lord's Day and other most celebrated Christian days, especially because on the Eighth Day of holy Easter the people gather more at the Circus than at church."[45]

In his Sunday sermons Augustine frequently attacked paganism, but he was heard by relatively few people because in fifth-century North Africa there were not many churches and most were small. Christians who wanted to go to church on the Lord's Day could not always do so. Augustine's congregation in Hippo "was made up of the upper classes of landowners, merchants, and officers. . . . The bulk of the Christian population made do without the weekly inoculation of ritual."[46]

What about the people who heard Augustine preach? Some attended church out of curiosity rather than piety; they wanted to hear a famous preacher. Describing Augustine's sermons, Peter Brown says that "one senses in them the constant presence of the unpersuaded, the indifferent and the downright disobedient. . . . Indeed, the very urgency and trenchancy of their tone betrays how little authority Augustine actually wielded over his hearers."[47]

Augustine was a towering figure in Christian thought, but many of the people who heard him preach on Sunday were wavering Christians who paid little heed to what he said about observing the Lord's Day.

Observing Sunday: Caesarius

One hundred years after Augustine, Caesarius, the Bishop of Arles, preached frequently on Sundays and other holy days. In many of his sermons he described how he thought Christians should conduct themselves on the Lord's Day.

Arles was a Roman city that Constantine designated the capital of Gaul. (He also established an imperial·residence there.) Before Constantine, there were few Christians in Arles. During his reign Christianity expanded rapidly in the city and its environs, but pagan spectacles remained popular with most Christians, who went to the theater, the circus, and also the amphitheater, where men fought wild beasts. In the fifth century church leaders wanted to destroy a pagan theater to use its materials to embellish a church, but the theater remained in use for another century. The surrounding rural population was more pagan than Christian. Many worshiped Celtic gods as well as a wide variety of other gods, including Mithras.

When Caesarius became bishop in 502, there also were two strains of Christianity. The Visigoths, who had conquered Arles in 476, were Arian Christians, but they did not persecute Catholic Christians. (The Arians denied the full divinity of Christ.) Caesarius did not try to combat the Arian heresy. To do so would have been risky while the Visigoths held power. His main concern was twofold: admonishing Christians to observe Sunday in a sabbatarian way and persuading them that pagan rites and customs were ineffectual and corrupting.

Caesarius' view of Sunday observance was more rigorous than Augustine's. He was strongly against going to spectacles on Sunday. The Lord's Day, he said, should be devoted to prayer, worship, and the avoidance of all "secular pursuits," including agricultural work. Christians should prepare themselves for worship by giving alms to the poor, settling disputes, and confessing their sins. And they should bring offerings of bread or wine for Communion and when possible the tithes of the harvest.[48]

Christians also should abstain from having sex on Sunday. "If a man has sexual relations with his wife . . . on Sunday or on any other feast day, the children conceived at that time will be born as lepers or epileptics, or possibly even possessed by the devil."[49] Christians who planned to receive Communion should avoid sexual relations for several days before Sunday. Perhaps because the requirements were so rigorous, Christians in Gaul took Communion infrequently, but they were required to take Communion at Christmas, Easter, and Pentecost.

(Most Jewish commentators say that Jews are encouraged to have sex on the Sabbath, but some disagree. They say that those engaging in intercourse could not be at rest, and that touching semen renders both participants impure. Herold Weiss says that "eventually, rabbinic halakah [law] established that the bliss of conjugal ecstasy was not just permitted but almost required as part of Sabbath observance. But the issue was not easily resolved and remained a matter of debate for centuries.")[50]

Caesarius thought Christians should attend church every Sunday and stay until the service ended. He was angry one Sunday when several members of the congregation began to leave before he gave the sermon. To make sure that churchgoers heard his sermon to the end, he often locked the church's doors. Caesarius also warned against improper behavior during the Mass. "The devil . . . tries to involve us in fruitless thoughts and idle talk in the church itself."

Churchgoers who are guilty of engaging in gossip are filled with "empty, vain, and perhaps even bitter conversations and sordid thoughts." A person who gossips in church offers "a kind of poison or sword to other people, since he neither hears the word of God himself nor permits others to hear it."[51]

Caesarius was disturbed that on Sundays the church had become a meeting place for people to conduct secular business. While Mass was being held, men gathered in other parts of the church or outside the church in order to gossip, quarrel, and carry on business, including "pleading and hearing lawsuits."[52] (On a visit to a remote area of Brazil in 1932, Evelyn Waugh reported that the men congregated near a church on Sunday but did not go inside. "They did not come into the Church, for that is contrary to Brazilian etiquette, but they clustered in the porch, sauntering out occasionally to smoke a cigarette.")[53]

Many peasants, who often had to work on Sunday, did not agree with Caesarius that Sunday should be a day of rest. One peasant complained to him: "I am a peasant, and I am completely occupied in working the land; I am not able to listen to or read the scriptures." Even if a peasant could find time to attend church on Sunday, there were few churches in rural Gaul. Recognizing this problem, a church council, which met in 506 at the port city of Agde and was chaired by Caesarius, said that on most Sundays it was permissible for peasants to attend Mass in private chapels on the estates of nobles, but on major Christian holy days they must attend Mass at a cathedral or parish church. A lack of churches, especially in rural areas, remained a problem in the West for centuries.[54]

In many sermons Caesarius tells Christians to give up their pagan habits. "It is gratifying to us, dearest brothers, and we give great thanks to God, that we see you faithfully coming to church. . . . [Yet] we know that some of you are frequently going to the ancient worship of idols, like godless pagans bereft of the grace of baptism. We have heard that some of you are making vows at trees, praying at springs, and practicing diabolical divination." Caesarius also complained that some Christians were celebrating holidays dedicated to Christian martyrs in a pagan fashion: getting drunk, dancing, and singing shameful songs. He also attacked those "unfortunate and miserable people who not only are unwilling to destroy the shrines of the pagans but even are not afraid or ashamed to build up those which have been destroyed. . . . What are these unfortunate and miserable people doing? They are deserting the light and running to darkness. . . . Why did they receive the sacrament of baptism—if afterwards they intended to return to the profanation of idols?"[55]

Caesarius was especially angered by Christians who followed the pagan custom of regarding Thursday as a holy day. "No one should refuse to work on Thursdays in honor of Jupiter. No man or woman, brothers, should observe this custom at any time, lest the Lord judge those who sacrilegiously transfer to Jupiter's day what they ought to observe on the Lord's day, [and choose] to be pagans rather than Christians."[56] Some Christians did not celebrate Thursday, but they participated in Celtic rites that included ritual bathing as well as sun worship—doing so in the belief that it would ensure a successful harvest.

For four decades Caesarius told churchgoers that they should observe the Lord's Day and avoid pagan rites and spectacles. His sermons were popular because they were in the vernacular Latin spoken by his audience. Caesarius thought most Christians could be weaned from their pagan habits by effective preaching. He called upon bishops to preach "not only on the most important feasts, but every Sunday."[57]

Caesarius warns errant Christians that they "will be tortured by eternal fire without any remedy." He also tells landowners that they should punish serfs who indulge in pagan practices. Caesarius also uses a carrot as well as a stick; he says that Christianity is the path to better health. "Anyone who runs to church in sickness will receive both bodily health and forgiveness of sins. Since we can find a double advantage in church, why do wretched people bring multiple evils upon themselves through enchanters, through springs, trees, and diabolical amulets, or through soothsayers . . . diviners, and fortunetellers?"[58]

The argument that being an observant Christian will improve your health could backfire. In England in 664 (according to the Venerable Bede) a major epidemic caused many East Saxons to return to paganism. They "deserted the sacraments of the Christian faith and apostasized. . . . They began to restore the derelict temples and to worship images, as if they could protect themselves by such means from the plague."[59]

A central question for Caesarius and all church officials was: "How much of the pre-Christian past should the church tolerate?" Caesarius was more hostile than some clerics to anything that smacked of paganism. He wanted to abolish the traditional pagan names for the days of the week. "Let us brothers, who are known to have hope . . . in the living and true God, judge no day worthy of the name of demons. . . . Let us disdain to speak those most sordid names and never let us say 'Mars's day,' 'Mercury's day' or 'Jupiter's day,' but rather 'first day,' 'second day,' or 'third day.'" His project failed. Of all the Romance languages, only Portuguese names the days of the week according to Caesarius' formula. Peter Brown wittily says: "By Caesarius' high standards, Portugal must count as the only fully Christianized country in Europe!"[60]

(Many Scottish Presbyterians in the seventeenth and eighteenth centuries would have agreed with Caesarius. In *The Heart of Midlothian* the narrator describes a radical Presbyterian who objects to pagan names for the days and months. "This ardent and enlightened person and his followers had also great scruples about the lawfulness of bestowing the ordinary names upon the days of the week and the months of the year, which savoured in their nostrils so strongly of paganism, that at length they arrived at the conclusion that they who owned such names as Monday, Tuesday, January, February, and so forth, 'served themselves heirs to the same, if not greater punishment, than had been denounced against the idolaters of old.'")[61]

Pope Gregory the Great was more flexible than Caesarius. Though he lamented that some Christians had been "led astray by the wiles of the Devil and now serve idols under the guise of the Christian religion," he told church officials on a mission to England to be somewhat lenient about the pagan practices of new converts to Christianity. "It is doubtless impossible to cut out everything at once from their stubborn minds: just as the man who is attempting to climb to the highest place, rises by steps and degrees and not by leaps." Yet even Pope Gregory would not have condoned the persistence of these practices over generations. An anonymous ninth-century sermon warns churchgoers about practicing divination as well as going shopping or hunting on Sundays. It also criticizes Christians who like to swear by the sun and the moon.[62]

In the church no one view of the pre-Christian past prevailed. In late antiquity and early medieval times, one historian says, "there was a spectrum of definitions of what it meant to be Christian." Augustine strongly condemned Christians who celebrated the Kalends of January, a holiday that included the exchange of gifts: "Do not mix yourselves with pagans by similarity of customs and deeds," he told churchgoers. "They give New Year's gifts; you should give alms." By contrast, Peter Chrysologus, Bishop of Ravenna in the fifth century, said the festival of Kalends lacked any religious significance. It was "but a wish for sportive enjoyment. It is the joy over a new era, not the folly of the old; it is the beginning of the year, not a pagan outrage."[63]

In late antiquity and the early Middle Ages many Christians ignored the sermons of Caesarius and other priests, for they continued to offer prayers to pagan gods as well as to the Christian God. Christian farmers often chose "a broad-spectrum approach to eliminating hail, simultaneously invoking archangels, saints, and Satan while mixing prayers, incantations, and adjurations in a powerful cocktail of diverse traditional practices and local wisdom." In 580 a Spanish ambassador shocked Gregory, Bishop of Tours, when he said: "We have a saying, that no harm is done when a man passing between pagan altars and a church of God, offers veneration to both."[64]

Paganism's strength should not be exaggerated. Though the pagan past was not eradicated, paganism was a weak force compared to Christianity. Christianity was a universal religion with a sacred text, whereas paganism comprised a wide variety of local religions with no text. Pagan places of worship were not impressive structures but a riverbank, an open field, or a tree. Moreover, Christianity was associated with Latin, a language that united different peoples in the West. By the sixth century paganism was a spent force intellectually. Christians saw the church as a force for order and stability.

Christianity was a strong force for another reason: the calendar was Christianized. In the first millennium of Christianity, Sunday worship was less important for most Christians than the celebration of major Christian holidays. A leading historian of the early Middle Ages says: "We shall perhaps be closer to the truth if we cease to think in terms of Sunday worshippers . . . and see popular religion as a system of ceremonies and stories for great occasions."[65]

One such great occasion was Christmas, which is not mentioned before the middle of the fourth century. The origins of Christmas are obscure, but we know that December 25 was a Roman holy day dedi-

When Elizabeth ascended to the throne in 1558, the English people were weary of so many changes in worship. The new queen did not follow either Edward's or Mary's policies. She promoted Calvinist Protestantism, though not the radical variety. She forbade private meetings for prayer and Bible study, and she also made it illegal for Catholics to worship. The Act of Uniformity (1559) required "all and every person and persons inhabiting within this realm" to attend church on Sundays and holy days—both the main morning service and evening prayer. Bishops were supposed to appoint three or four "discreet men" in every parish to make sure the act was enforced, though the requirement to attend evening worship rarely was.[6]

Elizabeth wanted to make sure that Catholicism would never again be a strong force in England. Though she kept many traditional rituals and restored most of the saints' days that had been observed under Henry VIII, she began an extended campaign to eradicate "monuments of superstition." As a contemporary put it, the new queen wanted to make sure that "there remain no memory of the same [traditional religion] in walls, glasses, windows, or elsewhere within their churches and houses."[7]

In 1571 William Shakespeare, age seven, watched men knock out the stained-glass windows of the Guild Chapel in Stratford, replacing it with plain glass. A radical Protestant reformer said: "Popery may creep in at a glass window as well as at a door." A few months before Shakespeare was born, Stratford's governing council had ordered a massive "defacing [of] images." The paintings that covered the chapel's interior had been whitewashed.[8]

The most obvious change in Sunday observance in England was not the defacing of churches; it was the banning of Catholic worship. Catholics could choose to be recusants—that is, to stay home on Sunday. But if they did so, they would be fined. If they held a secret Mass, they could be sentenced to prison. If they harbored a priest, they could be executed. Henry Donne, John Donne's younger brother, was arrested for harboring a priest. He died in prison from the plague. When Elizabeth died in 1603 Catholics numbered approximately 5 percent of the population.

Most Anglicans agreed with Elizabeth's anti-Catholic policies, but some did not think her reforms went far enough. They wanted more changes in Sunday worship, and they wanted the Lord's Day to be observed in a sabbatarian manner. "The institution of Sunday as the Lord's day, . . . the regulation of sabbath activities, and the penalties for sabbath abuses were contentious issues that were never fully resolved."[9]

In the course of three decades (from 1584 to 1614) at least ten sabbatarian bills were debated in Parliament. In 1563 Parliament debated a bill to close taverns, alehouses, "and other unruly places" on the Lord's Day. It did not pass. Nor did a bill in 1566 against Sunday trading. Sabbath bills introduced in the 1570s and 1580s mainly focused on church attendance—what kind of fine was appropriate for recusants—but none passed into law. "The main obstacle to these bills," Kenneth Parker says, "was the royal veto; for Elizabeth and James seemed unwilling to allow parliament to meddle in religious matters."[10]

By the end of the sixteenth century, the Anglicans who pushed for more reforms were usually called Puritans. The *OED's* first definition of "Puritan" is: "A member of a group of English Protestants of the late sixteenth and seventeenth centuries, who regarded the reformation of the Church under Elizabeth I as incomplete and sought to remove any remaining elements of church practice (such as ceremonies, church ornaments, the use of musical instruments, and in some cases Episcopal authority) which they considered corrupt, idolatrous, or unscriptural." Since "Puritan"—like "pagan"—was initially a pejorative term, some historians are wary of using it, or prefer to put quotation marks around it. The Puritans called themselves the "godly." Yet "Puritan" gradually came to be used neutrally to describe an Anglican who was dissatisfied with various aspects of traditional Anglican worship. Puritans were also called "Precisians." The poet Michael Drayton sarcastically speaks of "our Precisions [*sic*] . . . Who [see] . . . some Crosse or Saint in the window" and therefore want to "pluck downe all the Church."[11]

In the first two decades of the seventeenth century, most Puritans remained within the fold of the Anglican church, but some did not. Separatists, who numbered in the thousands, refused to accept the authority of the church. In their view a church hierarchy was a corrupting force. Each person should converse with God by reading the Bible with the help of a minister who had been chosen by fellow Bible readers. Separatists held conventicles—secret meetings where they read the Bible—but in doing so they risked being arrested for sedition. Many Separatists fled to Holland, including the Pilgrim Fathers, who in 1608 went to Holland and in 1620 sailed for Plymouth, Massachusetts.[12]

Puritans and Separatists usually took a strict view of Sunday observance. They complained that many Anglicans thought attending church on Sunday morning was their only Sabbath duty. Such Anglicans—Puritans said—were behaving like Papists, who "thinke if they heare Masse in the morning, they may do what they list all the day after." Puritans also criticized "cold statute Protestants"—men and women who went to church on Sunday only because the Act of Uniformity required them to do so. Such indifferent churchgoers, one writer said, were "idle and fruitless hearers" who forgot what the preacher had said as soon as the service was over.[13]

John Northbrooke

Many Puritans were disturbed that sabbatarian laws were enforced in a lax manner. According to Humphrey Roberts, the author of *Ear-*

nest Complaint of Divers Vain, Wicked and Abused Exercises Practised on the Saboth Day (1572), "so little care have Officers and Magistrates to their charge and office, in punishing of the offenders, that to abuse the Sabbath day, is counted either no offence at all, or a very light crime."[14]

The Puritan John Northbrooke said that if sabbatarian laws were "executed justly," then "this dung and filth of ydleness would easily be rejected and cast oute of thys common wealth" (76).[15] In his tract, first published in 1577, Northbrooke lists many traditional pastimes that he thinks should be proscribed on the Sabbath, but he is not against all pastimes. "A faithful Christian doe sometimes play and sport himselfe, so that such play and pastime be in lawfull and honest things, and also done with moderation" (52). Honest recreation, he says, "is invented for man, and for his health, which maketh us the better, and more devout to serve God" (51–52).

Northbrooke approves of many traditional sports: "lifting and throwing of the stone, barre, or bowle, with hande or foote; casting of the darte, wrastling, shooting in long bowes, crossebowes, handgunnes" (107). He also approves of "ryding, trayning up men in the knowledge of martiall and warrelike affairs and exercises, knowledge to handle weapons, to leap and vault; running, swimming . . ." (107). Northbrooke also endorses hawking, hunting, and "playing at tennice." "These exercises are good, and have been used in ancient times, as we may read in Genesis" (107). (Where are the tennis players in Genesis?)

Northbrooke's treatise is in the form of a dialogue between two vaguely defined characters: Youth and Age. The former asks questions. The latter, who is Northbrooke's spokesman, supplies the answers. Like all Puritans, Age talks about the evils of popery. He accuses the pope of promoting idleness by coining many "holydays," or saints' days, which "traine up the people in ignorance and ydleness, whereby halfe of the year . . . was overpassed [spent] . . . in loytering and vaine pastimes . . . [and] in restrayning men from their handy labors and occupations" (44). These festival days were pagan in origin, for they were "never appointed nor commanded by God" (44).

Youth is puzzled by a seeming contradiction: The Sabbath is the day of rest, yet isn't rest a form of idleness? Age says there is good idleness and bad idleness: "The ydleness of the Sabboth day was commended for another purpose, that is for the studie and diligent desire of religion. . . . We must not cease from such workes as pertaine unto the true worshipping of God. . . . That is: First—in reading, interpreting, and hearing of Scriptures. Secondly—in prayers, public and private, in celebrating and receyving of sacraments. Thirdly—in collecting and gathering for the poor and indigent. Fourthly—in visiting and distributing to the poore, and making peace and unitie among neighbours, where any controversie was" (63–64).

Referring to a Sabbath question that preoccupied the ancient Jews, Age also says that it is lawful on the Sabbath "to fight in defense, that we may preserve the creature of God" (64). And it is lawful to perform any labor that is necessary to sustain life.

Youth is disturbed by what happened to a man in the Old Testament who broke the Sabbath. "Why then did Moses and Aaron commande the congregation to stone to death that man that was founde gathering stickes upon the Sabbath day?" (65). According to Age, the harsh punishment was merited because the man did not gather sticks out of necessity but out "of set purpose. . . . Obstinately, and stubbornely didde [he] breake and violate this commandment of God. . . . He was put to death for his contempt against the Lorde" (65).[16]

The main topic of the first section of the treatise is not idleness but playgoing. Age attacks spectacles of any kind, including the Roman spectacles that Augustine attacked, but he is mainly concerned about the plays produced on the London stage. "To speake my minde and conscience plainly . . . they are not tollerable, nor sufferable in any common weale, especially where the Gospell is preached" (84).

Age says that a Christian should not go to plays on Sunday—or any day. Playhouses are the haunt of thieves and prostitutes, so public plays should be outlawed. Playhouses should be "forbidden, and dissolved, and put downe by authorities, as the brothell houses and stewes are" (86). Other Puritan writers agreed. Describing the theater as the "chappel of Satan," one says that whoever visits it "shal finde there no want of yong ruffins, nor lacke of harlots, utterlie past al shame."[17] Respectable women were not supposed to go to playhouses.

Age does not want to banish all plays. Schools should be allowed to put on plays—preferably Latin plays—so long as the plays are free from ribaldry or profanity. Shakespeare would not pass muster with Northbrooke, nor would any other Elizabethan or Jacobean playwright. Youth is persuaded by Age's argument. He says he will absent himself "from such places and theatres, and shall provoke others to doe the like also" (103).

It was not only Puritans who disliked the theater. In 1596 the inhabitants of the Blackfriars district of London petitioned the London Privy Council to prevent Blackfriars Playhouse from reopening—saying that it would draw large crowds, which could result in the spread of disease, and that it would attract "all manner of vagrant and lewde persons."[18] They were not opposed to playgoing in general; they were opposed to having a theater in their neighborhood.

The petitioners also said that the plays disturbed Sunday worship. "The playhouse is so neere the Church [St. Paul's] that the noyse of the drummes and trumpetts will greatly disturbe and hinder both the ministers and parishioners in tyme of devine service and sermons." The petition did not succeed, for the playhouse reopened. Going to the theater was a popular Sunday activity. A Puritan writer said: "If you resorte to the Theatre . . . and other places of playes in the citye, you shall, on the Lorde's day, have these places so full as possibly they can throng." John Field, a Puritan writer, lamented that after so much preaching "theatres should be full, and churches be emptie." Theatergoing was very popular. Between 1567 and 1642, "some twenty three professional theatres were built in and around London. . . . Up to 20,000 people a week patronized them."[19]

In some parts of England Puritan sentiment was much stronger than it was in London, and playgoing was restricted or forbidden. When Shakespeare was growing up, traveling players were allowed to put on plays in Stratford, yet a few decades later Stratford's governing body forbade the staging of plays. In 1594 and 1595 Stratford had suffered two terrible fires. The plays were staged on the Sabbath, so the city leaders may have been persuaded by Puritan arguments that the fires were signs of God's wrath. The whole town, it was said, "hath been twice burnt for the breach of the Sabbath by the inhabitants."[20]

After discussing playgoing, Youth and Age briefly discuss music and dicing (gambling). Age disapproves of dicing. He approves of music, yet he thinks music should not play a major part in worship. According to Age, the "Papists" rely too much on music. "Singing [should] be not so much used and occupied in the church, that there be no time . . . left to preach the worde of God and holye doctrine; where by it cometh to passe that the people depart out of church full of musicke and harmonie, but yet hungerbaned and fasting, as touching heavenly foode and doctrine" (113). Age also says that the Mass, with its emphasis on ritual and ceremony, is like a play. Some Christian people "doe runne unto the church as to a stage playe, where they may be delighted with pyping and singing" (114).

It was commonplace for Puritans to associate everything they dis-liked with Catholics. A Puritan preacher, in a sermon given in 1608, says: "The ungodly Playes and enterludes so rife in this nation: what are they but a bastard of Babylon . . . a hellish device (the divels owne recreation to mock at holy things) by him delivered to the Heathen, from them to Papists, and from them to us."[21]

Age and Youth also discuss dancing, which Age calls "the vilest vice of all." Age attacks dancing on Sundays, but it is clear that he is against dancing in general. Youth is puzzled, since in the Bible "we have so many examples . . . of those that were godly, and daunced" (147). Age says that he is not against men and women dancing sepa-rately in order to celebrate God. He also does not disapprove of men dancing to stir up martial camaraderie—dancing "whereby men were exercised in warrelike affayres" (145). He is against contempo-rary dancing, where the sexes are mixed. The dances in the Bible, he says, "were spirituall, religious, and godly; not after our hoppings and leapings, and interminglings men with women" (150).

Youth remains unconvinced. He notes that the English aristoc-racy loves to dance. "What should move you to be so earnestly bent against this merye and pleasant pastyme of dauncing, sithe so many noblemen, gentlemen, ladies, and others, use it continuallye?" (155). Age says that contemporary dancing makes people lustful rather than merry. "And why are women so desirous rather to choose this man than that man to daunce withall . . . but onely to declare thereby how they are inflamed eche to other in filthie concupiscence and lust" (161). Age cites Augustine. "Saint Augustine sayth, It is much better to dygge . . . than to daunce (upon the Sabbaoth daye). Again he sayth, It is better that women should picke wool or spinne upon the Sabbaoth day, than they should daunce impudently and filthily" (165).

Age, like most Puritans, is angry that dancing remains a popular pastime in England—especially on Sunday. "What wold these [church] fathers say now, if they were presently alive, to see the wanton and filthie daunces that are now used, in this cleare day and light of the Gospell? What Sabboth dayes, what other days are there, nay, what nights are overpassed without dancing among a number at this time?" (175).

After deciding that Age is right about dancing, Youth repeats a question that he had asked in the first section of the treatise: What activities are appropriate on the day of rest? Age does not now mention sports and pastimes. He implies that the only appropriate activities on the Lord's Day are singing psalms and hymns, reading edifying works of history, and studying Scripture.

Perhaps Northbrooke now seems to advocate strict sabbatarianism because in the course of writing the treatise he learned that thousands of Protestants had been murdered in France. The St. Bartholomew Day's massacre, which began in Paris on August 24, 1572, and continued for several months in the provinces, resulted in the deaths of thousands of Protestants. Age asks: "Is it now (thinke you) a time to be mery, dice, daunce, and playe, seeing before our eyes how the blouddie Papistes murther and slaughter in all places rounde about us our poore brethren that professe the gospell of Jesu Christ?" (179).

Age speaks of the "dangerous times that we are in" (179). By "we" he means Protestants. Northbrooke, it seems, thought English Protestants needed to take a more sabbatarian view of the Lord's Day in order to strengthen their Protestant faith and make them better able to withstand the dangers posed by despotic Catholic countries.

Age ends with a dire warning: if England does not reform, especially with regard to observing the Sabbath, it will perish. "Excepte thou Englande, amende thy manners, and bring forth better fruites of the Gospell, thou wilte likewise perishe also" (179–180). England's "iniquitie," he says, will provoke God's wrath. He seems to have forgotten that French Protestants were being murdered because of their religious convictions—not because of their "iniquitie."

A decade after Northbrooke's tract was published it was reprinted, so it may have been popular. But it is unlikely that it was read by mainstream Anglicans, who disliked sabbatarianism. The *OED* quotes John Donne, who said "a sabbatarian righteousness is no righteousness." It also quotes another seventeenth-century writer who complains about "the rigour and strictnesse of Sabbatarian Ministers, in denying People recreations on the Sunday."

It would be wrong to say that mainstream Anglicans completely disagreed with Puritans about Sunday observance. They too decried certain activities on the Lord's Day. An Anglican divine lamented that on the Lord's Day "taverns, alehouses, and other unruly places be full, but the Lord's house [is] empty." Another warned that Sunday should not be misspent idly "in banqueting, in dicing and carding, in dancing and bearbaiting, in bowling and shooting, in laughing and whoring, and in such like beastly and filthy pleasures of the flesh."[22]

Ignoring the sermons of Puritan and mainstream Anglicans, many English men and women enjoyed a wide variety of sports and pastimes on Sunday—especially dancing. Dancing parties were held in private houses or in taverns and inns (with minstrels supplying the music). One dancer said: "The pox on them that fynd fault with them that daunce on the sabaoth dayes."[23]

During the reign of James I (1603–1625) about 20 percent of the population were not observant Christians, so they didn't care what Anglican divines said. They did not go to church on the Lord's Day—or they went only reluctantly to avoid paying a fine. Keith Thomas says that "a certain proportion [of the English population] remained throughout their lives utterly ignorant of the elementary tenets of Christian dogma." Church nonattendance varied by region. In some localities the penalty for not attending church was harsher than in others. In Ipswich sabbatarian laws were strictly enforced. "Paupers who stayed away from church went without poor relief."[24]

Puritans, who comprised roughly 15 percent of the population, had a high rate of literacy. They wrote many tracts about the Lord's Day, which they always called the Sabbath. In all their writings Puritans bewailed the state of religion in England. One said that most Englishmen would rather "sit at cards on the Sabbath by a hot fire than . . . sit at a Sermon with God in a cold church." Another complained that "heapes of our people"—meaning fellow Protestants—had abandoned popery while remaining in "an utter ignorance of the truth."[25] Puritan accounts of the dire state of religion in Elizabethan and Jacobean England must be regarded with caution, since Puritans tended to call Anglicans ungodly if they did not strictly observe the Lord's Day.

James I

When James I became king differences over Sunday observance had not come to the boiling point. All Anglicans—Puritan and mainstream—agreed that a despotic Catholic foreign power (either Spain or France) might attempt to restore a Catholic to the English throne. Jacobean Englishmen, Patrick Collinson says, wanted "to defend the integrity of the protestant church and nation against what was perceived to be a fearful popish enemy, partly intestine, partly identified with the pope himself and the powers of catholic Europe."[26]

James, like many Englishmen, was interested in the Sabbath question. In 1599, four years before he became king, he wrote a tract (*Basilikon Doron*) in which he defended traditional pastimes on Sundays and major holidays. He said they promoted cheerfulness, thereby defusing the political anger of the lower orders, who were prone to "judge and speake rashly of their Prince." Traditional pastimes are a "forme of contenting the peoples minds." There was nothing wrong with "playes and lawful games" on Sundays and holidays, provided that "the Sabboths be kept holy, and no unlawfull pastime be used."[27]

James did not clarify what he meant by an "unlawful" pastime. After ascending to the throne, James issued a proclamation that listed the pastimes he regarded as unlawful. "We are informed that there hath been heretofore great neglect in the kingdom of keeping the Sabbath day: For better observing of the same, and avoiding all impious prophanation, we do straightly charge and command, that no bear-baiting, Bull baiting, Enterludes, Common Plays, or other like disorders or unlawful Exercises or Pastimes, be frequented, kept, or used at any time, hereafter upon the Sabbath-day."[28] An interlude is a light skit or entertainment. A popular interlude was a jig, which was a short comic routine, usually bawdy, that concluded publicly staged plays. Jigs were also performed independently.

In this proclamation James takes a more sabbatarian view of Sunday observance than he did in 1599. According to one historian, James's views were shaped by his Scottish past. His proclamation was "consistent with the actions of the king who presided over Scottish assemblies and convocations that issued orders against profanations of the Sabbath in the 1590s."[29] Scottish Presbyterians were strong sabbatarians.

James, who was known for his irresolution, took a somewhat different view of Sunday observance in 1614. He vetoed "an act for the keeping of the Saboathe" that was passed by the so-called Addled Parliament. (That session of Parliament was called addled because it accomplished nothing. James dissolved it two months after it had convened.) James probably vetoed the bill because he thought Parliament was attempting to undermine his royal prerogative to decide upon the way Sunday should be observed—and undermine his power in other ways as well.

Concerned about the growing political strength of Puritans, James may have enlisted Ben Jonson to write an anti-Puritan play, *Bartholomew Fair*, which was staged in 1614. Jonson, who had been a Catholic, was known for his anti-Puritan views. In Jonson's play *The Alchemist* (1610), Ananias, a self-righteous and very gullible Puritan, makes it clear that he hates all traditional ritual and ceremony. "I hate *Traditions*. . . . They are *Popish*, all." Another character, Subtle, implies that Puritans are obsessed with the question of Sunday observance. They worry about "whether a Christian may hawk or hunt" on the Sabbath.

In 1618 James made another attempt to prescribe how Sunday should be observed. In a three-page declaration that came to be known as *The Book of Sports*, James says that many pastimes are lawful on Sunday, and he encourages his subjects to enjoy them. "As for our good people's lawful recreation, our pleasure likewise is, that after the end of divine service, our good people be not disturbed . . . or discouraged from any lawful recreation, such as dancing, either men or women, archery for men, leaping, vaulting, or any other such harmless recreation, nor from having of May-games, Whitsun-ales, and Morris-dances; and the setting up of Maypoles."[30]

James issued *The Book of Sports* in an attempt to address a problem that had arisen in Lancashire, where many Catholic recusants lived. An Anglican bishop complained that recusants were engaging in traditional pastimes on Sunday in order to disrupt Anglican services. He spoke of a popish plot "to keep the people from Church by dancing and other recreations, even in the time of divine service, especially on holy dayes, and the Lords day in the afternoon." In *The*

Book of Sports James warns the recusants that if they do not attend
church, they will not be allowed to enjoy traditional pastimes. "We
bar from this benefit and liberty [i.e., the enjoyment of traditional
pastimes] all such known Recusants, either men or women, as will
abstain from coming to church or divine service, being therefore un-
worthy of any lawful recreation after the said service, that will not
first come to church and serve God."[31]

The main reason James issued *The Book of Sports* was not to warn
recusant Catholics that if they stayed away from church on Sunday,
they would not be allowed to enjoy traditional pastimes. This was an
unenforceable threat. The main reason was to make it clear to the
English people that it was the king's prerogative to define Sunday
observance, so James required *The Book of Sports* to be read by ministers from the pulpit. But the requirement met with so much opposition that it soon was dropped. Moreover, some parishes enforced
sabbatarian laws against dancing and other pastimes. In 1618 the
Somerset bench ordered the mother and reputed father of a bastard
to be flogged "till their bodies shall be bloody" and two fiddlers to
play before the couple to "make known their lewdness in begetting
the said base child upon the Sabbath day coming from dancing."[32]

The Book of Sports inflamed sabbatarian sentiment, and it may
have increased tensions between Anglican priests and their Puritan
parishioners. Some Anglican priests thought mixed dancing was acceptable on Sunday so long as it did not interfere with divine service. In *The Spanish Curate* (1622), a play by Beaumont and Fletcher,
a parson probably reflects the sentiment of many moderate priests
when he deplores the fact that parishioners have "Puritan hearts"
and have "spurned . . . all pastimes." The parson thinks Sunday pastimes, including dancing, are good, for they encourage the healthy
mingling of the sexes and thereby promote marriage.[33]

During James's reign the Anglican hierarchy was generally conciliatory toward Puritans. An influential bishop was said to be "apter to reconcile differences rather than make them." But it became increasingly difficult to reconcile differences between Puritans and mainstream Anglicans. When a mainstream Anglican praised *The Book of Sports* and teased his Puritan neighbor by asking him "if he would go dance with him the nexte sunne day," the Puritan neighbor replied: "Take heede that you be not dancing in Hell before that daye." In 1622 the Bishop of Exeter warned that "there needs no prophetical spirit to discern [that] . . . there is a storm coming towards our Church."[34]

When Charles I became king in 1625, Puritans were hopeful that he would address some of their concerns, and at first he did. He signed a bill proscribing bear- and bullbaiting, interludes, and common plays on Sunday. A year later he signed a Sunday observance law that restricted travel and butchering on Sunday. Yet it soon became apparent that Charles would not be sympathetic to the concerns of Puritans, for he made William Laud, an Anglican bishop with strongly anti-Puritan views, his main advisor. Laud regarded Puritans as the enemies of the church and state. "Puritanisme," a Laud supporter said, "[is] the roote of all rebellions and disobedient intractableness in Parliaments etc. and all schisme and sauciness in the Countrey, nay in the church, itself."[35] Laud and his supporters labeled Puritan anyone who questioned their view of royal authority.

Laud, who became Archbishop of Canterbury in 1633 (he was an influential advisor for several years before assuming this post), defended traditional Anglican ritual and attacked sabbatarianism. Insisting on conformity, Laud prosecuted Puritan pamphleteers for sedition, and he removed priests from their pulpits if they did not follow his prescription for Sunday worship and Sunday observance. In Laud's view "Calvinist" and "Puritan" were interchangeable terms.

(Queen Elizabeth would not have agreed with this view.) The Church of England, he said, was Arminian, not Calvinist. In the seventeenth century, mainstream Anglicans often were called Arminians, after the Dutch theologian Arminius. English Arminians, like their Dutch counterparts, rejected Calvin's doctrine of predestination. English Arminians considered the Anglican church to be the bulwark of English political stability. In their view radical Protestants were potentially seditious because they lacked respect for the Anglican hierarchy. Calvinists opposed the king's policies whereas Arminians generally supported them.

After Laud became powerful, a cynical riddle made the rounds: "What do the Arminians hold?" That is, what are the theological views of Arminians? The answer: "All the best deaneries and bishoprics."[36.] Laud drew up a list of prominent divines—labeling them either P. for Puritan or O. for Orthodox. Those labeled P. were denied a high position in the church.

It was not only Puritans who objected to Laud's attempt to enforce conformity in Sunday worship and Sunday observance. Many mainstream Anglicans suspected that Charles, whose wife was Catholic, wanted the Anglican church to reconcile with the Church of Rome. Worried about Charles's religious views, Parliament passed a bill in 1628–29 stating that "whosoever shall bring in innovation in religion, or . . . seek to extend or introduce Popery or Arminianism, or any other opinion disagreeing from the true and orthodox Church, shall be reputed a capital enemy to this kingdom and commonwealth."[37]

George Herbert

In 1630, when George Herbert was ordained, many Puritans had given up hope that the Anglican church could be reformed. They especially objected to Laud's view of Sunday observance. Hugh Peter, a Puritan who was ordained into the Anglican church in June 1623, said that "truly, my reason for myself and others to go [to New England]" was the king's policy about Sunday observance: "*Had not the Book for Encouragement of Sports on the Sabbath come forth, many had staid*" (emphasis added).[38] In July 1635 Peter left for New England, where he became of one of the first governors of Harvard College.

Taking up the post of a country parson was a radical career change for Herbert, offspring of a powerful and wealthy family that was closely associated with the court of James I. Herbert's mother, Lady Magdalen, who bore ten children (George was the fifth of seven sons), was an intellectual as well as a close friend of John Donne, who dedicated a cycle of poems to her. Herbert's career began auspiciously. At Cambridge he held the prestigious post of University Orator, and soon after graduation he was a member of Parliament. When Charles I ascended to the throne in 1625, the Herbert family fell out of favor, so Herbert's governmental career was over.[39]

Did Herbert become a parson because he had failed to gain a government post or because he felt a calling for the position? It seems he requested ordination in 1624 (a year before James died), so he may have wanted to become an Anglican priest for some time. In the small village of Bemerton there would be little opportunity for the kind of conversation he enjoyed at court or at his mother's house—what he calls the "quick returns of courtesy and wit." Donne said that Lady Magdalen's house was a court where one heard "the conversation of the best."[40] Yet Herbert appears to have been a dedicated country parson. He restored the church in Bemerton and he wrote *The Country Parson*, which suggests that he thought a great deal about what a parson should do, especially about what a parson should do on Sundays, which he calls his "day of joy."

Herbert says a good Christian should go to church twice on Sunday, and he should refrain from working. *"They labor profanely,"* Herbert says, *"when on the Lord's day they do unnecessary servile work"* (218).[41] Herbert thinks a parson should try to be a good preacher. "The Country Parson preacheth constantly: the pulpit is his joy and his throne" (204). The preacher should remember that his parishioners may often have other things on their minds than what he has to say; many "come with less prepared hearts than they ought" (207). A good preacher tells stories, "for men heed and remember [them] better than exhortations, which though earnest, yet often die with the sermons" (204). .

Herbert also says that parishioners should not leave early. Some parishioners "oftentimes go·out of church before he hath blessed them" (253). The country parson should also instruct "his people how to carry themselves in divine service . . . by no means enduring either talking or sleeping, or gazing, or leaning, or half-kneeling, or any undutiful behaviour in them, but causing them when they sit or stand or kneel, to do all in a straight and steady posture" (203). A good Christian, he says in the poem "The Church-Porch," should not let his mind wander during the service: "Let vain or busy thoughts have there no part."

Though Herbert exhorts his parishioners to go to church twice on Sunday, he also tells those who do so that they should not assume they will always be in the "peaceable state"—that is, free from sinful temptations. Churchgoers should be "very vigilant, and not to let go the reins as soon as the horse goes easy" (248). Herbert stresses that a Christian's life is a constant struggle against the powers of darkness, which he calls "the manifold wiles of Satan." Going to church on Sunday fortifies the soul in its struggle against these dark forces, but there is also the danger that churchgoing may become a Sunday habit devoid of meaning. Parishioners should "take heed lest their quiet [peaceable state] betray them (as it is apt to do) to a coldness and carelessness in their devotions. . . . [They need] to labour still to be . . . fervent in Christian duties" (248).

The country parson should also warn parishioners about two temptations: the feeling that there is no God, that "all goes by chance or wit"; and the feeling that there is a God but they are lost to him—"God doth forsake and persecute them, and there is none to deliver them" (248).

Does Herbert also worry about the persistence of pagan practices, including sun worship? In *The Country Parson* Herbert makes the same point Augustine made: God controls the sun. "It is observable that if anything could presume of an inevitable course and constancy in its operations, certainly it should be . . . the sun in heaven. . . . Yet when God pleased, the sun stood still" (239). In the poem "Sunday" Herbert says: "This day my Saviour rose,/And did enclose this light for his." The Savior's light trumps the sun's light. In "Misery" Herbert says that God's light is never eclipsed, whereas the sun's light occasionally is; for this reason, "the sun holds down his head for shame,/Dead with eclipses." Herbert, Ann Pasternak Slater says, sees divine providence in every movement of the sun.[42]

It is unlikely that Herbert worried a great deal about sun worship in England, yet in "Ungratefulness" he implies that if it weren't for Jesus' sacrifice Christians would be sun worshipers:

> Lord, with what bounty and rare clemency
> Hast thou redeem'd us from the grave!
> If thou hadst let us run,
> Gladly had man ador'd the sun.

Sun worship is a temptation for humankind. Many pagan practices continued to exist in rural parts of England. In 1628 Sir Benjamin

Rudyerd told the House of Commons that there were parts of northern England and Wales "which were scarce in Christendom, where God was little better known than amongst the Indians."[43]

There is a debate among historians about "pagan survivalism." Jean Delumeau says that "on the eve of the Reformation, the average westerner was but superficially christianized." Eamon Duffy disagrees. Acknowledging that some prayers and practices lay outside the bounds of fifteenth-century orthodoxy, he says that they "cannot sensibly be called pagan. . . . They represent the appropriation and adaptation to lay needs and anxieties of a range of sacred gestures and prayers. . . . This is not paganism, but lay Christianity."[44]

Herbert is more worried about disorder in the church than about the survival of pagan practices. In the first stanza of "Church-Rents and Schisms," the church is a rose that has been attacked by a worm. In the second stanza the church is his mother who has become sick.

> Debates and fretting jealousies
> Did worm and work within you more and more,
> Your colour faded, and calamities
> Turned your ruddy [face] into pale and bleak:
> Your health and beauty both began to break.

In the third stanza the church is a structure that is being torn apart by the winds of schism.

Herbert's religious views continue to be the subject of scholarly controversy, but it is clear from many poems that his view of worship is different from that of most Puritans. For one thing, Herbert called the Lord's Day Sunday, not the Sabbath, and a decade before he became parson he attacked a Scottish Presbyterian who had written a savage criticism of the Anglican church. W. H. Auden points out that Herbert "took enormous pains to explain to his parishioners, most of whom were probably illiterate, the significance of every ritual act in the liturgy, and to instruct them in the meaning of the Church Calendar."[45]

In "The Windows" Herbert praises stained-glass windows, which Puritans thought were idolatrous.

> Lord, how can man preach thy eternal word?
> He is a brittle crazy glass:
> Yet in thy temple thou dost him afford
> This glorious and transcendent place,
> To be a window, through thy grace.
>
> But when thou dost anneal in glass thy story,
> Making thy life to shine within
> The holy Preacher's; then the light and glory
> More rev'rend grows, and more doth win:
> Which else shows watrish, bleak, and thin.
>
> Doctrine and life, colours and light, in one
> When they combine and mingle, bring
> A strong regard and awe: but speech alone
> Doth vanish like a flaring thing,
> And in the ear, not conscience ring.

"Anneal in glass" means "make into stained-glass windows." Herbert says the stained-glass windows promote "a strong regard and awe." Though Herbert took preaching seriously, he did not think preaching and the reading of Scripture should be the only components of worship. To strengthen faith the church cannot rely on "speech alone." It also needs "colours and light."

Herbert also disagrees with the Puritans about the role of music in worship. The last two lines of "Church-Music" are: "But if I travel in your [music's] company, / You know the way to heaven's door." Twice a week Herbert went to the cathedral church in Salisbury to hear its choir and organ. Izaak Walton, Herbert's first biographer, says that "at his return [he] would say that his time spent in prayer and cathedral music elevated his soul." He also played music regularly with a group that met in Salisbury. "The Sunday before his death, he rose suddenly from his bed or couch, called for one of his instruments," and sang a stanza from a poem that he had set to music. The poem was "Sunday."[46]

"Sundays observe," Herbert enjoins in "The Church-Porch." How should Sundays be observed? The last stanza of "Sunday" begins, "Thou art a day of mirth." Puritans disliked the word "mirth" because they associated it with the traditional pastimes they deplored. In several of Herbert's poems "mirth" means sensual pleasure, but in "Sunday" mirth is associated with the Resurrection. Herbert implies that the absence of mirth is akin to the Christian sin of despair. In "Affliction (1)" he says: "My mirth and edge was lost; a blunted knife / Was of more use than I." In "Dullness" he begins:

> Why do I languish thus, drooping and dull,
>   As if I were all earth?
> O give me quickness, that I may with mirth
>   Praise thee brim-full!

For Herbert the Lord's Day is a day of mirth. According to Walton, Herbert "would often say . . . [that] religion does not banish mirth, but only moderates and sets rules to it."[47]

What about the "honest mirth or recreation" that James I advocates in *The Book of Sports*? In *The Country Parson* Herbert says nothing about *The Book of Sports*, but he does say the parson should respect "Old Customes." Herbert discusses mirth in a one-paragraph chapter entitled "The Parson in Mirth." Mirth is a social disposition the parson cultivates in order to be an effective leader of his parish. Herbert begins by saying that "the Country Parson is generally sad because he knows nothing but the Cross of Christ . . . [and] he meets continually with two most sad spectacles, Sin and Misery" (236). Yet the parson knows "that nature will not bear everlasting droopings, and that pleasantness of disposition is a great key to do good. . . . Wherefore he condescends to [shows an understanding of] human frailties both in himself and others and intermingles some mirth in his discourses occasionally, according to the pulse of the hearer" (236). Or, to put it another way, a sense of humor is helpful when the parson is talking to his parishioners.

Herbert talks about mirth in other chapters of *The Country Parson*. A parson should use mirth to defuse quarrels among parishioners. "If he perceive in company any discourse tending to ill, either by the wickedness or quarrelsomeness thereof, he either prevents it judiciously, or breaks it off seasonably by some diversion. Wherein a pleasantness of disposition is of great use, men being willing to sell the interest and engagement of their discourses for no price sooner than that of mirth" (222). An injection of mirth enables people to back away from their stubbornly held positions.

In "The Church-Porch" Herbert suggests that mirth is the soil in which conversation grows.

> Pick out of mirth, like stones out of thy ground,
> Profaneness, filthiness, abusiveness.
> These are the scum, with which coarse wits abound.

Profaneness, filthiness, abusiveness are stones in that soil—i.e., enemies of conversation. In the poem Herbert makes a number of related points about conversation. One should command one's temper and one should avoid quarrelsomeness. "Be calm in arguing: for fierceness makes / Error a fault, and truth discourtesy."

Herbert, a biographer says, "was exactly the kind of holy, dedicated minister that King Charles and Bishop Laud longed to see in every parish church in England."[48] Yet Herbert's approach to dissent was different from Laud's. "The Country Parson, if there be any of his parish that hold strange doctrines, useth all possible diligence to reduce them to the common faith" (231).

When talking to parishioners who hold "strange doctrines"—he is referring to Papists and schismatics (Puritans)—the parson should "fit his discourse to them that it may effectually pierce their hearts and convert them" (231). The work of persuasion is not easy, but the parson has "two great helps and powerful persuaders on his side: the one, a strict religious life; the other, an humble and ingenuous search of truth, being unmoved in arguing, and void of all contentiousness" (232). In other words, the parson should treat Papists and Puritans with respect; he should never berate them or consider them immoral for holding "strange doctrines."

The parson hopes to persuade a Papist to become an Anglican by discussing the question of whether a church "be a rule to itself," as is the Catholic church, or whether it should submit to sovereign authority, as the Anglican church does. He would take a different approach when talking to a schismatic. The discussion should center on what to do about scandal, since Puritans thought the Anglican church was rife with corruption. Schismatics, Herbert says, should keep in mind that a concern with scandal should not be the reason for disobeying authority, "especially since in disobeying there is scandal also" (232).

What if a Papist or schismatic continues to disagree with him? Herbert doesn't address this question, but he stresses the importance of talking to one's parishioners. Talking is more important than preaching, for "at sermons and prayers men may sleep or wander, but when one is asked a question he must discover what he is" (226). Parsons should read Plato's Socratic dialogues in order to learn how to rigorously yet politely discuss questions.

Herbert thought the country parson should work hard to heal divisions in the community. After fulfilling his public duties on Sunday—"having read Divine Service twice fully, and preached in the morning, and catechized in the afternoon"—the parson should spend the remainder of the day "either in reconciling neighbours that are at variance, or in visiting the sick, or in exhortations to some of his flock" who have not heard his sermons (207). Why are the neighbors at variance? There could be many reasons, including differences over religion.

The parson should also meet with his parishioners on Sunday evening. "At night, he thinks it a very fit time, both suitable to the joy of the day and without hindrance to public duties, either to entertain some of the neighbours or to be entertained of them" (207). What does the parson talk about at these informal gatherings? "He takes occasion to discourse *of such things as are both profitable and pleasant, and to raise up their minds to apprehend God's good blessing to our Church and state—that order is kept in the one, and peace in the other, without disturbance or interruption of public divine offices*" (207; emphasis Herbert's). He wants his parishioners to recognize that it would be a terrible thing if religious differences undermined England's political order.

Thus, Sunday is for Herbert not only a day for celebrating the Resurrection; it is also a day for promoting harmony in his parish through prayer, preaching, and conversation. "The Country Parson desires to be all to his parish, and not only a pastor, but a lawyer also, and a physician" (228). Because he is a physician to his parish, the country parson should also talk to his parishioners on weekdays, when they are more likely to be candid and forthcoming. "For there he shall find his flock most naturally as they are, wallowing in the midst of their affairs; whereas on Sunday it is easy for them to compose themselves to order, which they put on as their holy-day clothes" (217). The country parson should visit everyone in his parish—going to "the poorest cottage, though he even creep into it, and though it smell never so loathsomely; for both God is there also, and those for whom God died" (219).

Herbert's parson cultivates mirth and seeks out conversation with his parishioners because he is preoccupied with reconciling differences. By contrast, Laud, who was "neither an agreeable nor a convivial character," disliked discussion. His biographer says that Laud always tried to stifle dissent. "The way to secure orthodoxy was . . . to enforce it, and to silence all disputation which tended to reopen a closed question."[49]

In 1633, six months after Herbert died, Laud tried to enforce religious conformity in England. He reissued *The Book of Sports* and required it to be read in all churches. Laud warned the English people that if they did not take part in traditional pastimes on Sunday, they would be viewed as seditious.

Puritans and many mainstream Anglicans were appalled by Laud's insistence that *The Book of Sports* be read in church, and many refused to do so. "When our minister was reading it," one wrote, "I was seized with a chill and horror not to be described. Now, thought I, iniquity is established by a law, and sinners are hardened in their sinful ways! What sore judgments are to be expected upon so wicked and guilty a nation!" Clerics who defied Laud lost their parishes and their flock. Some became Separatists—holding secret conventicles. Others left for America. A leading Puritan remarked that "ministers [were] driven out of England for not reading the booke of sports, and they are now separatists beyond [the] sea."[50]

Public opinion was polarized. There were tracts for Laud's policies and tracts against them. Puritan authors often thundered that God had already begun to punish England for breaking the Sabbath. In *A Divine Tragedie Lately Acted or . . . Gods Judgements upon Sabbath-Breakers* (1636), Henry Burton describes many calamities that England had suffered since 1633, including fires, bad harvests, murders, and grotesque deaths. A prominent Puritan predicted that "such dreadfull divisions will be amongst God's people . . . as will equalize the greatest persecutions."[51]

It is clear that Laud's rage for order fomented disorder. The assertion of royal power to regulate the Sabbath soon weakened royal power. "There is considerable evidence," Leah Marcus says, "that *The Book of Sports* exacerbated contemporary opposition to the central government rather than defusing it as the Stuart kings had hoped." On September 8, 1641, the House of Commons defied Laud's policy. It resolved that "the Lord's day should be duly observed and sanctified; that all dancing, or other sports either before or after divine service be forborne and restrained." Twenty months later Parliament ordered *The Book of Sports* to be publicly burned.[52] In December 1644 it found Laud guilty of high treason. He was beheaded in early January 1645.

The anti-Laudians triumphed, yet some Englishmen refused to observe the Lord's Day in a sabbatarian manner. In 1646 Thomas Laurence, who was Herbert's successor at Bemerton, was "sequestered" (removed from office) by Parliament. It was alleged by local Puritans that in Laurence's churchyard on "every Saboth day" there was bowling and kittling (that is, playing skittles or nine-pins). There was also dancing on Sunday "in his own howse, wch hee Countenanced, with the presence of him selfe and family & maynteined it to bee very fitt for Recreation."[53] For Laurence and his family Sunday was a holiday as well as a holy day.

Chapter Four

Sunday in Eighteenth-Century England and Scotland

*O*ne hundred years after Archbishop Laud tried to enforce uniformity in the Church of England and prescribe how Sunday should be observed, the English religious landscape had changed dramatically. "This is the land of sects," Voltaire says in *Letters on England* (1733). "An Englishman, as a free man, goes to Heaven by whatever route he likes." In his brief survey of religion in England, Voltaire discusses Quakers, Anglicans, Presbyterians, Socinians, Arians, and anti-Trinitarians. Voltaire thought it was politically healthy for a country to have many religious sects. "If there were only one religion in England there would be [the] danger of despotism, if there were two they would cut each other's throats, but there are thirty, and they live in peace and happiness."[1]

Voltaire exaggerated the religious diversity of England. Most Englishmen—roughly 85 percent—were Anglicans. Dissenting Protestants accounted for approximately 8 percent of the population, whereas Catholics had dwindled to 1 percent. A Dissenter—also known as a Non-Conformist—was a Protestant who did not subscribe to the Thirty-Nine Articles of the Church of England. The

Toleration Act (1689) made it possible for Dissenters to worship publicly, but they were penalized in other ways. They could not vote, be elected to Parliament, hold civil office, attend Oxford or Cambridge, or be called to the bar. They could hold civil office if they practiced "occasional conformity" by taking Communion in the Anglican church once a year.

The Toleration Act was a boon for Dissenters. In the next two decades more than 2,500 new meeting-houses, where Dissenters worshiped, were licensed. (There were about 9,500 Anglican parish churches.) Many Protestants came to England from abroad. Fifty thousand Huguenots emigrated from France after the revocation of the Edict of Nantes in 1685; a much smaller number of Moravians came from Germany and Moravia in 1728. There were also many home-grown Protestant sects, including Independents, Congregationalists, Baptists, and Philadelphians.[2] The Philadelphians (who had nothing to do with Franklin's City of Brotherly Love) were a small Protestant sect that was influenced by the German mystic Jacob Boehme.

The Toleration Act did not extend to Catholics, Quakers, anti-Trinitarians, Jews, or Muslims. By law they were not allowed to worship, yet these laws were rarely enforced. As a French visitor said, "there are a great many Acts of Parliament . . . against Popery and Papists; but those laws are not strictly executed."[3] When Boswell came to London, Catholics, Quakers, and Jews worshiped openly. In 1750 there were roughly 8,000 Jews in England.[4]

Voltaire did not like Presbyterians. They were responsible for "the sanctification of Sunday in the three kingdoms [England, Scotland, Ireland]. On that day both work and play are forbidden, which is double the severity of Catholic Churches. There are no operas, plays or concerts in London on Sunday; even cards are so expressly forbidden that only people of standing and what are called respectable people, play on that day. The rest of the nation goes to the sermon, the tavern, and the ladies of the town."[5] The lack of things to do on Sunday, Voltaire suggests, increases immorality.

Voltaire is wrong to suggest that only Presbyterians were sabbatarians. According to another French visitor, Henri Misson de Valbourg, who came to England in 1698, "The English of all Sects, but particularly the Presbyterians, make Profession of being very strict Observers of the Sabbath Day."[6] The Presbyterians were by all accounts the strictest sabbatarians, but Samuel Johnson's mother, an Anglican, had the same view of Sunday observance as James Boswell's mother, a Presbyterian.

After the Restoration in 1660, sabbatarianism became a weaker force, yet Parliament continued to debate sabbatarian legislation. It was mainly concerned with the regulation of commerce—not with the restriction of sports and pastimes. In 1677 the Sunday Observance Act was passed. It prohibited Sunday work and trade, "excepting acts of necessity and mercy, sale of milk, dressing of meat in inns, cookshops and victualling houses." It also limited Sunday legal proceedings and restricted Sunday traveling. In 1698 two acts were passed that allowed the Sunday sale of mackerel before and after divine service, and allowed forty Thames watermen to ply for hire on Sundays.[7]

At the end of the seventeenth century, societies for the reformation of manners were founded to ensure that sabbatarian laws were enforced. In 1708 the London Society for the Reformation of Manners initiated 1,187 prosecutions for Sabbath breaking. Many Englishmen resented its efforts, claiming that it targeted the poor, who often had to work on Sunday. In 1724 the number of those arrested declined to 600. It is possible that fewer arrests were made because Sabbath breaking had become less common, but it is more likely that the authorities were increasingly reluctant to enforce these laws. In 1738 the society issued its last report.[8]

William Law

In the first half of the eighteenth century, support for sabbatarianism was waning in England, but it was given a boost by William Law, an Anglican divine who translated Jacob Boehme and wrote a bestseller: *A Serious Call to a Devout and Holy Life* (1728).[9] Law's book had a profound effect on Samuel Johnson, who told Boswell that he became religious after reading it when he was a student at Oxford. Law's book also influenced John Wesley, the founder of Methodism. By 1816 twenty editions of *A Serious Call* had been published.

Law received holy orders, but he was a nonjuror so he could not pursue a career in the Anglican church. A nonjuror was a citizen who refused, for a variety of reasons, to take the oath of loyalty to the reigning monarch. Law became tutor to Edward Gibbon, the father of the historian. In his autobiography, Gibbon says that Law's "vigorous mind [had] been clouded by enthusiasm."[10] By "enthusiasm" Gibbon means religious fanaticism. After leaving the Gibbon household, Law led a quasi-monastic life dedicated to charitable works, particularly the education of the poor.

In *A Serious Call* Law disapproves of Christians who regard the Lord's Day as a holiday as well as a holy day. He also questions the devoutness of many churchgoing Christians. He supports his argument with brief character sketches—giving his characters Latin names that describe their predominant passion.

Penitens, a prosperous businessman who has become a devout Christian on his deathbed, feels remorseful that he went to church only when it did not interfere with business or pleasure. "It is true,

I have lived in the communion of the Church and generally frequented its worship and service on Sundays, when I was neither too idle or not otherwise disposed of by my business and pleasures." Had he put Christianity at the center of his life, he would have acted differently. "I had been oftener at church, more devout when there, and more fearful of ever neglecting it" (27).

Calidus, a rich businessman, thinks of Sunday as a holiday. (Calidus—Latin for "hot"—signifies a man who is "fervent in business.") Calidus also talks about Saturday as a day off. "Calidus will tell you, with great pleasure, that he has been in this hurry for so many years, and that it must have killed him long ago, but that it has been a rule with him to get out of the town every Saturday and make the Sunday a day of quiet and good refreshment in the country" (35). In the late seventeenth century rich merchants began to go away to weekend villas.[11] According to Law, many "trading people" are like Calidus. "You see them all the week buried in business, unable to think of anything else, and then spending the Sunday in idleness and refreshment, in wandering into the country, in such visits and jovial meetings as make it often the worst day of the week" (36).

There is also Flavia—a spoiled rich woman who is catty and shallow. (Flavia, which derives from the family name of several Roman emperors, stands for "worldly pomp, half innocent, half vicious.")[12] She goes to church on Sunday but spends the rest of the day in idle conversation. "If you visit Flavia on the Sunday, you will always meet good company, you will know what is doing in the world, you will hear the latest lampoon, be told who wrote it, and who is meant by every name that is in it" (63). Flavia thinks of herself as a strict observer of Sunday, but she is deceiving herself. "Flavia thinks they are atheists that play at cards on the Sunday, but she will tell you the nicety of all the games, what cards she held, how she played them, and the history of all that happened at play, as soon as she comes from church" (63).

Flavia is not only shallow; she is also cruel. She wields sabbatarianism as a stick to hurt those who are dependent upon her. "But still she has so great a regard for the holiness of the Sunday, that she has turned a poor old widow out of her house as a profane wretch for having been found once mending her clothes on the Sunday night" (63). Even though Flavia goes to church "most Sundays in the year . . . she has no grounds from Scripture to think she is in the way of salvation. For her whole life is in direct opposition to all those tempers and practices which the Gospel has made necessary to salvation" (64).

Law reproves Flavia for gossiping on Sunday, but he disapproves of gossip on any day of the week. "Whatever raises a levity of mind, a trifling spirit, renders the soul incapable of seeing, apprehending, and relishing the doctrines of piety" (66). He criticizes those who "fancy that they must be grave and solemn at church, but may be silly and frantic at home; that they must live by some rule on the Sunday, but may spend other days by chance" (47). If a person has some free time, he should use it to pray, read Scripture, or help others. "He that truly knows why he should spend any time well, knows that it is never allowable to throw any time away" (47).

Law's view of Sunday observance is similar to the views of John Northbrooke and other sixteenth- and seventeenth-century Puritans. Christians, Law says, should "abstain on the Lord's day from any innocent and lawful things, as traveling, visiting, common conversation, and discoursing upon worldly matters, as trade, news, and the like" (68). Instead, they "should devote the day, besides the public worship, to greater retirement, reading, devotion, instruction, and works of charity" (68). Law wants to purify Christianity. Christians are devout "when there is the same spirit in us that there was in the Apostles and primitive Christians, when we feel the weight of religion as they did" (151). Law, unlike most Puritans, praises Constantine—claiming that Christianity was "in its greatest glory and purity" during his reign, "when the faith of our Nicene Creed was established" (87).

According to Law, purity is less about what Christians do than about "the inward state of our minds." Many people call themselves Christians but they are heathens insofar as they are mired "in self-love and indulgence, in sensual pleasures and diversions, in the vanity of dress, the love of show and greatness" (11). The fact that they go to church on Sunday is of no consequence. "They who add devotion to such a life, must be said to pray as Christians but live as heathens" (11).

Reassuring his readers that he is not asking them to become saints, Law says that his description of a devout and holy life "is not intended to possess people's minds with a scrupulous anxiety and discontent in the service of God" (23). Yet he sets the bar for being a devout Christian very high. Devout Christians possess "such a humility of spirit as renders us meek and lowly in the whole course of our lives, as shows itself in our dress, our person, our conversation, our enjoyment of the world" (41).

In a journal entry for a Sunday in December 1793, Boswell says that he is reading *A Serious Call* because it is "the book which I have mentioned as having made Dr. Johnson first think earnestly of religion after his childhood." Boswell soon decides that he does not like *A Serious Call*. "I wondered at his [Johnson's] approbation of it." *A Serious Call*, he says, is unrealistic: "The scope of it is to make a religious life inconsistent with all the feelings and views which animate this state of being, and in short to make us ascetics upon the monastic plan. It had a dreary influence on my mind, at present disposed to be gloomy." Boswell read passages from *A Serious Call* to his son James, who "very sensibly observed: 'Such books do a great deal of harm.'" Though Boswell "resolved to read it through," he never mentions it again.[13]

Johnson read *A Serious Call* when he was twenty, but he continued to admire it when he was older. In the fourth edition of his *Dictionary* there are almost 200 citations from Law's work. According to Henry Hitchings, "Law more than any other quoted author can be thought of as a spokesman for Johnson's most cherished views."[14] Yet Johnson's view of Sunday observance was not the same as Law's. Johnson was not a strict sabbatarian. He enjoyed Sunday afternoon dinners with friends, where the conversation ranged freely over many questions, sacred and profane.

Johnson admired *A Serious Call* because he agreed with Law that the Christian God was a God of judgment—a God to be feared—whereas most of his friends preferred to think of God as benevolent. *A Serious Call*, Law says, is intended to give readers "a just fear of living in sloth and idleness and in the neglect of such virtues as they will want at the day of judgment" (23). In a diary entry for August 1777 Johnson says: "Faith in some proportion to Fear."[15]

Joseph Addison

Reading *A Serious Call* changed Johnson's life, but in his view of Sunday observance Johnson is much closer to Joseph Addison. (Addison, like Johnson, came from Lichfield, where his father was dean of Lichfield Cathedral.) In his journal Boswell quotes Johnson as saying that "Addison . . . was a great man. His learning was not very deep, but his morality, his humour, and his elegance of writing set him very high." In the *Life of Addison*, Johnson says: "If any judgement be made, from his books, of his moral character, nothing will be found but purity and excellence." He also notes that Addison's "religion has nothing in it enthusiastick or superstitious." In the eighteenth century "superstitious" was often a code word for Catholic. Johnson means that Addison's religious views are moderate. "His morality is neither dangerously lax, nor impracticably rigid."[16]

In the eighteenth-century English-speaking world, the essays Addison and his collaborator Richard Steele wrote for the *Tatler* and the *Spectator* were considered required reading by every educated person, and they were also considered a guide for conduct. Soon after Boswell arrived in London he wrote in his journal: "I felt strong dispositions to be a Mr. Addison." In the journal of his first year in London Boswell mentions the *Spectator* eleven times. One Sunday, after returning from church, he went to his friend William Temple's chambers "and we read some of Mr. Addison's papers in *The Spectator* with infinite relish."[17]

The essays that constitute the *Spectator*, which were published without attribution, were written under the byline of a Mr. Spectator. Addison and Steele don't define him very carefully. He is a genial man who is interested in many aspects of English life, from London coffeehouses to country life. Addison wrote most of the essays in which Mr. Spectator examines literary and aesthetic questions; he also wrote a number of essays on religion.

Spectator 112 is about Sunday worship in a rural church. Law was disturbed that many churchgoers were not devout, but Addison thinks churchgoing is a good thing whatever one's state of mind. Mr. Spectator says: "I am always very well pleased with a Country *Sunday*; and think, if keeping holy the Seventh Day were only a human institution, it would be the best Method that could have been thought of for the polishing and civilizing of Mankind." Addison, like many people, assumes that Sunday is the seventh day of the week because it is for Christians the day of rest.[18]

Communal worship on Sunday, Addison suggests, is a civilizing force. "It is certain the Country-People would soon degenerate into a kind of Savages and Barbarians, were there not such frequent Returns of a stated Time, in which the whole Village meet together with their best Faces, and in their cleanliest Habits, to converse with one another upon indifferent Subjects, hear their Duties explained to them, and join together in Adoration of the supreme Being." Churchgoing enables people from various walks of life to get together, not only to celebrate the Resurrection but also to engage in conversation.

Churchgoing is good for another reason: it takes people out of their ordinary routines. "*Sunday* clears away the Rust of the whole Week, not only as it refreshes in their Minds the Notions of Religion, but as it puts both the Sexes upon appearing in their most agreeable Forms, and exerting such Qualities as to give them a Figure in the Eye of the Village." Going to church is likely to strengthen people's faith—and make them more sociable. Addison worried about political disorder, which he called the "rage of Party." If the English became more sociable, the chances of violent political discord would decrease. Addison's fears were not excessive, for many observers thought English politics were heating up to a dangerous degree.

Mr. Spectator refers to Sir Roger de Coverley, who is the landlord of the "whole Congregation." The church is on Sir Roger's estate, and the members of the congregation are tenants to whom he leases property. Sir Roger is a mildly eccentric English gentleman who is the most well-known creation of Addison and Steele. Fifteen essays mention Sir Roger, who is introduced in *Spectator* 2 (written by Steele) as a man "now in his Fifty sixth Year, cheerful, gay, and hearty, [who] keeps a good House both in Town and Country; a great Lover of Mankind."

In *Spectator* 112 Sir Roger is called a "good Church-man [who] has beautified the Inside of his Church." He has also instructed his parishioners in the niceties of worship. "He has often told me . . . that in order to make them kneel and join the Responses, he gave every one of them [his parishioners] a Hassock and a Common-prayer Book; and at the same Time employed an itinerant Singing-Master . . . to instruct them rightly in the Tunes of the Psalms." Like Herbert, Addison was a great lover of music, and he thought music played an important part in worship. Music, he says in *Spectator* 405, "strengthens Devotion. . . . It lengthens out every act of Worship and produces more lasting and permanent Impressions in the Mind, than those which accompany any transient Form of Words that are uttered in the ordinary Method of Religious Worship."

Addison takes Sunday worship seriously, but not solemnly. Mr. Spectator pokes fun at Sir Roger's attempt to make sure that all of the parishioners are attentive when the sermon is being delivered. "Sir Roger keeps them in very good Order and will suffer no Body to sleep in it besides himself; for if by Chance he has been surprized into a short Nap at Sermon, upon recovering out of it he stands up and looks about him, and if he sees any Body else nodding, either wakes them himself, or sends his Servants to them."

In *Spectator* 122 Mr. Spectator speaks of Sir Roger's "usual Chearfulness." In the eighteenth century cheerfulness did not mean mindless pleasantness. It meant a disposition to be agreeable—to regulate one's antisocial passions. In several essays Addison talks about the importance of cheerfulness, which he calls a "*Moral* Habit of the Mind" (*Spectator* 387). In *Spectator* 494 he says that "the true Spirit of Religion cheers, as well as composes the Soul." By contrast, Law speaks of "the sobriety of the Christian spirit."[19]

Englishmen, Addison says, need to make a special effort to be cheerful because "Melancholy is a kind of Demon that haunts our

Island" (*Spectator* 387). Referring to the Puritans—and perhaps to writers such as Law—Addison says that many religious Englishmen have wanted to be gloomy. "About an Age ago it was the Fashion in *England* for every one that would be thought religious, to throw as much Sanctity as possible into his Face, and in particular to abstain from all appearances of Mirth and Pleasantry" (*Spectator* 494). Though gloomy sanctity is not as popular as it once was, there still are many persons "who, by a natural Unchearfulness of Heart, mistaken Notions of Piety, or Weakness of Understanding, love to indulge this uncomfortable Way of Life. . . . Superstitious Fears, and groundless Scruples, cut them off from the Pleasures of Conversation, and all those social entertainments which are not only innocent but laudable; as if Mirth was made for Reprobates" (*Spectator* 494). Like Herbert, Addison praises mirth.

Gloomy Christians, Addison also says, give religion a bad name. Such people should consider "whether such a Behaviour does not deterr Men from a religious Life, by Representing it as an unsociable State, that extinguishes all Joy and Gladness, darkens the Face of Nature, and destroys the Relish of Being itself" (*Spectator* 494). Man, Addison concludes, "has an Heart capable of Mirth, and naturally disposed to it." The only people who have a reason to be gloomy, he says, are atheists. Cheerful Christians are also less likely to be dogmatic and intolerant about political differences. The "mirthful" Sir Roger is a Tory, but he gets along with Sir Andrew Freeport, a fellow club member who is a Whig.

Cheerfulness must be cultivated, but there are aids to cheerfulness. Englishmen are likely to be more cheerful if they attend a traditional Anglican service every Sunday. They are also likely to be more cheerful if the weather is good. Though Addison of course is not a sun worshiper, he associates cheerfulness with the sun. "The Sun, which is as the great Soul of the Universe, and produces all the

Necessaries of Life, has a particular Influence in chearing the Mind of Man, and making the Heart glad" (*Spectator* 387).

Johnson praises Addison for arguing that religion is not an enemy of cheerfulness. "He has dissipated the prejudice that had long connected gaiety with vice, and easiness of manners with laxity of principles." Addison, he adds, "separated mirth from indecency, and wit from licentiousness." Modern readers may find Addison's cheerful Christianity superficial, but Johnson thought Addison had a profound understanding of the passions that animate humankind. Addison, he said, "knew the heart of man from the depths of stratagem to the surface of affectation."[20]

Addison's essays were very popular, but so was Law's *Serious Call*. Most Continental visitors thought an English Sunday was more influenced by Law's views than Addison's. They had the same complaints that Voltaire had; they could not understand why museums, art galleries, and theaters were closed on Sunday but pubs were open. A German visitor remarked that "the law prohibits on the only day on which the labourer and the tradesman can enjoy the open air and divert himself, all musick and dancing; so that the public gardens, the taverns, the bagnios and all public places, swarm with people, who without dancing, run to every sort of excess."[21] Like many foreign visitors, he thought sabbatarian laws promoted immorality. Foreign observers may have exaggerated the dullness of an English Sunday, for sabbatarian laws were haphazardly enforced. Oliver Goldsmith said: "Scarce an Englishman who does not almost every day of his life, offend with impunity against some express law."[22]

What is most striking about a mid-eighteenth-century English Sunday is not the strength of sabbatarianism but the freedom of worship that Englishmen had. Paul Langford speaks of "the religious pluralism and the sense of almost boundless intellectual choice which marked the period."[23] Religious choice made for a great deal of religious ferment, which worried some Anglicans, yet theological questions did not generate as much heat as they had a century earlier. Theological disputes are ridiculed in two major eighteenth-century novels: *The Vicar of Wakefield* and *Tom Jones*.

A sign of the times was the lack of strong anti-Catholic feeling among elites, though anti-Catholicism remained a strong force among many Protestant sects, especially the Methodists, and among the uneducated. In his biography of Alexander Pope, a Catholic, Johnson notes that Pope was a successful social-climber who had many friends among "the great." A century earlier a Catholic writer would have been regarded with suspicion as someone who was likely to be an agent of France or Spain.

Many educated people were not regular churchgoers, but they remained nominal Christians. Though the law requiring church attendance remained on the books until 1791, it was not enforced. The Toleration Act made it unenforceable, because a parishioner did not have to explain why he was not at a local parish church. If asked, he could say that he was at the meeting-house of a Dissenter sect. In some areas there were not enough Anglican places of worship, so it was difficult to go to a parish church even if one wanted to.

Undoubtedly, some people went to church because there was social pressure to do so. Addison implies as much in his essay on churchgoing in rural England. When the service is over Sir Roger "walks down from his Seat in the Chancel . . . and every now and then enquires how such an one's Wife, or Mother, or Son or Father do whom he does not see at Church; which is understood as a secret Reprimand to the Person that is absent" (*Spectator* 112). A secret reprimand was a smaller price to pay than a fine, which is what people who did not go to church had had to pay a century earlier, though enforcement of the law was spotty even in Elizabethan times.

In eighteenth-century England the idea of requiring people to go to church had few supporters. Henry Fielding, who was a London magistrate, made such a proposal in a policy paper he wrote in 1753 entitled: *Proposal for Making an Effectual Provision for the Poor, for Amending Their Morals, and for Rendering Them Useful Members of the Society*. Fielding, like most eighteenth-century British writers, thought irreligion abetted immorality, so his plan required those who lived in urban workhouses to attend services morning and evening. Fielding's proposal, his biographer says, "was never taken very seriously even in friendly quarters."[24]

In sum, eighteenth-century Britons observed Sunday in a variety of ways. In Scotland most people regarded Sunday the way Law did—as a holy day. In England most people regarded Sunday the way Addison did—as a holy day and a holiday. Most of the urban and rural poor did not follow either Addison's or Law's prescription for Sunday. In their view Sunday was a holiday—a day for drinking, dancing, and various forms of gambling, especially cock-fighting, which was praised by one observer (in 1705) as a "noble and heroic recreation."[25]

Samuel Johnson

Johnson thought a great deal about Sunday observance. According to Boswell, "Dr. Johnson enforced [urged] the strict observance of Sunday." Boswell quotes Johnson as saying: "It should be different . . . from another day. People may walk, but not throw stones at birds. There may be relaxation, but there should be no levity."[26] Was Johnson serious or was he teasing Boswell—exaggerating his view of Sunday observance because Boswell's questions about religion often annoyed him? Or did Boswell misquote Johnson, since he liked to make Johnson appear more dogmatic than he really was?

Whatever we make of the remark, Johnson—a devout Anglican—regarded Sunday as the Lord's Day, and he thought Christians should observe it as the Sabbath. When he was dying he told a friend: "Remember to observe the Sabbath. Let it never be a day of business, nor wholly a day of dissipation." Traveling in France, Johnson notes with disapproval that in Paris "so many shops open that Sunday is little distinguished."[27]

Johnson, though, did not take a strict view of Sunday observance. Mrs. Thrale (Johnson's close friend) reports that when an acquaintance "lamented the enormous wickedness of the times, because some bird-catchers were busy one fine Sunday morning," Johnson criticized him for self-righteous moral posturing: "While half the Christian world is permitted . . . to dance and sing, and celebrate Sunday as a day of festivity, how comes your puritanical spirit [is] so offended with frivolous and empty deviations from exactness. Whoever loads life with unnecessary scruples . . . provokes the attention of others on his conduct, and incurs the censure of singularity without reaping the reward of superior virtue."[28]

Johnson disliked the "puritanical spirit" for its censoriousness and rigidity, and he thought Puritanism had been a destructive political force. The Puritans, he said, were guilty of enthusiasm, which he defines as "a vain belief of private revelation; a vain confidence of divine favour or communication." Johnson often praises activities that most Puritans regard as immoral. According to Mrs. Thrale, "Cards, dress [fancy clothes] and dancing . . . all found their advocates in Dr. Johnson, who inculcated, upon principle, the cultivation of those arts, which many a moralist thinks himself bound to reject, and many a Christian holds unfit to be practised."[29] It goes without saying that Johnson, who edited Shakespeare's plays and numbered among his friends David Garrick—the greatest actor of the age—disagreed with Puritan strictures against playgoing.

Nevertheless, there is a Puritan strain to Johnson's thought. Like many Puritans, Johnson kept a diary in which he scrutinized his conduct. "The modern type of confessional diary," Diarmaid Mac-Culloch says, "emerged as a literary genre among English Puritans around 1600: these were journals intended to examine oneself for proofs of genuine election by God." In many prayers Johnson sounds like a Puritan. He asks God to "purify my thoughts from pollutions" so that he can attain "purity of mind."[30]

Johnson, though, was not a sabbatarian. In his *Dictionary* Johnson defines "sabbatism"—a variant of "sabbatarianism"—as "observance of the Sabbath superstitiously rigid." Johnson said (in Boswell's paraphrase) that "he would not have Sunday kept with ritual severity and gloom, but with a gravity and simplicity of behaviour." Johnson, though, was not always grave on Sundays. "One Sunday, when the weather was very fine, [Topham] Beauclerk enticed him, insensibly, to saunter about all the morning. They went into a church-yard, in the time of divine service, and Johnson laid himself down at his ease upon one of the tomb-stones." On a Sunday in France Johnson raced his friend Giuseppe Baretti and beat him.[31]

Johnson even qualified his view that Sunday should be a day of rest. When Boswell asked him if it was all right to "go to a consultation with another lawyer upon Sunday," Johnson replied: "Why, Sir, when you are of consequence enough to oppose the practice of consulting upon Sunday, you should do it: but you may go now. It is not criminal. . . . The distinction is clear between what is of moral and what is of ritual obligation."[32] Sunday observance is a ritual obligation, not a moral one. If Boswell needs to consult with another lawyer on Sunday in order to build a successful practice, he should do so. But once he is successful—once he is "of consequence"—he should refrain from working on Sunday.

Johnson's view of Sunday observance—and of Anglicanism in

general—is similar to George Herbert's. Like Herbert, whose writings Johnson cites frequently in his *Dictionary,* Johnson stresses the importance of public worship. Johnson was not a parson, but he wrote forty sermons—many of them for his friend Dr. John Taylor. Like Herbert, Johnson was tolerant toward non-Anglicans. Boswell says that Johnson once "argued in defence of some of the peculiar tenets of the Church of Rome."[33] Compared to most mainstream Anglicans, Johnson was also more sympathetic to Methodists, who in many respects were the heirs of the Puritans.

Johnson's Sundays were different from Herbert's for the obvious reason that Herbert was a parson, but they were different in another way: Johnson often lacked the mirth that Herbert thought Christians should have on the Lord's Day. On Sunday mornings Johnson usually reviewed the conduct of his life and he often came to the conclusion that he was not a good Christian. Two things disturbed him greatly: he wasted time because he rose late on Sunday (and on other days as well), and he rarely went to church on Sunday though he always went during Easter Week and he usually went on the anniversary of the death of his wife, Elizabeth (known as Tetty), who had died in 1752.

Johnson's diary entries often take the form of a prayer. Johnson asks God to strengthen his will to keep his resolutions. The entry for Sunday, July 13, 1755, is typical in its concerns, though somewhat longer than most entries.

> Having lived hitherto in perpetual neglect of publick worship & though for some years past not without an habitual reverence for the Sabbath yet without that attention to its religious duties which Christianity requires I will once more form a scheme of life for the day such as alas I have often vainly formed which when my mind is capable of settled practice I hope to follow.

1. To rise early and in order to [do] it go to sleep early on Saturday.

2. To use some extraordinary devotion in the morning.

3. To examine the tenour of my life & particularly the last week & to mark my advances in religion or recession from it.

4. To read the Scripture methodically with such helps as are at hand.

5. To go to church twice.

6. To read books of divinity either speculative or practical.

7. To instruct my family.

8. To wear off by meditation any worldly soil contracted in the week.[34]

The list of resolutions suggests that Johnson thought of Sunday mainly as a holy day.

On Sundays Johnson usually rose late, read the Bible or a work of theology, and went to dinner at a friend's house. One Sunday (January 5, 1766) he "rose at 8," went back to bed, and later "dined at Hawkins's." (John Hawkins was a good friend who would become his literary executor.) Then he went to another friend's house, where he read a work of theology, and returned home. On another Sunday (March 24, 1782) he says: "I rose not early." That afternoon several friends visited him, and then he went out to dinner. "Dinner at Strahan's. Came home, and chatted with Williams, and read Romans IX in Greek."[35] William Strahan, a printer and publisher, was a friend of Johnson's. Anna Williams, a blind poet, lived in Johnson's household for many years; he took her in because she was destitute.

These two entries for Sunday show that Johnson generally kept one of his resolutions: to read the Bible and a work of divinity on Sunday. For brief periods Johnson kept his resolution to go to church regularly. In April 1772 he writes: "I have, I think, been less guilty of neglecting publick worship than formerly. I have commonly on Sunday gone once to church." Yet a year later he says: "I did not regain the habit of going to church, though I did not wholly omit it."[36]

The failure to keep his resolutions upset Johnson deeply. On Good Friday 1775 he says: "When I look back upon resoluti[ons] of improvement and amendments, which have year after year been made and broken, either by negligence, forgetfulness, vicious idleness, casual interruption, or morbid infirmity, . . . why do I yet try to resolve again? I try because Reformation is necessary and despair is criminal. I try in humble hope of the help of God."[37]

Though Johnson did not stop making resolutions, he thought it was a mistake to burden the mind with many resolutions. On Easter Sunday 1776 he says: "I will resolve henceforth to rise at eight in the morning, so far as resolution is proper." On Good Friday 1777 he says: "I have this year omitted church on most Sundays, intending to supply the deficience in the week. So that I owe twelve attendances in worship." Then he decides that it is foolish to try to calculate how he can make up his deficiency in church attendance. "I will make no more superstitious stipulations which entangle the mind with unbid[den] obligations." In his late sixties Johnson generally cut back on the number of resolutions he made. On his seventy-third birthday he made only two, but one is the same resolution that he had made three decades earlier: "More frequent attendance on publick Worship."[38]

For approximately three decades Johnson made a resolution to go to church on Sunday—and for the most part he did not keep it. He had trouble keeping other resolutions as well. The editor of Johnson's *Diaries, Prayers, and Annals* says: "Johnson's resolution to go to church every Sunday . . . was little better kept than the others."[39]

Why did Johnson find it so hard to go to church regularly? The main reason is: he did not enjoy public worship. In April 1773 he says: "I hope in time to take pleasure in publick Worship." When he was a child he disliked going to church. "The church at Lichfield," he writes Boswell, "in which we had a seat, wanted reparation, so I was to go and find a seat in other churches; and having bad eyes, and being awkward about this, I used to go and read in the fields on Sunday. This habit continued till my fourteenth year; and still I find a great reluctance to go to church."[40]

Churchgoing required rising early, which was difficult for Johnson. When he did go to church, he frequently was late, which probably embarrassed him. And because he usually stayed up very late on Saturday, he occasionally fell asleep in church. Johnson also found it difficult to pay attention in church—mainly because he was hard of hearing. While attending a divine service one Sunday, he wrote this note to himself: "If I can hear the sermon to attend [to] it, unless the attention be more troublesome than useful."[41] He implies that sometimes the sermon is not worth hearing.

Johnson occasionally pleads illness as the reason for not going to church. He has a bad cough, "which would have interrupted both my own attention and that of others." In one entry he admits that he may be looking for excuses for not going. "I came home late, and was unwilling to carry my Rheumatism to the cold church in the morning, unless that were rather an excuse made to myself." In church one Sunday he seems to have been bored, for he wrote down the amount of time different parts of the service took. The sermon, he says, took thirty minutes. "The whole [service] one hour, thirty three minutes."[42]

A word that continually comes up in Johnson's Sunday diary entries is "scruples." On Easter Sunday 1750 he writes a fervent prayer: "O Lord, who wouldst that all men should be saved, and who knowest that without thy grace we can do nothing acceptable to thee, have mercy upon me. Enable me to break the chain of my sins, to reject sensuality in thought, and to overcome and suppress vain scruples." Thirty-four years later, on a Sunday, he prays that "my resolutions of amendment may be rightly formed and diligently exerted, that I may be freed from vain and useless scruples."[43]

The *OED's* first definition of "scruple" is: "a thought or circumstance that troubles the mind or conscience; a doubt, uncertainty or hesitation in regard to right and wrong, duty, propriety, etc; esp. one which is regarded as over-refined or over-nice." Johnson told Mrs. Thrale: "Scruples would . . . certainly make men miserable, and seldom make them good." He tells several friends: "I do not like to read any thing on a Sunday, but what is theological; not that I would scrupulously refuse to look at any thing which a friend should shew me in a news-paper."[44] Johnson implies that it is foolish to think that reading a newspaper on Sunday is profaning the Sabbath.

When Johnson speaks of "vain scruples," he is mainly thinking about those who worry excessively about how they observe Sunday and worry excessively about minor aspects of their conduct. The *OED* defines "vain" as "devoid of real value, worth, or significance; idle, unprofitable, useless, worthless." People who are burdened with vain scruples torture their conscience unnecessarily; they also tend to be what we call "judgmental"—disapproving of other people's conduct. In Johnson's view those who have the "puritanical spirit" are burdened with "vain scruples."

When Johnson talks about scruples, he is occasionally thinking about something else: his religious doubts. The *OED's* third definition of "scruple" is: "A doubt or uncertainty as to a matter of fact or allegation; an intellectual difficulty, perplexity, or objection." In Johnson's *Dictionary* "scruple" is a verb that means "to doubt; to hesitate." In his diary entry for March 29, 1766, which was Good Friday and also the day his wife had died, he says: "Scruples still distress me.

My resolution, with the blessing of God, is to contend with them, and, if I can, to conquer them." On March 5, 1777, he writes Boswell, who complained to him about suffering from melancholy: "I am very sorry that your melancholy should return. . . . Let me warn you very earnestly against scruples."[45]

When Johnson uses "vain" to modify "scruples," he is telling himself (and occasionally telling Boswell) that it is a mistake to think about whether or not Christianity is true—that pursuing this question will lead to despair. "Scruples distract me," he writes on Good Friday, "but at Church I had hopes to conquer them." Johnson also says that having scruples is a sign of one's intellectual vanity. Making notes for a book on prayer, Johnson lists eleven reasons why people become religious skeptics; one is that skeptics "study not for truth but vanity." Johnson told Boswell that "Hume, and other skeptical innovators, are vain men."[46]

In his diaries Johnson is circumspect about his religious doubts, but he occasionally admits that his belief in Christianity is not firm. On the day before Easter Sunday in 1766, he prays: "O God, grant me repentance, grant me reformation. Grant that I may be no longer disturbed with doubts and harassed with vain terrors." Johnson told the Scottish writer James Beattie that he often was tormented by religious doubts. Johnson hoped to win the battle against despair by going to church regularly. Yet even in church he was assailed by doubts. In September 1768 he writes: "I have now begun the sixtieth year of my life. . . . This day has been past in great perturbation. I was distracted at Church in an uncommon degree, and my distress has had very little intermission."[47]

On Easter Sunday 1778 Johnson made the following resolution: "To serve and trust God, and be cheerful." But it was very hard for Johnson to be cheerful on Sunday. His diary is a record of despair about his inability to reform his conduct and his inability to banish vain scruples. There are matter-of-fact entries about his travels and his Sunday dinners and reading, but only one Sunday entry is cheerful. On Sunday, May 16, 1784, seven months before he died, he says: "Afternoon spent cheerfully and elegantly, I hope without offence to GOD or man; though in no holy duty yet in the general exercise and cultivation of benevolence."[48] Addison would have approved.

Johnson did not remain cheerful. On August 12, 1784, he composed a lengthy prayer: "O Lord, my Maker and Protector, . . . enable me to drive from me all such unquiet and perplexing thoughts as may mislead or hinder me in the practice of those duties which thou hast required." On October 31, six weeks before he died, Johnson scribbled several pages of notes for the book he was writing on prayer. On one page there are only two words: "Against Despair."[49]

Johnson's last prayer, written a week before he died, suggests that he had overcome his scruples and driven out despair. He says: "Forgive and accept my late conversion." By conversion, he doesn't mean a change of religion; he means a "change from reprobation to grace, from a bad to a holy life." This is one of the definitions of "conversion" in Johnson's *Dictionary*. "This last prayer," the editor of Johnson's *Diaries* says, "shows Johnson calm, no longer troubled by scruples, and ready to meet death, which came on 13 December."[50]

Just as Johnson was of two minds about making resolutions, he was of two minds about reviewing his conduct on Sundays and holy days. He thinks a good Christian should review his conduct, but he also tells Boswell that it is important to "divert distressing thoughts, and not combat them." When Boswell asks: "May not he think them down," Johnson replies: "No, Sir. To Attempt to *think them down* is madness." A person burdened with distressing thoughts needs to "contrive to have as many retreats for his mind as he can."[51] Yet on Sundays Johnson did not retreat. He entered the arena of his mind—determined to conquer vain scruples and perplexing thoughts.

Drive away, overcome, suppress, conquer, combat: these are the verbs Johnson uses when talking about "vain scruples" and "perplexing thoughts." Johnson thought life was a struggle—a struggle to "have the management of the mind," a struggle to make Sunday a day of mirth rather than a day of despair.

Chapter Five

Varieties of Sunday Observance

~ *Boswell and His Contemporaries*

*I*f Johnson tried without success to be a regular churchgoer on Sunday, James Boswell went to church regularly, and he enjoyed the experience. Boswell was a moderate sabbatarian who traveled and wrote on Sunday. He did not agree with his son James, who said it was inappropriate to dine out on Sunday. Yet he thought it was wrong to play cards on Sunday. He notes that one Sunday evening he "played whist with some compunction as *contra bonos mores* [against good morals] in this country."[1] He had "some compunction," but not enough to stop him from playing.

When Boswell did not go to church, he often read a religious work. One Sunday he was too late for church, so he read the Bible. Few people, he says, read the Bible. "It is a strange thing that the Bible is so little read. I am reading it regularly through at present. I dare say there are many people of distinction in London who know nothing about it." On another Sunday he was sick, so he read the lives of several leading Anglicans, including John Donne, Richard Hooker, and George Herbert. His reading put him "in the most placid and pious frame."[2]

Boswell usually was pious on Sunday but rarely was he placid. He was often despondent because he remembered the gloomy Sundays of his childhood. Though he loved his "extremely pious" mother, he did not like the God-fearing Presbyterianism she tried to drum into him—telling him that if he was not a good Christian "the eternity of punishment" awaited him.

Boswell's parents were strict sabbatarians. On Sunday the young James had to go to church twice, and in the evening he had to read the Bible and learn his catechisms. After Boswell's mother died, his father remarried (on the same day that Boswell married). The father remained a sabbatarian. Boswell found it a burden to spend Sundays with his father. One Sunday dinner, Boswell says, was "the usual constraint joined with the usual small conversation."[3] Boswell, though, was a dutiful son, so when he was in Edinburgh he attended church with his father and went to his father's estate for Sunday dinner.

Did Boswell's Presbyterian upbringing contribute to the depression he suffered from throughout his life? Boswell thought it did. "The whole vulgar idea of the Presbyterian worship . . . made me very gloomy." But he also blamed his depression on heredity—saying that melancholy "was hereditary in our family."[4]

In London Boswell's Sundays were less gloomy, which is one reason Boswell always looked forward to leaving Edinburgh. On a Sunday in London in January 1763 (he did not go to church that day) Boswell was annoyed because his brother paid him a visit. His brother "brought many low old Sunday ideas when we were boys into my memory." Even in London Boswell was disturbed by the "low old Sunday ideas." An entry for a London Sunday in May 1763 reads: "I was so bad this day that I could not settle to go to public worship." By "bad" he means depressed—filled with what he calls gloomy or vexing thoughts. In an entry for a London Sunday in December 1792, he notes that in church "I had real satisfaction from the whole solemnity though inwardly melancholy." He adds: "Mrs. McAdam dined and drank tea with us. I passed as dull a day as if I had been in Edinburgh."⁵

Boswell's upbringing led him to reject Presbyterianism, but he never became a skeptic like David Hume. When he was a young man he sought a divine service that was the opposite of Presbyterian worship, so he went to London and began instruction in the Catholic faith. An emissary from his horrified father persuaded Boswell to change his mind about becoming a Catholic, yet for the rest of his life he occasionally went to Catholic Mass.

On Easter Sunday in 1772 Boswell worshiped at the chapel of the Sardinian ambassador. "The solemnity of high mass, the music, the wax lights, and the odour of the frankincense made a delightful impression upon me. I was divinely happy." In May 1790 he took a close friend who was an Anglican parson to the Neapolitan ambassador's chapel, so that his friend "might hear High Mass for the first time."⁶ Catholic worship still was publicly forbidden (the law would be repealed in 1792), but one could attend Mass at the private chapels of Catholic aristocrats and at the chapels of the embassies of Catholic countries.

Boswell became an Anglican. He liked the architecture of Anglican churches, and he liked the Anglican liturgy. He thought Anglican priests were convivial, and he revered Johnson, the most famous Anglican writer of the age. Yet Boswell was a restless soul who was curious about the varieties of worship—not only Christian worship. Arriving in London in 1762, "I took a whim to go through all the churches and chapels in London, taking one each Sunday." Six months later, on a Sunday in July 1763: "In the forenoon I was at a Quakers' meeting in Lombard Street, and in the afternoon at St. Paul's, where I was very devout and very happy." On a Friday night and Saturday morning in 1772 he and a friend went to two synagogues. He says nothing about the service, but he is disturbed by the way Jews are treated. "I could not help feeling a kind of regret to see the certain descendants of venerable Abraham in an outcast state and sneered and abused by every fool, at least to a certain degree." In January 1790 he is still trying new churches. "Went by accident (to try a new chapel) to St. Mary's, Park Street, and heard an excellent discourse by a Dr. Steevens on the truth of Christianity."[7]

When Boswell was in Edinburgh he usually worshiped at New Church, which is the church he had attended as a child. In his journal entries for 1774, he says that he went there "both forenoon and afternoon." In between services he went to dinner at his father's. The sermons at New Church were more interesting than those he had heard in his childhood because they usually were delivered by Hugh Blair, a moderate Presbyterian who was a friend of Hume's.

On a Sunday in June 1774 Boswell notes that he heard three sermons. "Was all day at the New Church; Dr. Blair [preached] in the forenoon, _____ in the afternoon. At my father's between sermons. . . . In the evening sauntered with my wife and Mrs. M., with intention to go to the Methodists' meeting, or Lady Glenorchy's Chapel to hear some remarkable evening sermon. [Lady Glenorchy's chapel preached evangelical Protestantism.] They went to the latter; I went in only for a little, and heard a Mr. Davidson from England. I went home by myself." It was a good Sunday for Boswell, for he was not mired in depression. "It is amazing how all impressions of gloom upon a Sunday evening, which used formerly to hang so heavy on my mind, are quite effaced."[8]

Churchgoing usually lifted Boswell's spirits and helped to strengthen his belief in the truth of Christian doctrine. In St. Paul's on Easter Sunday 1773 the preacher "gave us a neat and clear deduction of the evidence of Christianity. I was struck and elevated as usual by the service." He still is plagued by doubts, but he is not gloomy: "Though I did not feel that firm conviction which I have done at different periods of my life . . . yet my heart and affections were pious, and I received the Holy Sacrament with considerable satisfaction. I was above three hours in church today."[9]

When Boswell was not in church, the gloomy thoughts often returned—especially gloomy thoughts about death and the afterlife. "I myself," he wrote in 1779, "have frequently been terrified and dismally afflicted in this way nor can I yet secure my mind against it at gloomy seasons of dejection." Boswell often asked Johnson about "futurity," but it was a subject that Johnson did not like to discuss. "Poor Boswell," a friend wrote in 1791, "is very low and dispirited and almost melancholy mad."[10]

Boswell was haunted by the possibility that Christianity was an illusion, but he also worried that Christianity was the truth and that he would suffer an eternity of punishment because of his failure to be a good Christian. On a Sunday in November 1793, eighteen months before he died, he had a strange dream: a statue stepped down from its pedestal and he ran from it in fear. Was he thinking of the last scene in Mozart's *Don Giovanni*, where Don Giovanni goes to hell? The opera was not performed in London until March of the following year, but it had been performed on the Continent and Boswell may have known about it.[11]

It makes sense for Boswell to compare himself to Don Giovanni, for he was a compulsive womanizer. Though Boswell sought out prostitutes and made assignations on any day of the week, he seems to have had sex on his mind more frequently on Sunday than on other days. In a journal entry for November 1762 he admits that when he was attending service in St. James church he was thinking about sex. "What a curious, inconsistent thing is the mind of man. In the midst of divine service I was laying plans for having women, and yet I had the most sincere feelings of religion." Frederick Pottle, the editor of Boswell's *London Journal*, notes that Boswell "had made plans for both church and fornication in his memorandum written that morning." A month later Boswell planned the same Sunday activities: first going to church, then having sex.[12]

Boswell tried to reform. A journal entry for a Sunday in May 1783 mentions attending Mass in the Portuguese chapel: "Was devout as I could wish; heavenly and happy. Vowed before the altar no more *filles* while in London."[13] Did he reform or did he simply become more discreet about what he put in his journal? A number of journal entries are crossed out.

In the last decade of his life Boswell probably had fewer casual sexual partners than he'd had when he was younger because his sexual drive was not as strong, owing to poor health. He still talks about beautiful women but now he sounds more like a connoisseur of beauty than a sexual predator. On a Sunday in May 1793 he sees a very attractive woman while attending church. "Went in the morning to High Mass at the Spanish Ambassador's Chapel. . . . For the first time for many months I was struck with the face, person, dress, and manner of a lady, who seemed to be a foreigner. . . . She inspired once more those sensations and irradiations of fancy which have innumerable times in my life been experienced by me." After the service he follows her "at a becoming distance." He resolved "to inquire afterwards in the neighborhood who she was," but he never mentions her again.[14]

Two years earlier Boswell had been infatuated with a woman he saw in church—a Miss Upton. He even wrote a dreadful poem about it, "Love at Church." Here is the first stanza.

> When in St. George's hallowed dome,
>
> Upton, thy pleasing form I see,
>
> My fluttering thoughts, too apt to roam,
>
> Are wholly fixed on heaven and thee.

Three years later he sees the woman in church again, but now he realizes that nothing will come of this infatuation. "Attended part of the morning service, standing in the passage where I could see Miss Upton, who looked as elegant as ever and suggested pleasing imaginations, which, however, reflection told me could hardly be realized."[15]

In the last decade of his life Boswell's main Sunday activity after attending church was heavy drinking, unless he was suffering from a hangover from the previous night. On a Sunday in June 1783 his friend William Temple writes in his journal: "Called on Boswell. Went to church. Bl. [Boswell] irregular in his conduct and manners, selfish, indelicate, thoughtless. . . . Seems often absurd and almost mad, I think. . . . Boswell came to us [Temple was lodged with a friend] in the evening in his usual ranting way and stayed till 12, drinking wine and water, glass after glass."[16]

In the last four years of his life, after the publication of the *Life of Johnson* in 1791, Boswell often was drunk. A journal entry for a Sunday in March 1794 reads: "From having drunk too much yesterday I lay long today." He went out to a coffeehouse to get tea and a muffin, but came home too late for afternoon service. He went out to dinner. "But I drank too freely."[17]

Boswell had three ways of dealing with a gloomy Sunday: going to church, having sex, and drinking heavily. He often resorted to all three. At times going to church did not relieve his depression, but on most occasions it did. On a Sunday in January 1763 he says: "I heard service and sermon in the New Church in the Strand, which insensibly relieved me from my cloudy spirits." Two months later he says: "I heard prayers and sermon at Spring Garden Chapel; I felt a calm delight in again being at divine service." On a Sunday in August 1793 Boswell wakes up feeling "that inexplicable disorder which vexes a great part of my life." Yet in church later that morning he "had some relief by pious exercise." And he adds: "It is no small comfort to me that in all situations my religion still continues."[18]

For Boswell Sunday was both the low point of the week and the high point. It was the low point because it reminded him of the Sundays of his childhood. It was the high point because attending public worship often relieved his depression. A journal entry for a Sunday in April 1774 reads: "I went to St. Paul's and heard the latter part of an excellent sermon by Mr. Sturges, one of the prebendaries. Then assisted at some prayers, stayed the communion, and received the Holy Sacrament in that grand edifice. I was elevated and bettered." A week later he worshiped at Westminster Abbey. "The solemnity of the grand old building, the painted glass windows, the noble music, the excellent service of the Church and a very good sermon, all contributed to do me much good."[19] But the "low old Sunday ideas" always returned.

Joshua Reynolds

If Boswell went to church regularly, his good friend Joshua Reynolds, to whom he dedicated the *Life of Johnson,* never went to church. On Sundays Reynolds painted. He said that "the pupil in art, who looks for the Sunday with pleasure as an idle day, will never make a painter." Reynolds' nephew claimed that his uncle "has not seen the inside of a church for years." On Sunday evenings Reynolds usually went to dinner at the Society of Dilettanti, an English dining club for those who had made the Grand Tour.[20] It was mainly an occasion for heavy drinking.

James Northcote, Reynolds' apprentice, said: "I do not know his Religion [but] he never goes to church, which miss Reynolds [Frances] thinks is very wrong of him." Reynolds broke off relations with his sister Frances in part because she often nagged him "that He was a Clergyman's Son & that it was very improper for Him to set the example of *painting on a Sunday.*"[21] Reynolds did not like his sister's telling him what he should do on Sunday.

When Johnson was dying, he asked Reynolds, whose company he greatly enjoyed, not to paint on Sunday. (He also asked Reynolds to read the Bible regularly.) Reynolds promised Johnson that he would refrain from painting on Sunday. According to one report, he did not paint on Sunday "for a considerable time, breaking it only when someone eager for a sitting persuaded him that 'the Doctor [i.e., Johnson] had no title to exact such a promise.'"[22]

Though Reynolds painted on Sunday, he disliked public attacks on Christianity. When he was president of the Royal Academy, he told an artist who had submitted a caricature of two monks carousing before a crucifix that he would not allow it to be exhibited. Yet in a letter Reynolds implies that religious people are weak. "I am of opinion a man may be a good member of society and even a man of sense in other things . . . tho' he may be weak enough to be a believer in—or even a Christian." Yet Reynolds did not think the devout Johnson was weak. Johnson, he said, "formed my mind . . . and brushed off from it a great deal of rubbish."[23]

Reynolds came from a religious family. His father was a country parson like Herbert. Did Reynolds turn away from religion because of the gloomy Sundays of his childhood? This seems unlikely. There is no evidence that his father was a strict sabbatarian. Moreover, Reynolds' two sisters—Frances and Elizabeth—were observant Christians. Elizabeth, like Frances, disapproved of her brother's irreligion and his habit of painting on Sunday. Elizabeth wrote him: "Thy soul is a shocking spectacle of poverty." She refused to let her second son live with Sir Joshua because she was afraid he might become as irreligious as his uncle.[24]

Reynolds was not opposed to religion; he was indifferent to it. A painter, he said, should think about painting all the time. "Whoever is resolved to excel in painting . . . must bring all his mind to bear on that one object, from the moment he rises till he goes to bed." According to Frances Reynolds, who was also a painter, most painters were irreligious. "Miss Reynolds," James Northcote recounts, "said one day it was almost a pity the science [of painting] had ever been known, [since] it so entirely employed the mind of those who have ever made great painters that they neglected every other thing in this life and very seldom thought of the future; [she was] alluding to the neglect of the Church, which is disagreeable to her."[25]

Thomas Gainsborough said that he never painted on Sunday. "I generally view my Works of a Sunday, tho: I never touch." Yet on a Sunday in November 1782 Gainsborough apparently did paint (or draw), for Reynolds came to his house for a preliminary sitting for his portrait.[26]

When Reynolds was dying, Boswell wrote an Anglican divine: "I am very sorry that he did not imbibe christian piety from Johnson. No clergyman attends him; no holy rites console his languishing hours." Reynolds' indifference to religion had no effect on his career. In London's cultural world there was no stigma attached to being an unobservant Christian. A clubbable man whose dinner parties were very popular, Reynolds had a wide range of friends—from Edmund Burke, who was an observant Christian, to John Wilkes, a notorious rake and libertine. Burke, who wrote Reynolds' obituary, praised Reynolds for "social virtues" that put him at "the centre of a very great and unparalleled variety of agreeable societies."[27]

Oliver Goldsmith

Reynolds greatly admired Johnson but the man he was closest to was Oliver Goldsmith, who also was a good friend of Johnson's. During the last ten years of Goldsmith's life—he died in 1774—Reynolds and Goldsmith were constantly in one another's company. One of the few days that Reynolds did not paint was the day Goldsmith died. Northcote writes that Reynolds "did not touch the pencil for that day, a circumstance most extraordinary for him."[28]

If Reynolds painted on Sunday, Goldsmith probably wrote on Sunday. In a literary career that spanned two decades, he wrote continually—poems, plays, essays, one novel, works of history—because he was always in debt, mainly owing to his taste for expensive clothes and his habit of gambling. Goldsmith, like Reynolds, was the son of an Anglican clergyman. His father was the curate of a parish in Ireland. Goldsmith's religious views were similar to Reynolds'. He was not observant but he defended the Church of England.

In "The Deserted Village" (1770), a long poem that Goldsmith dedicated to Reynolds, he describes traditional Sunday sports and pastimes in a way that would have earned the approval of Archbishop Laud. The speaker remembers his happy youth in a village that is now deserted. He remembers "the decent church that topped the neighbouring hill." A "decent" church is a church that is appropriate in size and style for such a village.[29]

After mentioning the church, the speaker describes the traditional Sunday pastimes that he enjoyed as a child.

> How often have I blessed the coming day [i.e., the Sabbath]
> When toil remitting lent its turn to play,
> And all the village train, from labour free,
> Led up their sports beneath the spreading tree.
> While many a pastime circled in the shade,
> The young contending as the old surveyed;
> And many a gambol frolicked o'er the ground,
> And sleights of art and feats of strength went round;
> And still as each repeated pleasure tired,
> Succeeding sports the mirthful band inspired.[30]

Sports, pastimes, mirth: it seems as if we are back in the 1630s, when debates about Sunday observance tore the country apart. But in late eighteenth-century England the words "sports," "pastimes," and "mirth" no longer carried a strong charge. They stirred nostalgia rather than anger. Goldsmith's poem is a pastoral idyll—not a realistic portrait of a rural village. Everyone is happy, everything is pleasant.

In his description of Sunday in a rural village, Goldsmith mentions the church but he says nothing about worship. "The Deserted Village" is not about religious faith. It is a lament for a lost world. "I see the rural Virtues leave the land." It is also a political poem—an attack on Luxury (commercial expansion), which in Goldsmith's view has been a destructive force, driving people from villages to cities. Addressing the "sweet smiling village," he says: "Thy sports are fled" and "rural mirth and manners are no more."[31] When Goldsmith speaks of mirth, he does not mean the religious joy that comes from celebrating the Resurrection. He means the mirth that comes from rural sports and pastimes on a Sunday afternoon.

The Vicar of Wakefield (1766), Goldsmith's only novel, touches in part on the same theme—that commercial expansion is destroying traditional England. The vicar and his wife move to a "little neighborhood" that has not yet been touched by commerce. In this "retreat" the farmers are faithful to the traditional Christian calendar. "They wrought with chearfulness on days of labor; but observed festivals as intervals of idleness and pleasure." This rural world, Goldsmith suggests, is fast disappearing.

The vicar does not sound like Herbert's country parson. He is very vague about his Sunday duties. "I always loved to be at church a good while before the rest of the congregation." On his first Sunday as vicar, he complains about the clothes his wife and daughters are wearing. Admonishing them for their vanity, he asks them to change their clothes, which they do. He is also vague about Christian doctrine. "To religion then we must hold in every circumstance of life for our truest comfort; for if already we are happy it is a pleasure to think that we can make that happiness unending, and if we are miserable, it is very consoling to think that there is a place of rest. Thus to the fortunate religion holds out a continuance of bliss, to the wretched a change from pain."

What is striking about this sermon is the blandness of the vicar's religious language. He says "religion," not Christianity. He refers to "the author of our religion" instead of Christ. He refers to "providence" rather than God. In a previous passage he uses "Being" when describing the prayers of his staff at sunrise: "We all bent in gratitude to that Being who gave us another day." The vicar's religious language is very different from Herbert's and Johnson's. Johnson occasionally uses the word "religion" for Christianity, but his prayers are always addressed to "Almighty God" or "Almighty and most merciful Father."

The vicar does not discuss Christian doctrine, but two young men dispute theological questions. Their exchange is comical because the language is gobbledygook. One says: "Very well, the premises being thus settled, I proceed to observe that the concatenation of self existences, proceeding in a reciprocal duplicate ratio, naturally produce a problematical dialogism, which in some measure proves that the essence of spirituality may be referred to the second predicable." His opponent thinks these absurd remarks make sense, for he says: "I deny that: Do you think I can thus tamely submit to such heterodox doctrines?" The exchange sounds like a debate between Groucho and Chico in a Marx Brothers movie.

In an essay Goldsmith says that he has no patience with works of theology. "Thus, for the soul of me, I could never find courage nor grace enough to wade above two pages deep into *Thoughts upon God and Nature* or *Thoughts upon Providence*, or *Thoughts upon Free Grace*, or indeed into Thoughts upon any thing at all."[32] The titles he cites are undoubtedly made up, but they bear a close resemblance to the titles of many works of theology.

Goldsmith's "religious convictions," Ricardo Quintana says, "were of the simplest but deeply rooted." What is deeply rooted in Goldsmith is a strong belief in maintaining the established Church of England and a vague belief in the existence of a future state. Goldsmith spends more time discussing the evils of luxury than the rewards of providence. In the dedication to "The Deserted Village" he says: "For twenty or thirty years past, it has been the fashion to consider luxury as one of the greatest national advantages; and all the wisdom of antiquity in that particular, as erroneous. Still however, I . . . continue to think those luxuries prejudicial to states, by which so many vices are introduced, and so many kingdoms have been undone."[33] Johnson disagreed with Goldsmith, and he frequently defended luxury. At meetings of Johnson's famous club, the question of luxury was discussed far more frequently than sabbatarianism.

Thomas Gray and Hugh Blair

In the late eighteenth century, most educated Britons believed in God, but many were losing interest in traditional worship. Many thought God was more likely to be found on a mountaintop than in a church. As a contemporary observer put it, "All the noblest convictions and confidences of religion may be acquired in the simple school of nature."[34] Those who found God in nature often called their experience "sublime."

One of the most influential proponents of the sublime was Thomas Gray, a popular poet whose poems were praised by most contemporary critics. When Gray was twenty-three, his friend Horace Walpole said that he would pay Gray's expenses if he accompanied him on an extended trip to France and Italy. On the Grand Tour, which lasted almost two and a half years, Gray was a dedicated tourist—too dedicated for Walpole, who wanted to go to more parties and do less sightseeing. (They eventually quarreled and Gray went back to England by himself.) Though Gray admired many churches and many paintings, what impressed him the most were the Alps. After he first crossed them, he wrote a friend: "Not a precipice, not a torrent, not a cliff but is pregnant with religion and poetry. There are certain scenes that would awe an atheist into belief, without the help of other argument."[35]

Crossing the Alps again on his way back to England, Gray marked the occasion by writing a poem in Latin, in which he says: "We perceive God closer to us among pathless rocks, wild ridges, and precipitous ravines, and in the thundering of the waters and the darkness of the woods, than if, kept under a roof of citrus-wood, He glowed with gold even from the hand of Phidias." Gray is saying that even the work of Phidias, the ancient Greek sculptor, is not as good a path to God as the Alps are. William Gilpin, who wrote popular travel guides to England's Lake District, said that "no man was a greater admirer of nature than Mr. Gray."[36]

Gray, though, was not an enemy of traditional religion. In some respects he was a conventional Anglican who regarded Sunday as a holy day and a holiday, though he did not go in for sports and pastimes. (He told his uncle that he preferred to go for long walks rather than ride or hunt.) When Gray was a student at Cambridge, he attended church every Sunday because his scholarship required him to sing in the chapel choir. After graduation Gray probably attended church occasionally. Gray's biographer says that when Gray visited his mother he "almost certainly, on the Sunday following his arrival in Buckinghamshire [where his mother lived], attended regular services at the parish church." Visiting an Anglican priest who was a close friend, Gray says: "We went twice a-day to church."[37]

Though Gray is an occasional churchgoer, he devalues the importance of communal worship: he says that the place where one is most likely to find God is on a mountaintop. Gray's nature worship is not communal; most of the time he went for walks by himself. Traveling to the Scottish Highlands in 1765, Gray says: "In short since I saw the Alps, I have seen nothing sublime till now." Looking for the sublime, he suggests, is a religious quest. "The mountains [in the Highlands] are ecstatic, and ought to be visited in pilgrimage once a year. None but those monstrous creatures of God know how to join so much beauty with so much horror." According to Gray, those who don't make a pilgrimage to sublime mountains are missing a profound religious experience. "A fig for your poets, painters, gardeners and clergymen, that have not been among them."[38]

On a three-week walking tour of the Lake District in England, Gray describes an experience he had on a Sunday morning. He is looking from a distance at a group of people who are leaving a small white chapel after they have gone to Sunday morning service. "From the shore a low promontory pushes itself far into the water, & on it stands a white village with the parish-church rising in the midst of it . . . & just opposite . . . is a large farm-house at the bottom of a steep smooth lawn embosom'd in old woods which climb half way up the mountain's side, & . . . above them a broken line of crags, that crown the scene."[39]

Instead of going to church that Sunday morning, Gray viewed a church from the distance. The church was part of a landscape that was both sublime and picturesque. (A sublime landscape has a terrifying aspect, whereas a picturesque landscape is charming.) Was Gray's Sunday morning experience religious or aesthetic? It was both. Gray usually suggests that viewing a sublime landscape is at the same time an aesthetic and a religious experience.

Gray was not the first Englishman to describe a trip to the mountains as a sublime experience. In the last decade of the seventeenth century the English literary critic John Dennis said that his trip across the Alps was "sublime." But the vogue for finding God in mountains began in earnest in the second half of the eighteenth century, when touring the Lake District in England became fashionable. In *The Excursion* (1814) William Wordsworth describes a solitary herdsman: "In the mountains did he feel his faith."

During the nineteenth century the idea that one finds God in the mountains remained popular. In *The Way of All Flesh* (1903) Samuel Butler makes fun of the vogue for nature worship. One Sunday while traveling in the Alps, George Pontifex, the pompous main character, writes a dreadful poem in a visitors' book:

> Lord, while these wonders of thy hand I see,
> My soul in holy reverence bends to thee.
> These awful solitudes, this dread repose,
> Yon pyramids sublime of spotless snows . . .

Was finding the sublime the same thing as finding God? Though the two words were not used interchangeably, they often were associated with each other.

Another enthusiast for the sublime was Hugh Blair. Blair was more than an occasional churchgoer like Gray; he was the most prominent clergyman in the Church of Scotland. For thirty-five years Blair preached most Sundays in the High Church, the church Boswell attended when he was in Edinburgh. Though Blair had a weak voice, he was a popular preacher. His sermons, which were published in four volumes between 1777 and 1794 (he died in 1800), were highly regarded by many people, including Johnson. Disliking the gloomy Calvinism of the more orthodox wing (the Calvinism of

Boswell's parents), Blair saw nothing wrong with going to the theater, playing cards, or dancing.

Four years after Blair became a minister at the High Church, he was appointed Regius Professor of Rhetoric and Belles-Lettres at Edinburgh University. (He still remained a clergyman.) His lectures on rhetoric and belles-lettres were published in 1783, but he first achieved fame in 1765, when he published "A Critical Dissertation on the Poems of Ossian." Ossian purportedly was a third-century blind pagan Scottish bard whose epic poems (*Fingal* and *Temora*) were "discovered" and translated from the Gaelic by James Macpherson. Blair compares Ossian to Homer and says that in some respects Ossian is a better poet than Homer.[40]

Though Blair—like Boswell and Gray—greatly admired Ossian, he was disturbed by the "total absence of religious ideas" in *Fingal*. The poem, he says, "would have been much more beautiful and perfect, had the author discovered some knowledge of a supream Being." Yet ten pages later Blair suggests that the warriors in *Fingal* are perfect moral specimens. "We behold no debasing passions among Fingal's warriors; no spirit of avarice or of insult; but a perpetual contention for fame; a desire of being distinguished and remembered for gallant actions; a love of justice. . . . Such is the strain of sentiment in the works of Ossian."[41]

Blair is not recommending that Christians read Ossian rather than the Bible on Sunday. And he is not saying that people should devote Sunday to finding the sublime in nature. Yet he downplays the importance of Christian worship in shaping moral conduct. "Particularly in all the sentiments of Fingal, there is a grandeur and loftiness proper to swell the mind with the highest ideas of human perfection." What Britons need to make them more moral are infusions of the "sublime"—a word that Blair uses innumerable times in his essay on Ossian. "Sublimity . . . coincides in a great measure with magnanimity, heroism, and generosity of sentiment." Blair also celebrates ethnic mystique. Fingal's heroes are distinguished by "a zealous attachment to their friends and country."[42]

Blair's essay on Ossian and the writings of Ossian were immensely influential in Europe. They stirred an interest in finding the ancient verse—folksongs as well as epics—of a particular culture. In an essay on Ossian, the influential German philosopher Johann Gottfried Herder says: "All unpolished peoples sing and act. . . . Their songs are the archives of their people, the treasury of their science and religion."[43] Herder argued that cultural identity is a stronger and more important force than religious identity.

Herder was a cultural puritan—i.e., a nationalist. In his view, a nation can be strong and healthy only if it is not polluted by other cultures. A culture gains strength if it drinks deeply from its ancient poetry and its folk culture. Throughout Europe, many educated people subscribed to Herder's ideas. And many became more interested in cultural questions than religious questions.

For many cultural puritans in nineteenth and twentieth-century Germany, Sunday was a day to enjoy the natural world and celebrate Germany's distinctive culture—a day to be spent hiking in the mountains and singing folksongs. Such were the main activities of the neo-pagan *Wandervogel* movement—a German nationalist youth group founded in the early twentieth century that became popular during the Weimar Era. "Many expounded a pantheistic love of nature and mystical love of the fatherland."[44]

Many nineteenth-century Englishmen also liked to spend their Sundays outdoors. In the middle of the nineteenth century, the word "outing," which first meant (according to the *OED*), "the action of going out or forth," or "the action of putting or driving out," came to mean "an excursion, esp. one lasting a (part of) a day." If families had the means, they went on Sunday outings—to the countryside, the mountains, or the seashore. In England cultural puritanism was not as strong a force as it was in Germany. It generally took the form of insularity, a conviction that other countries, as Mr. Podsnap says in Dickens' *Our Mutual Friend*, are "a mistake."

It would be wrong, though, to assume that in nineteenth-century Britain nature worship had triumphed over Christianity. In the poem "Dover Beach," published in 1867, Matthew Arnold speaks of the "melancholy, long, withdrawing roar" of the "Sea of Faith," but in the first half of the nineteenth century faith was not withdrawing. The rise of evangelicalism in the last two decades of the eighteenth century reanimated Christianity in Britain. There was a renewed interest in enforcing existing sabbatarian laws and in passing new laws that would further restrict activities on Sunday.

Chapter Six

The Rise and Decline of the Victorian Sunday

While some Englishmen were finding God in the mountains, others were finding Jesus in an open field. In February 1739 George Whitefield, a powerful speaker, had begun to preach outdoors. A month after Whitefield began preaching outdoors, John Wesley followed suit, though at first he was reluctant to do so. "I could scarcely reconcile myself . . . to this strange way of preaching in the fields of which [he] set me an example on Sunday."[1]

Open-air preaching was not new. It had been done occasionally a century earlier by the Quakers and other Dissenting sects, but it was new for Anglicans. Whitefield, an Anglican minister, played down the importance of Anglican liturgy. "It was best," he said, "to preach the new birth, and the power of godliness, and not to insist so much on the form." Many Anglicans were outraged. Whitefield's outdoor preaching, a contemporary said, was "a shocking departure from Church rules and usages."[2]

Like Whitefield, Wesley was an Anglican priest, but he gradually built up a "Connexion," as it was called, within the Church of England. In England Methodism did not become a separate denomination until after Wesley died in 1791, though in the United States the break occurred in 1784. In 1741 Whitefield split with Wesley over theological differences, but both stressed the importance of being born again and both thought Sunday was a holy day that should be strictly observed. In 1745 Wesley wrote that England was "on the brink of utter destruction . . . because of our sins." The first sin he listed was "sabbath breaking."[3]

Wesley spent fifty years preaching both outdoors and in meeting-houses—a popular print shows Wesley preaching in a church grave-yard—but Methodism grew slowly. In 1791 there were only 79,000 Methodists in England, but in the ensuing decades Methodism gained many new adherents, as did evangelical Christianity in general. Historians speak of the period as the Evangelical Revival. In the United States it is called the Second Great Awakening.

Thus, in the last two decades of the eighteenth century two very different currents of thought were growing stronger in Britain. One was Romantic primitivism, which manifested itself in the Ossian craze; the other was evangelicalism, a movement that affected all Christian denominations. Romantic primitivists were not interested in the question of Sunday observance. Evangelicals were deeply interested in this question, for most were sabbatarians. The Sunday Observance Society was founded in 1775 and the Society for Promoting the External Observance of the Lord's Day was founded in 1831.

Hannah More

One of the leading figures in the Evangelical Revival was Hannah More. Born in 1745—six years after Whitefield and Wesley began preaching outdoors—More was a prolific author (poems, stories, plays, and tracts), a founder of many Sunday schools, and a tireless fundraiser for many charitable undertakings. If Wesley rode all over

England in search of new places to preach—he could read books on horseback—More often could be seen traveling "on horseback [in the greater Bristol area] in all weathers through country roads that were muddy and dusty in order to teach ragged children to read and to set up friendly societies for their mothers."[4] More remained an Anglican all her life, but she was on good terms with many Methodists, who she believed made the best Sunday-school teachers.

The young More was an unlikely candidate for evangelicalism—confessing to a friend that "my natural gaiety of temper is not favourable to religion." She enjoyed reading poems and plays, especially Shakespeare. She "durst not read him after supper, as he shook my nerves so, as by his power of excitement to prevent my sleeping."[5] When More was thirteen she attended a school founded by an older sister (she was one of five sisters), and eventually became a teacher there. At the school she learned Italian, Spanish, and French. In her twenties she was a successful local author in Bristol—publishing a long poem and a play.

In May 1774 More moved from Bristol to London with two of her sisters to pursue a literary career. Soon she met David Garrick, who suggested improvements for a play she had written. She also met other leading figures in London's cultural world, including Burke, Reynolds, Johnson, Gibbon, and Elizabeth Montagu. A literary critic, Montagu was the "Queen of the Blues"—an informal group of women writers called bluestockings. In 1783 More wrote "The Bas Bleu: Or, Conversation," a mildly amusing poem in rhymed couplets about the conversational world of the bluestockings. The poem was admired by literary London. Johnson called it "a very great performance." In More's introduction to "The Bas Bleu" we can see a strain of sabbatarian earnestness; she says that the conversation of the bluestockings was "little disgraced by calumny, levity, and the other censurable errors with which it is too commonly tainted."[6]

By any measure More was a success in London. In 1776 she was invited to live with the Garricks, who treated her as if she were their daughter. In 1777 More's tragedy, *Percy*, had a successful run of nineteen performances. She frequently enjoyed the company of Johnson, who gave her a tour of Oxford in 1882. Yet she was not completely happy in London's cultural world. She disliked the raciness of its conversation and she was disturbed by its indifference to religion. Even before she became an evangelical, she was a sabbatarian. One Sunday evening in the summer of 1777 Garrick told her that she did not have to participate in a musical soirée. "You are a *Sunday woman*; retire to your room—I will recall you when the music is over."[7]

More wished London's cultural world would be more religious. She agreed with Boswell that no one read the Bible. She told Reynolds, "I hope the poets and painters will at last bring the Bible into fashion, and that people will get to like it from taste, though they are insensible to its spirit, and afraid of its doctrines."[8] In 1782 she published *Sacred Dramas*—a collection of biblical stories meant for young people. It also included a poem, "Sensibility," which advocated a religion of the heart. The book became an evangelical classic.

More revered Johnson. (Johnson was irritated by her frequent praise of him.) When Johnson died, More said that he had "a zeal for religion which one cannot but admire." More mistakenly thought Johnson had an evangelical conversion on his deathbed. She may have been eager to regard Johnson as an evangelical because she was moving in that direction herself—influenced by the example of James Stonhouse, a family friend who had undergone a conversion experience after a dissolute youth. Like most evangelicals, Stonhouse, who became a clergyman as well as a doctor, was a sabbatarian. In 1775 he chastised More for going to a bluestocking gathering on a Sunday.[9]

More also admired Beilby Porteus, a poet and Anglican bishop whom she first met in 1776. Though Porteus was not an evangelical, he agreed with the evangelicals that Sunday should be observed in a sabbatarian manner. He was concerned about the growth of London debating societies, which usually met on Sunday evenings. In 1780 he introduced a bill to ban them, and a year later the bill passed. In 1787 he was approached by friends to form a society for the reformation of manners—especially to combat "all the various Profanations of the Lord's Day." Serving as the king's chaplain, Porteus may have persuaded George III to issue a sabbatarian proclamation in 1788. It prohibited "all our loving subjects . . . from playing on the Lord's Day at dice, cards, or any other game whatsoever, either in public or in private houses."[10] The aristocracy ignored the unenforceable proclamation.

In London in the 1780s More often heard Thomas Scott preach. A self-educated sheep farmer turned evangelical clergyman, Scott became chaplain to the Lock Hospital for venereal diseases. Situated at Hyde Park Corner, the Lock had become a prominent evangelical pulpit in London. More recollected that Scott had a strong northern accent and very plain manners, but what he said was animated by "sound sense and sound piety."[11]

John Henry Newman, one of the leaders of the "High Church" Oxford Movement, which leaned toward Catholicism, also admired Scott. Born a generation after Scott, Newman praised Scott's autobiography, *The Force of Truth* (1779), which had a wide circulation. Scott, Newman said, was a writer "who made a deeper impression on my mind than any other."[12]

The Anglican intellectuals who founded the Oxford Movement in 1833, the year More died, were called Tractarians because they wrote ninety *Tracts for the Times* in the hope of reforming a church that in their minds was suffering from spiritual lethargy. They wanted to make the Church of England more closely resemble the Church of Rome in both its structure and its worship. Newman said that the Church of England was actually "the Catholic Church in England," the true church that descended directly from Saint Peter.[13] In 1845 Newman would shock England's political and intellectual world by becoming a Catholic.

Though some Tractarians, including Newman, came from evangelical backgrounds and had been sabbatarians, they "abandoned Sabbatarianism as they established the Tractarian movement." John Keble, a leading Tractarian, liked to play cricket with his congregation on summer Sundays after Evensong. Keble wrote *The Christian Year: Thoughts in Verse for the Sundays and Holy Days throughout the Year* (1827). The book of 107 devotional poems arranged according to the Sundays and feast days of the liturgical calendar was a bestseller, which suggests that most Englishmen—sabbatarian or not—regarded Sunday as the Lord's Day. Newman said "it is not necessary . . . to praise a book which has already become one of the classics of the language."[14]

More, who disapproved of "high-fives" (handball) on Sunday, would certainly have disapproved of cricket on Sunday. In any case, she belonged to an older generation. In 1787, almost a half-century before the Oxford Movement began, she befriended two influential evangelical Anglicans. One was William Wilberforce, the leading figure in the crusade to outlaw slavery. Wilberforce was a sabbatarian. In 1787 he said (in his diary): "God Almighty has set before me two great objects, the suppression of the Slave Trade and the Reformation of Manners." By "reformation of manners" he mainly meant the strict observance of the Lord's Day. The other new friend was John Newton, who wrote the famous hymn, "Amazing Grace." Newton's conversion story is well known. He was the first mate on a slave ship, but after surviving a storm at a sea and a severe fever he denounced slavery and decided to become an Anglican priest. More read Newton's *Cardiphonia,* a two-volume epistolary account of his religious progress. The book "did not secure More's immediate conversion," her biographer says, "but it helped set her feet on a new path."[15]

More never had a dramatic conversion experience, but during the late 1780s she gradually withdrew from the London literary world—preferring the company of evangelicals. After Garrick died in 1779, she spent more time in Bristol than London, and in 1785 she bought a house in Cowslip Green, which is near Bristol. Her cultural friends were dismayed by her new religiosity. Garrick's widow said that religion was spoiling More's "fine disposition." Her Bristol publisher said she was now "too good a Christian for an author." Horace Walpole, whom she met in 1780, noted with regret the growth of her "enthusiasm."[16]

In the eighteenth century "enthusiasm" was a word in transition. It was more often than not used in its modern positive sense, yet it still retained its old meaning of "religious fanaticism." Methodists were widely considered to be enthusiasts, and were suspected of being politically radical, though Wesley was a Tory. Many people used "evangelical" and "Methodist" interchangeably. More was called a Methodist though she remained an Anglican her entire life.

Johnson often defended Methodist preachers because he thought they reached people who never went to church. (He admired Wesley, whom he knew from his days at Oxford.) Yet Johnson was angry with a Methodist whom he met in church on Easter Sunday. "I invited home with me the man whose pious behaviour I had for several years observed on this day, and found him a kind of Methodist, full of texts, but ill-instructed. I talked to him with temper, and offered him wine which he refused. I suffered him to go without the dinner which I had purposed to give him." Johnson is annoyed with himself for losing his temper. "Let me not be prejudiced hereafter against the appearance of piety in mean persons, who, with indeterminate notions, and perverse or inelegant conversation perhaps are doing all that they can."[17]

Few mainstream Anglicans would have invited a Methodist to a Sunday dinner. George Horne, the president of Magdalen College at Oxford, said that Methodism, with its emphasis on lay preachers and Bible reading, was a religion of the mob that promoted *"Spiritual Republicanism."* Yet in England friendship often crossed religious lines, and Horne and More became good friends. When Horne died in 1792, More remembered him fondly: "How wise and how witty, how pleasant and how good he was."[18] She was grateful that Horne supported her efforts to establish Sunday schools.

More agreed with the Methodists that Sabbath breaking was a major problem in England. In 1788 she published *Thoughts on the Importance of the Manners of the Great to General Society*. In the pamphlet, which went through seven editions in three months, she attacked persons of rank and fortune for not observing the Sabbath. "They acknowledge the truth of the Christian religion," she says, yet they attend Sunday concerts and walk in public gardens on Sunday.[19]

More argues that if the Lord's Day is not observed as a holy day, Christianity will fade away. Sunday is "a kind of Christian Palladium"—a protection against the powerful forces of secularization. She also argues that sabbatarian legislation is enforced inequitably. "Will not the common people think it a little inequitable that they are abridged of the diversions of the public-house and the gaming-yard on Sunday evening, when they shall hear that many houses of the first nobility are on that evening crowded with company?"[20] Her main concern, though, is the fashionable world's indifference to sabbatarianism.

The novelist Fanny Burney praised *Thoughts*, but she had some major reservations about it. "The design is very laudable, and speaks a mind earnest to promote religion and its duties; but it sometimes points out imperfections almost unavoidable, with amendments almost impracticable." Horace Walpole disliked *Thoughts*. Accusing More of "Puritanism," he jokingly argued that the Fourth Commandment "was never intended for people of fashion, as they never do any thing on the other days."[21]

If *Thoughts* did not change the ways of the aristocracy, it boosted More's standing among evangelicals, and it cemented her connection with the Clapham Sect—a coterie of wealthy evangelical Anglicans, including Wilberforce, who lived in Clapham, a suburb of London. (They were also known derisively as the "Saints.") Many of these philanthropically minded evangelicals—they included bankers, government officials, and members of Parliament—would provide financial support for More's new project: establishing a network of Sunday schools in the Bristol area.

The Sunday school was a relatively recent development in England. In 1741 Wesley opened the first school in Newcastle in the largest Methodist meeting-house in England.[22] Sunday schools did not become widespread until the 1780s, when Robert Raikes, the editor of the *Gloucester Journal*, established several schools in the Gloucester area to teach elementary subjects as well as study Scripture. According to the *OED*, "Sunday school" was first used in the *Gloucester Journal* (November 1783): "Some of the clergy . . . bent upon attempting a reform among the children of the lower class, are establishing Sunday schools, for rendering the Lord's day subservient to the ends of instruction, which has hitherto been prostituted to bad purposes."

More and other evangelicals thought the Sunday school would help to change the view of the "lower class" that Sunday was mainly a holiday. In 1783 the Sunday School Society, an interdenominational group, was founded to give the schools financial support. Twenty years later the Sunday School Union was founded to provide books and other materials to the schools. In roughly a decade More and her sister Patty set up eleven Sunday schools in the Bristol area. By 1824 the schools had 1,000 pupils.

Sunday schools expanded rapidly in nineteenth-century England. By 1800 there were at least 200,000 working-class children enrolled in them. By the 1890s three-quarters of all English children attended Sunday schools.[23] The schools had a mixed reception. Some people thought they gave the poor ideas above their station. Others thought they were run by Methodists and therefore were seditious. A Tory journal, the *Anti-Jacobin,* made the unfounded claim that a "vast number" of former Sunday school pupils "were turned skeptics, and infidels and anarchists, and were spreading a malignant influence though the mass of the community."[24]

More and her sister were also accused of attempting to take away whatever pleasures the working poor had. More wanted children to enjoy Sunday school, so she told teachers to "try to make it pleasant by cheerful manners . . . and by avoiding corporal punishment." The teachers, More said, should abide by the following rule: "Whatever makes them [the children] hate Sunday is wrong."[25]

In "Sunday School," one of many didactic stories More wrote, she describes the trials and tribulations of someone who is setting up a Sunday school. Mrs. Jones—an energetic woman like More—asks a rich farmer for a charitable donation to her school. At first he refuses to give her money because he thinks that teaching the poor how to read will make them less conscientious workers, but she reassures him that if the workers read the Bible they will be more conscientious. The farmer remains skeptical, but eventually she persuades him to support the Sunday school.

In the story Mrs. Jones also sets up Sunday evening Bible-reading sessions for "grown-up youth." The classes, she says, were a big success. "And it was observed that as the school filled, not only the fives court [handball] and public house was thinned, but even Sunday gossiping and tea visiting declined." These remarks reveal More's ambitious sabbatarian goals: she even disapproves of Sunday "tea visiting."[26]

Yet in the sequel to the first story of Mrs. Jones, the narrator insists that Sunday should not be gloomy. "Religion must be made pleasant, and instruction must be carried on in a kind, and agreeable, and familiar way." More even tries to persuade her readers that attending a Sunday evening Bible study class is a holiday activity. "To attend Mrs. Jones's evening instructions was soon thought not a task but a holiday."[27] It is doubtful that those who attended Sunday evening classes thought they were enjoying a holiday.

Exhausted by her "punishing Sundays," More often spent Monday in bed, suffering from a migraine attack. A Sunday she spent with the newly married Wilberforce and his bride was especially grueling. Years later Barbara Wilberforce described what, in effect, was her honeymoon. The day began at More's house in Cowslip Green, where they had spent the night. The first stop was a church in Shipham, where parishioners strewed flowers on a gravel walk "in honour of the Bride." Then they went to Axbridge, where they called on a man whose wife was dying of cancer. The next stop was a Sunday school classroom, where they were confronted by "a furious dirty woman" who was noisily withdrawing her son because of "some petty punishment." Then they left for Cheddar, where they had a cold lunch. After attending a church service in Cheddar, they visited another schoolroom, where they heard children answer questions about the Bible. In the evening, after tea, they heard children read prayers, and then they returned to Cowslip Green.[28]

Though busy with her schools and the female clubs that she had

founded for adult women, More found time to write, and in the
1790s she published a number of works. *An Estimate of the Religion of
the Fashionable World* (1791) was similar to the sabbatarian tract she
had published three years earlier and similar to Law's *Serious Call*.
She said the fashionable world was guilty of *"practical irreligion"*—
paying only lip service to Christianity. Like her previous work, *An
Estimate* was widely read, going through five editions by 1793, but it
had little impact. Walpole said it was "prettily written but her enthusiasm increases."[29]

A year after *Estimate*, More wrote another tract, *Village Politics*.
Some observers called the work, which was published anonymously,
"Burke for Beginners" because its argument is similar to the argument in Edmund Burke's *Reflections on the Revolution in France*
(1791). *Village Politics* takes the form of a dialogue between a blacksmith who defends the British constitutional order and a mason who
is sympathetic to the French Revolution. The debate takes place in a
village where all the classes live in harmony. The resident squire,
who cares about the villagers, supports the local Sunday school.[30]

The blacksmith is not a conventional Tory, for he defends religious liberty. "Now, tho' some folks pretend that a man's hating a
Papist or a Presbyterian, proves him to be a good *Churchman*, it don't
prove him to be a good *Christian*. . . . I'd scorn to *live* in a country
where there was no liberty of conscience; and where every man
might not worship God his own way." More thought all Christians
should band together against the anti-Christians who held power in
France, for these zealots had repressed traditional religion, banned
the Lord's Day, and required everyone to worship the Supreme
Being.[31]

Village Politics was successful. Fanny Burney, who liked it, said that
"it makes much noise in London, & is suspected to be by some capital Author."[32] The fashionable world agreed with More about the

French Revolution, especially after the French king was executed in January 1793, but it was not interested in More's sabbatarianism.

More needed money for her projects, so she kept up her contacts in the fashionable world, even though she decried its "practical irreligion." Persuading Elizabeth Montagu to subscribe to the Sunday School Society, More said: "Your *name* will be the great thing." More was a good fundraiser—gaining "substantial sums of money." By contrast, Wesley disdained the fashionable world. He said: "To speak the rough truth, I do not desire intercourse with any person of quality in England."[33]

In order to gain financial support from the fashionable world, More was willing to soften her sabbatarianism. When the Duchess of Gloucester suggested that it would be a good idea to hold a Sunday concert for charitable purposes, More offered a temporizing reply. "I am inclined to think, that no *amusement*, however modified, can be made consistent with the Christian observance of that day, for though the act itself might, to a religious mind, be made even an act of piety; yet, as your Royal Highness observes, many difficulties respecting performers &c. would attend such a plan."[34] More doesn't rule out a Sunday concert, which might even be "an act of piety," but she thinks it might not be feasible to hold one, given the "many difficulties respecting performers."

More tried to promote sabbatarianism in another way: she helped to initiate a line of publications called Cheap Repository Tracts. These were inexpensive chapbooks—softcover books of four to twenty-four pages that often were illustrated with woodcuts. More embarked on this project, which she said "hardly leaves me time to eat," because she was disturbed that contemporary chapbooks were secular works that often were ribald. She told Hesther Piozzi that "30,000 Hawkers are maintain'd by this dissolute Traffic, and Boat loads of it [chapbooks] are sent away from the Trading Towns to infect the villages." She wanted to circulate "Religious and Useful Knowledge as an antidote to the poison continually flowing thro' the channel of vulgar and licentious publications."[35]

The "religious and useful knowledge" would be contained in short stories about "striking Conversions, Holy Lives, Happy Deaths, Providential Deliverances, Judgments on the Breakers of Commandments, Stories of Good and Wicked Apprentices, Hardened Sinners, Pious Servants &c." More wrote many tracts herself (they were published anonymously but those marked Z were written by her). The tracts are well written and often describe accurately the lives of the rural poor, but they always have a predictable ending. According to Anne Stott, More's biographer, "everything always turns out for the best provided one goes to church and keeps the sabbath."[36]

The project was a publishing success. By the end of 1795 two million tracts had been distributed, but the low price they were sold for did not meet the cost of paying authors, printers, and distributors. To make up the difference, More asked many people to become subscribers. The list of subscribers included the prime minister, William Pitt, who gave three guineas, as well as many of More's female friends.

In the last three decades of More's life she continued to push for the enforcement of sabbatarian legislation. She also wrote a wide variety of works. They include a collection of patriotic ballads, a book on female education, a work entitled *Christian Morals*, a study of Saint Paul, and a bestselling evangelical novel: *Coelebs in Search of a Wife* (1805). Jane Austen's sister Cassandra liked it, but Jane Austen said she was not interested in reading it. "You have by no means raised my curiosity about Caleb [*sic*]," and she added: "I do not like Evangelicals."[37]

There were many reasons Austen would have disliked evangelicals, but perhaps the main one is that most evangelicals—like their

Puritan forebears—disapproved of fiction that wasn't didactic and explicitly Christian. Most nineteenth-century English writers disliked evangelicals. George Eliot said about More: "I like neither her letters, nor her books, nor her character, nor her beliefs."[38]

More, though, never completely rejected the literary world that she had left. She republished her early plays, and she continued to read imaginative literature, especially Milton and Shakespeare. She read some contemporary literature—she mentions Walter Scott and William Wordsworth—but her favorite contemporary writer was the evangelical poet William Cowper. Reading Cowper's long poem *The Task,* she said: "I have found what I have been looking for all my life, a poet whom I can read on a Sunday."[39]

More continued to correspond with the deist Horace Walpole, who half-jokingly called her "Saint Hannah" or "Holy Hannah." His last gift to her was a three-volume edition of the Bible, inscribed "To his excellent friend MISS HANNAH MORE . . . as a mark of his esteem and gratitude." She told her sister Patty that she would miss Walpole's "unclouded kindness and pleasant correspondence." Nineteen years later she told an acquaintance that "I have not ceased to mourn [Walpole], not on account of his death but his unhappy prejudices against religion."[40]

Though More had no effect on Walpole's religious views, many observers thought she was a successful promoter of evangelicalism and sabbatarianism. In 1843 the publisher of the first complete American edition of More's work said that "no writer of the past or present age has equaled HANNAH MORE in the application of great talents to the improvement of society. . . . Her works have, indeed, in a very striking manner, and to an extraordinary extent, given a new and most important feature to the moral character of the nation she adorned. They have diffused vital religion." More did not think she was influential. She often complained that her writings had little impact. When Queen Charlotte died in 1817, More said that "not only our Nobles and Gentry but the middle classes" were "learning to desecrate the Sabbath."[41]

John Ruskin

If we think of religious views as geographic places, John Ruskin, the leading nineteenth-century British art critic, traveled in a different direction from Hannah More but not exactly in the opposite direction. In her thirties More went from the High Church Anglicanism of her parents to evangelicalism. In his thirties Ruskin said goodbye to the evangelicalism of his parents, yet he was not sure where he was going. It is difficult to chart Ruskin's turbulent religious life. He was a prolific writer (his collected works number thirty-nine volumes), and at times he took a religious position for argument's sake. He lamented his "incurably desultory character which has brought upon me the curse of Reuben, 'Unstable as water, thou shalt not excel.'"[42]

In *Praeterita*, the autobiography Ruskin wrote intermittently in the late 1880s but abandoned in 1889 because of a complete mental collapse, he describes his break with evangelicalism. His "final apostasy from Puritan doctrine"—"Puritan" and "evangelical" were often used interchangeably—took place on a Sunday morning in 1858, when he was worshiping in the chapel of a Protestant sect called the Waldensians. In the chapel—located on the outskirts of Turin—Ruskin realizes that he dislikes the preacher, whom he calls "a somewhat stunted figure . . . with a cracked voice" (441). (In an autobiographical essay written a decade earlier, Ruskin called the minister "a little squeaking idiot [who] was preaching to an audience of seventeen old women and three louts, that they were the only children of God in Turin.") The preacher, he says sardonically, "put his utmost zeal into a consolatory discourse on the wickedness of the wide world, more especially of the plain of Piedmont and city of Turin, and on the exclusive favour with God, enjoyed by the between nineteen and twenty-four elect members of his congregation" (441).[43]

Ruskin left the Waldensian church—he doesn't say whether he stayed until the service ended—and walked to Turin.

> I walked back into the condemned city [condemned by the preacher he disliked], and up into the gallery where Paul Veronese's Solomon and the Queen of Sheba glowed in full afternoon light. The gallery windows being open, there came in with the warm air, floating swells and falls of military music, from the courtyard before the palace, which seemed to me more devotional, in their perfect art, tune, and discipline, than anything I remembered of evangelical hymns. And as the perfect colour and sound gradually asserted their power on me, they seemed finally to fasten me in the old article of Jewish faith, that things done delightfully and rightly were always done by the help and in the Spirit of God. (441)

In this passage Ruskin turns an aesthetic moment—viewing the Veronese painting and listening to the military music—into a religious moment. Appreciating great art, Ruskin suggests, is a better form of divine worship than listening to a dreary Protestant sermon or singing an evangelical hymn.

In an earlier essay Ruskin speaks of the experience as a conversion. "I came out of the chapel . . . a conclusively *un*-converted man."[44] He was unconverted, that is, from evangelicalism. In *Praeterita* he puts it less dramatically: "Of course that hour's meditation in the gallery of Turin only concluded the courses of thought which had been leading me to such end through many years. There was no sudden conversion possible to me, either by preacher, picture, or dulcimer. But, that day, my evangelical beliefs were put away, to be debated of no more" (441). Ruskin put away his belief in evangelicalism—not in Christianity.

The experience in the chapel may have led Ruskin to disavow evangelicalism, but he had already abandoned sabbatarianism. A few weeks before the fateful Sunday in Turin, he had begun to read French novels on Sunday—and also draw. Beneath his first Sunday sketch, he wrote (a decade later): "This drawing of orchises [orchids] was the first I ever made on Sunday: and marks, henceforward, the beginning of [a] total change in habits of mind."[45]

Ruskin had already concluded that the New Testament does not support the notion that Sunday should be observed in a sabbatarian fashion. "Gradually, in honest Bible reading, I saw that Christ's first article of teaching was to unbind the yoke of the Sabbath, while, *as* a Jew, He yet obeyed the Mosaic law concerning it; but that St Paul had carefully abolished it altogether, and that the rejoicing, in memory of the Resurrection, on the Day of the Sun, the first of the week, was only by misunderstanding, and much willful obstinacy, confused with the Sabbath of the Jew" (438). Ruskin, though, is still moved by passages about the Sabbath in the Hebrew Bible: "the great passages in the Old Testament regarding its [the Sabbath's] observance held their power over me, nor have ceased to do so" (438).

Although Ruskin left evangelicalism, his evangelical upbringing continued to color his thinking. In 1888, attempting to explain his religious views to a young woman whom he had befriended, Ruskin sounds like an evangelical—saying that "our God is a *consuming* fire." He also sounds like an evangelical when he worries that "the extreme forms of religious distress into which I continually fall, are manifestly diseased; possibly diabolic, temptations."[46] It is in the evangelical grain to fear that one may be suffering from diabolical temptations.

In different ways Sunday remained a special day for the "unconverted" Ruskin. A year after he went to the art gallery in Turin, he began to write letters on Sunday to the girls who attended Winnington School, where he taught art, divinity, and many other subjects. The long semiformal public "Sunday letters" are mainly about interpreting the Bible, but he also discusses current affairs, books, and art; and he addresses remarks to particular girls—answering questions they raised. The letters, which he wrote for roughly five years, were read aloud and copied.[47]

In later years, when Ruskin became mentally unstable, Sunday became a day when he thought special things would happen to him, both good and bad. In 1877, a year before his first mental breakdown, he speaks obsessively of Sunday in his diary: "On this morning of Sunday 24th, last but one of the year's Sundays." He also writes: "First day. Sunday the 24th began . . . with crashing rain, intense darkness, and I utterly languid—no, *very* languid. I had been praying, but with languor inconceivable to myself, yet languor earnest enough in its feebleness somehow—or at least, real and honest prayer, what little there was—for a new sign from Rose."[48]

Rose is Rose La Touche—a deeply religious young woman whom Ruskin had proposed to in 1866, when he was forty-seven and she was seventeen. (Because she was in poor health, she had not fully matured, so she looked younger than seventeen.) Shocked by Ruskin's proposal, Rose's parents refused to let their daughter correspond with Ruskin or see him. Yet six years later they relented, and let him see Rose again. While Ruskin and Rose were walking to a village church one Sunday, he gave her a letter that intimated they might be married some time in the future. She did not open it. Perhaps Ruskin told her about the contents of the letter, for later that day (on a train) Rose broke down—screaming at him and telling him what a vile man he was. Rose returned to Ireland, where she lived with her parents. A few weeks later, when Ruskin was about to enter a different church one Sunday morning, he was handed a packet. It included his letter to Rose—unopened. Furious, Ruskin turned back from the church porch. He did not attend church that Sunday.[49]

The unopened letter turned Ruskin against Rose and her parents—and turned him temporarily against religion. On a Sunday morning Ruskin wrote Joan Severn (the woman who took care of his ailing mother and would take care of him when he descended into madness): "When the thing one is meant to pray for turns out not worth prayer—what is one to do?" Ruskin's anger soon metamorphosed into an obsessive longing to be in contact with Rose. On Sundays he often looked for signs from Rose. In 1867 he wrote Severn that "in the calm sky of last Sunday morning—there may have been the word of God to me," by which he probably meant a vision of Rose.[50] Rose died in 1875, but Ruskin continued to look for signs from her.

According to Ruskin, Sunday had always been a difficult day for him. In *Praeterita* he claims that "the inveterate habit of being unhappy all Sunday" was the effect of a childhood spent in a sabbatarian household (438). "The horror of Sunday," he says in the opening chapter, "used even to cast its prescient gloom as far back in the week as Friday" (23). In a later chapter he refers to gloomy Sunday again: "the gloom, and even terror, with which the restrictions of the Sunday, and the doctrines of the *Pilgrim's Progress*, the *Holy War*, and Quarles' *Emblems*, oppressed the seventh part of my time" (114). He is referring to books that warn of eternal damnation for those who profane the Sabbath. His mother told him about "a wicked boy [who] had fallen into the pond on Sunday, and forthwith the soul of him into a deeper and darker pool" (79).

Sunday, Ruskin says, meant hours of boredom in church. "I found the bottom of the pew so extremely dull a place to keep quiet in, (my best story-books being also taken away from me in the morning,)" (23). Sunday also meant being asked to recite an impromptu sermon for his mother's friends in the afternoon. And it meant being examined in Scripture in the evening by his mother—and discussing a sermon of Hugh Blair's that his father had read. One Sunday afternoon, while enjoying a walk with his father, he felt "some alarmed sense of the sin of being so happy among the hills, instead of writing out a sermon at home" (84).

Though Ruskin says that Sunday was "the only form of vexation which I was called on to endure," there were other aspects of his childhood that disturbed him (114). Twice he notes that he was whipped if he was troublesome. He also says that he "was never permitted for an instant to hope, or even imagine, the possession of such things as one saw in toy-shops" (19). When he was five, he played with a bunch of keys. A year later he played with "two boxes of well-cut wooden bricks." His main pleasures were quasi-aesthetic. He enjoyed "tracing the squares and comparing the colours of my carpet;—examining the knots in the wood of the floor, or counting the bricks in the opposite houses. . . . The carpet, and what patterns I could find in bed-covers, dresses, or wall-papers to be examined, were my chief resources" (19–20).

Ruskin's portrait of his sabbatarian childhood is plausible, since Scotland was the most sabbatarian country in Europe, but it is not accurate. Ruskin's parents were not strict sabbatarians. They went to church only once on Sunday, and they often entertained on Sunday evenings. At these dinners wine was served, which is not surprising since Ruskin's father was an importer of wine (mainly sherry). The young Ruskin was not deprived of toys. He had a rocking-horse and all the books and drawing materials he wanted. He also had dogs and a pony.[51]

Ruskin's father was a voracious reader who liked Shakespeare,

Cervantes, Pope, and Johnson. He also read Byron, a writer evangelicals abhorred, and he went to the theater—often taking his son with him. The family frequently toured the Continent, where they visited many cathedrals (though they never traveled on Sunday). While traveling they would read Johnson's essays aloud. Like Johnson, Ruskin's father distrusted enthusiasm. When Ruskin was in his twenties, his father warned him that "too much enthusiasm in Religion ends in Selfishness or Madness."[52]

Ruskin's mother was more religious than her husband—she never went to the theater—but she was not a strict sabbatarian. In *Praeterita* Ruskin says she was not like Esther Summerson's religious aunt in Dickens' *Bleak House*, who went to church three times on Sunday and never smiled. His mother had a hearty, frank, and irrepressible laugh. "She and my father enjoyed their *Humphrey Clinker* extremely, long before *I* was able to understand either the jest or gist of it" (129). Evangelicals rarely read novels, let alone Smollett's racy picaresque novel.

Ruskin's parents were evangelicals insofar as they read Scripture every day and they distrusted churches that emphasized liturgy more than Bible reading. They required their son "by steady daily toil, to learn long chapters of the Bible by heart" (13). Ruskin was grateful. "To that discipline—patient, accurate, and resolute—I owe, not only a knowledge of the book . . . but much of my general power of taking pains, and the best part of my taste in literature" (13–14). Ruskin claimed that he read the Bible every day.

Why does Ruskin, who has great affection for his parents, misrepresent his childhood—making the Sundays of his childhood gloomier than they were? Perhaps he does so because he wants to make the case that evangelicalism damaged his psyche. In *Praeterita* he speaks of "the falseness of the religious doctrines in which I had been educated" (430). In a letter to his father, written in 1864, he complains: "You thwarted me in all the earnest fire of passion and life." Ruskin blames evangelicalism more than he blames his father: "for I thought it my duty to be thwarted—it was the religion that led me all wrong there."[53] Evangelical religion, he says, made him deeply neurotic.

In "The Mystery of Life and Its Arts," a lecture Ruskin gave in 1869, he makes the same point. "I will not speak of the crimes which in past times have been committed in the name of Christ, nor of the follies which are at this hour held to be consistent with obedience to Him; but I *will* speak of the morbid corruption and waste of vital power in religious sentiment, by which the pure strength of that which should be the guiding soul of every nation, the splendour of its youthful manhood . . . is averted or cast away."[54] By "religious sentiment" he clearly means evangelicalism.

Ruskin's intense dislike of evangelicalism and sabbatarianism led him to express religious views that he did not really hold. In the 1860s he told people he was a pagan. He wrote a clergyman that he was a sun worshiper and that he hoped to become a believer in the Greek gods. "My personal experience of spiritual treatment has been chiefly from sun, moon, wind, and water. . . . And I've got the greatest possible desire to 'believe' in Apollo and Diana—and in Neseus [*sic*] and in water-symbols—and I do, very nearly; so that just a little touch of strong will will do it."[55]

Ruskin never came to believe in Apollo, Diana, or Nessus. He said he was a pagan because he wanted to shake up British Protestantism, which he called a "dull-droning drowsing inanity." British Protestantism, he suggests, needs a dose of paganism to make it less insular. In *The Queen of the Air* (1869) he argues that the Greek gods have much to teach British Protestants about the world, especially the natural world. Carlyle applauded Ruskin's remarks about paganism. Rose La Touche did not. She was disturbed by his letters to her mother in which he talked about his "heathenism." She asked him: "How could one love you, if you were a pagan?"[56]

To irritate British Protestants, especially evangelicals, Ruskin also praises Catholicism. In *Praeterita* he contrasts the French Catholic Sunday with its Scottish Protestant counterpart. "For here [in Abbeville] I saw that art . . . religion, and present human life, were yet in perfect harmony. There were no dead six days and dismal seventh in those sculptured churches" (140). He also talks about a "purely Catholic village and valley" in the Alps, where the Sunday services are "much pleasanter and prettier than the Sunday services . . . in England, which exhaust the little faith we have left" (427).

In *Praeterita* Ruskin claims that his father disliked going to church—and he has the same view as his father: "I knew very well that he liked going just as little as I did" (426). In the 1860s Ruskin occasionally went to church on Sunday—his paganism notwithstanding—but he usually preferred solitary acts of worship. In 1867 he writes that he is "not much inclined to go to church" but he will do so in order to please Rose. He tells Joan Severn that "I always—even in my naughtiest times—had a way of praying on hill summits, when I could get quiet on them." Angry with Rose's father for turning Rose against him, he notes in his diary that on a mountaintop he "knelt down to pray that it [the sun] might not go down on my wrath."[57]

Ruskin's love of mountains was as strong as Gray's. "My most intense happinesses have of course been among mountains" (141). Anticipating his first sight of the Alps, he writes: "The chain of the Alps! Within one's grasp for Sunday! What a Sunday—instead of customary Walworth and the Dulwich fields!" (99). The Ruskin family often worshiped in a chapel in Walworth and went for a stroll in

Dulwich fields. Traveling in the Alps, Ruskin talks about "the spiritual power of the air, the rocks, the waters" (149). In the following passage he seems to be describing a conversion experience. "But the Col de la Faucille [a pass in the Alps], on that day of 1835, opened to me in distinct vision the Holy Land of my future work and true home in this world. My eyes had been opened, and my heart with them, to see and to possess royally such a kingdom!" (150).

Ruskin says that mountain rhapsodists like himself have shaped Western culture. In *Praeterita* he talks about how in his first book, *Modern Painters*, "I tried to trace . . . the power of mountains in solemnizing the thoughts and purifying the hearts of the greatest nations of antiquity, and the greatest teachers of Christian faith" (423). He also mentions a brief exchange he had with a monk who took him on a tour of the Grande Chartreuse, a famous monastery in the Alps that Wordsworth writes about in *The Prelude*. He and the monk came to "a type of a modern Carthusian's cell, wherein, leaning on the window sill, I said something in the style of *Modern Painters*, about the effect of the scene outside upon religious minds. Whereupon, with a curl of his lip, 'We do not come here,' said the monk, 'to look at the mountains.' Under which rebuke I bent my head silently, thinking however all the same, 'What then, by all that's stupid, do you come here for at all?'" (424).

Ruskin thinks the monk is a fool for not realizing that someone with a "religious mind" strengthens his faith by gazing at the Alps. Is Ruskin saying, as Gray said, that to have a profound religious experience one should make a pilgrimage to the Alps or any spectacular mountain? He is, but with a major qualification. Before making the pilgrimage, Britons have to purify themselves of "coarse lusts." By "coarse lusts" he means what Goldsmith and other eighteenth-century writers meant by "Luxury." He uses the phrase in *Praeterita* when describing a major flaw in *Modern Painters*. "I did not then dwell then on what I had only felt, but not ascertained,—the destruction of all sensibility of this high order in the populations of modern Europe, first by the fine luxury of the fifteenth century, and then by the coarse lusts of the eighteenth and early nineteenth" (423).

Ruskin is telling his readers: Don't bother to make a pilgrimage to a mountain until you have purified yourself of coarse lusts. In many essays Ruskin, who never had to worry about money because his father was a successful businessman, attacks commercial Britain. In "Traffic" he says: "I think you will admit that the ruling goddess [of Britain] may be best generally described as the 'Goddess of Getting-On' or 'Britannia of the Market.'"[58] According to Ruskin, the "destruction of all sensibility"—a destruction caused by Britain's addiction to commerce—has affected religion. "Religious men themselves became incapable of education by any natural beauty or nobleness" (423). Even religious men, Ruskin says, have been tainted by the commercialization of British life. Ruskin, his biographer says, "disliked almost all clergymen."[59]

Ruskin dislikes evangelicalism, but he is a Puritan of sorts: he wants Britons to purify themselves of "coarse lusts." This is a sacred cause for him. He returns from a Sunday evening walk in the Alps "with my destiny fixed in all of it that was to be sacred and useful" (102). If Britons purify themselves, they will be able "to see clearly"—to appreciate what is great in nature and art. "To see clearly," he says in *Modern Painters*, "is poetry, prophecy, and religion,—all in one."[60]

Ruskin is antievangelical, antisabbatarian, and anticlerical, but he is not anti-Christian. "He never ceased to believe," his biographer says, "that the Christian God was his maker and that Jesus Christ was his saviour." If Ruskin had his way, purified Britons would still read the Bible on Sunday but they would not go to church—or go only occasionally. Instead, they would make a pilgrimage to a mountain or an art museum. "Pictures," he said, "will become gradu-ally as necessary to daily life as books."[61]

In a letter to his father, Ruskin says a great artist may be a better servant of God than a Protestant minister—especially a boring and shrill minister. "And is this mighty Paul Veronese, in whose soul there is a strength as of the snowy mountains, and within whose brain all the pomp and majesty of humanity floats in a marshalled glory, capacious and serene like clouds at sunset—this man whose finger is as fire, and whose eye is like the morning—is he a servant of the devil; and is the poor little wretch in a tidy black tie, to whom I have been listening this Sunday morning expounding Nothing with a twang—is he a servant of God?"[62]

Ruskin does not say that art is a substitute for religion, but he does say that appreciating art is a form of worship—a better form of wor-ship than attending church on Sunday. Ruskin praises George Her-bert and Samuel Johnson, yet Herbert and Johnson stress the im-portance of public worship whereas Ruskin prefers private worship. Johnson is disturbed that he attends church infrequently on Sunday; Ruskin proudly announces that he does not go to church. "I don't go to church—I cannot." By choosing not to attend church, Ruskin is showing his disdain for "false, formal Christianity."[63]

Though mainstream political observers disagreed with Ruskin's diagnosis that Britain needed to be purified of coarse lusts, Ruskin was a very influential writer who was admired by many people, in-cluding such English socialists as William Morris and R. H. Tawney. George Eliot called him "the finest writer living." She did not think much of evangelical preachers either. In an essay written in 1855, she sarcastically says:

> Pleasant to the clerical flesh . . . is the arrival of Sunday! Some-what at a disadvantage during the week, in the presence of working-day interests and lay splendours, on Sunday the preacher

becomes the cynosure of a thousand eyes. . . . The preacher is completely master of the situation; no one may hiss, no one may depart. Like the writer of imaginary conversations, he may put what imbecilities he pleases in the mouths of his antagonists, and swell with triumph when he has refuted them. He may riot in gratuitous assertions, confident that no man will contradict him.[64]

Many educated Englishmen agreed with Ruskin that the appreciation of art could be a religious experience, but few rejected Christianity altogether. Even agnostics declared their affection for the Church of England. The historian G. M. Trevelyan described himself as an agnostic, "but an Anglican agnostic." Philip Larkin made the same point sixty years later: "I'm an agnostic, I suppose, but an Anglican agnostic, of course."[65]

The artist J. M. W. Turner, whom Ruskin greatly admired, liked to paint on Sunday rather than go to church, yet when Turner was visiting a clergyman friend he would usually go to church. His biographer says that "there are many early drawings of church services." He does not say whether Turner sketched while attending the service.[66]

A few weeks before Turner died, he is reported to have said: "The sun is God." The source for this remark is Ruskin, but Ruskin was not present when it was made. Turner's biographer speculates that Turner "may equally have said, 'the Son is God,'" but this seems highly unlikely. For one thing, a devout Christian would probably not express his faith using this locution. Second, for most of his life Turner was preoccupied with painting sunlight, especially sunlight at dawn. "People talk a lot about *sunsets*," he told an acquaintance, "but when you are all fast asleep, I am watching the effects of *sunrise*, [which are] far more beautiful." A fellow painter recalled that Turner would ascend to the roof of his house "just before sunrise, and if there was a fair promise of an effective rising he would remain to study it, making pencil notes of the form of clouds, and writing in brief their tints of colour."[67] Though Turner was an occasional churchgoer, he may have been a pagan sun worshiper at heart.

Edmund Gosse

Edmund Gosse, the leading literary critic in late Victorian and Edwardian England, admired Ruskin—or at least he did when he was a young man. In *Father and Son* (1907), Gosse remembers "the zeal with which I snatched at a volume of Carlyle or Ruskin—since these magicians were now first revealing themselves to me—and the increasing languor with which I took up . . . my daily 'passage' [from the Bible]" (216). Living in an evangelical household, the young Gosse (he was in his early teens) was "scandalized" by his preference for the secular over the sacred. Yet a decade later he not only rejected evangelicalism; he argued that the pantheism Algernon Swinburne expressed in one of his poems "is at least as comprehensive and reasonable a creed as any other now presented to the human faculty of faith."[68]

Instead of going to church and reading the Bible on Sunday, the adult Gosse (and his wife) spent Sunday afternoons hosting tea parties that were attended by London's leading artists and writers. "One obvious reason why Gosse always entertained on Sundays," his biographer says, "was a determination to transform the dreary Sundays of his childhood."[69]

In the Victorian era many people who grew up in evangelical households made a determined effort to have fun on Sundays. A decade earlier George Eliot, who followed the same path Gosse did from evangelicalism to agnosticism, held Sunday gatherings with her companion, George Henry Lewes. Charles Darwin asked if he could bring his wife. Eliot said that of course he could. "Our hours of reception [on Sunday] are from 1/2 past two till six, & the earlier our friends can come to us, the more fully we are able to enjoy conversation with them. Please do not disappoint us . . . & bring Mrs. Darwin with you, the next time you are in town."[70]

Philip Gosse, Edmund's father, was a respected natural scientist who corresponded with Darwin. He wrote many books about marine life and zoology. He and his wife, Emily, also were members of the Plymouth Brethren, a Calvinist sect that was founded in 1827. According to Edmund, who wrote a biography of his father seventeen years before he wrote *Father and Son*, the "Saints," as the Brethren called themselves, were "extreme Calvinists . . . with no priest, no ritual, no festivals, no ornament of any kind, nothing but the Lord's Supper and the exposition of Holy Scripture."[71] They worshiped in a meeting-house called "the Room."

Philip Gosse did not think Sunday should be called the Sabbath. In *Father and Son* Gosse writes that his father "objected very strongly to the expression 'Sabbath-day,' as it is commonly used by Presbyterians and others. He said, quite justly, that . . . Sabbath was Saturday, the seventh day of the week," and that it was "a Jewish festival and not a Christian commemoration" (167). Although Philip Gosse did not think Sunday should be called the Sabbath, he thought Sunday should be observed in a sabbatarian manner. "His exaggerated view with regard to the observance of the First Day, namely, that it must be exclusively occupied with public and private exercises of divine worship, was based much more upon a Jewish than upon a Christian law" (168).

Gosse's parents were far more sabbatarian than Ruskin's. In *Father and Son* Gosse describes at length the gloomy Sundays of his childhood. "We came down to breakfast at the usual time. My Father prayed briefly before we began the meal; after it, the bell was rung, and, before the breakfast was cleared away, we had a lengthy service of exposition and prayer with the servants. If the weather was fine, we then walked about the garden, doing nothing, for about half an hour. We then sat, each in a separate room, with our Bibles open and some commentary on the text beside us, and prepared our minds for the morning service. A little before 11 A.M. we sallied forth, carrying our Bibles and hymn-books, and went through the morning-service of two hours at the Room; this was the central event of Sunday" (168).

Gosse's family worshiped three times on Sunday. "We then came back to dinner. . . . In the middle of the afternoon, my stepmother and I proceeded up the village to Sunday School, where I was early promoted to the tuition of a few very little boys. We returned in time for tea, immediately after which we all marched forth, again armed, as in the morning, with Bibles and hymn-books, and we went through the evening-service, at which my Father preached. The hour was now already past my week-day bedtime, but we had another service to attend, the Believers' Prayer Meeting, which commonly occupied forty minutes more. Then we used to creep home, I often so tired that the weariness was like physical pain, and I was permitted, without further 'worship,' to slip upstairs to bed" (168–169).

It was not only the long hours spent in worship that made Sundays "a very tedious occasion" for Edmund. It was also "the absence of every species of recreation on the Lord's Day" (167). Sundays were "so peculiarly trying . . . [because] I was not permitted the indulgence of any secular respite. I might not open a scientific book, nor make a drawing, nor examine a specimen. I was not allowed to go into the road, except to proceed with my parents to the Room, nor to discuss worldly subjects at meals. . . . I was hotly and tightly dressed in black, all day long, as though ready at any moment to attend a funeral with decorum. Sometimes, toward evening, I used to feel the monotony and weariness of my position to be almost unendurable, but at this time I was meek" (168–169).

Even on other days of the week, Edmund's activities were restricted. Because his parents did not want their son to be contaminated by "the World," Edmund was not allowed to have "young companions" or any of "the thousand and one employments provided for other children in more conventional surroundings" (23).[72] Gosse's mother, who was a successful writer of religious tracts, thought making up a story was a sin, so "no fiction of any kind, religious or secular, was admitted into the house" (18).

Philip Gosse did not let his religious views influence his scientific work. Yet in one book, *Omphalos* (1857), he tried to reconcile (Edmund says) "Scripture statements and geological deductions" (79). The book was attacked by the scientific community—and ignored by Darwin. Edmund says that "Darwin continued silent, and the youthful [Thomas Henry] Huxley was scornful" (79). Philip Gosse was crushed. "During that grim season, my Father was no lively companion" (79).

It seems unlikely that Philip Gosse was ever a lively companion. Though he belonged to several scientific societies, including the Linnean Society and the Royal Society, he was not clubbable. His parents, Edmund says, "received scarcely any visitors, never ate a meal away from home, [and] never spent an evening in social intercourse abroad. At night they discussed theology, read aloud to one another, or translated scientific brochures from French or German" (11).

Gosse's parents also spent many hours discussing the Book of Revelation—wondering when its prophecies would be fulfilled. When Emily Gosse was dying, she was convinced that certain events occurring in Italy at the time signified that the Church of Rome would soon collapse. Her conviction, Philip Gosse wrote in his diary, which

Edmund quotes, "irradiated her dying hours with an assurance that was like the light of the Morning Star, the harbinger of the rising sun" (51). For the rest of his life Philip Gosse continued to look for signs of end-times.[73]

After Emily Gosse died, Edmund's life became less restricted. A tutor was hired to teach him secular subjects and he was allowed to read some fiction—Dickens but not Scott. The young Ruskin was allowed to read Scott's novels, but many evangelicals disapproved of Scott, perhaps because Scott implied that strict sabbatarians were religious zealots. William Wilberforce said that he would sooner have written *The Shepherd of Salisbury Plain*, a tedious novel by Hannah More, than the works of Scott or Byron.[74]

A few years later Philip Gosse remarried, and Edmund was sent to a boarding school in a nearby town. His stepmother was a moderating influence. "She was a very well-meaning pious lady, but . . . not a fanatic" (156). Yet Sundays were still observed in sabbatarian fashion. Edmund had to come home from Saturday night to Monday morning, so "that there might be no cessation of my communion as a believer with the Saints in our village on Sundays" (186).

When Edmund was away at school, he began to read voraciously: Shakespeare, Keats, Wordsworth, Shelley. He also took an interest in religion, but not from his father's viewpoint. "I began to search the Scriptures for myself with interest and sympathy, if scarcely with ardour" (206). He asked his father many questions about his religious views, but he found his father's answers implausible—even repellent. "I could not sympathise, even in my then state of ignorance, with so rigid a conception of the Divine mercy. Little inclined as I was to be sceptical, I still thought it impossible, that a secret of such stupendous importance [Who shall be redeemed?] should have been entrusted to a group of Plymouth Brethren, and have been hidden from millions of disinterested and pious theologians" (206).

Though Gosse never broke with his father, he found it hard to forgive him for subjecting him to so many gloomy Sundays and to such narrow religious views. A few years after the seventeen-year-old Edmund moved to London in 1866 to work in the cataloguing section of the British Museum, he wrote his father: "I think you are the most difficult Father to satisfy in all the world." Yet Edmund continued to lead an evangelical life for roughly a decade. He lived with two older women who were members of the Plymouth Brethren (one had been a pupil at an academy run by Hannah More). He also worshiped with them at a meeting-house, and he taught in a Sunday school run by the sect. In 1871 he turned down invitations to dine with other writers on Sunday. Two years later he told his father that he no longer read religious books (except the Bible) and that his religious views had changed, yet he still taught at the Sunday school.[75]

In the late 1870s Gosse abandoned evangelicalism. In 1880 he threw a party on Sunday for a number of writers. For the rest of Gosse's life Sunday would mainly be a holiday. Yet he was not hostile to religion. Like Turner, he would go to church if he was staying with friends who were churchgoers.[76]

Did Gosse, like Ruskin, remain a Christian? In *Father and Son* Gosse says that when he was a schoolboy "in my hot and silly brain, Jesus and Pan held sway together, as in a wayside chapel discordantly and impishly consecrated to Pagan and to Christian rites" (209). The adult Gosse's religious views are difficult to determine because Gosse disliked talking about religion. In a letter to Robert Louis Stevenson he implies that he is not a Christian. "I have no anxiety about my soul—I am infinitely and sufficiently amused by the look of people, by the physical movement of things. . . . I am not without terror, sometimes, at the idea of this sensual sufficiency in life coming to an end; I have no idea how the spiritual world would look to me, for I have never glanced at it since I was a child and was gorged with it."[77]

Stevenson was a close friend of Gosse's. So were many other writers, including Henry James and Thomas Hardy. Many leading politicians were also friends of the clubbable Gosse, who often said what people wanted to hear. He wrote to the irreligious Hardy: "I would pray (if I knew any God to pray to)." To Lord Haldane, who probably was religious, he said: "The Lord bless you and keep you. The Lord make his face to shine upon you, and give you peace." When an acquaintance asked him what he believed, Gosse wittily replied: "Nothing supernatural, thank God!"[78]

Gosse, then, differs from Ruskin, who remained a Christian after he broke with evangelicalism. Gosse also differs from Ruskin in that he lacks moral fervor. It is not wise, he writes Stevenson, to be "too didactic in literature. It is the curse of the age, everybody from Ruskin and Matt. Arnold . . . scolding and preaching away. If you also take to preaching I shall sit down and howl."[79] In many respects Gosse is like Joshua Reynolds. Both were clubbable men who had innumerable friends, religious and irreligious. Both thought Sunday was a day when one could write or paint, but it was also a day for afternoon and evening gatherings with friends—a day for conversation rather than worship. Ann Thwaite entitles a chapter of her biography of Gosse "Sunday Talk."

Father and Son was a critical and commercial success. The first edition sold out, and there were fourteen printings in Gosse's lifetime. It was also translated into many languages. George Bernard Shaw told Gosse that his autobiography was "one of the immortal pages of English literature." A reviewer in the *Times Literary Supplement* disagreed. He said Gosse's portrait of his father was disrespectful. "The author of this book has no doubt settled it with his conscience how far in the interests of popular edification and amusement it is legitimate to expose the weaknesses and inconsistencies of a good man who is also one's father."[80]

Gosse did not write *Father and Son* "in the interests of popular edification." The book is not about the narrowness of an extreme Calvinist sect; it is about a son's growing resistance to his father's will. In a letter written to his father in 1874—eight years after Edmund had moved to London—he pleads with his father to leave him be. "If you will but restrain your natural instinct to mould and fashion the character of your own child . . . we may then lay down one another's letters with a sense of full enjoyment."[81]

If Gosse had wanted his book to be an exposé of the Plymouth Brethren, he would not have subtitled it *A Study of Two Temperaments*. Moreover, evangelicalism had already been losing strength in England, as Gosse himself suggests. His book, he says in the preface, offers a "diagnosis of a dying Puritanism" (3). Men like his father are no longer to be found—"so complete is the revolution which has overturned the puritanism of which he was perhaps the last surviving type" (214). Gosse also notes that "the observance of the Lord's Day has already become universally so lax that I think there may be some value in preserving an accurate record of how our Sundays were spent five and forty years ago" (168).

Gosse was right to say that the observance of the Lord's Day had become lax in 1907, when his autobiography was published. Sabbatarianism had been a strong force during the first half of the nineteenth century, when many Protestant Englishmen and Scotsmen thought France had suffered revolutionary upheaval because its citizens were either atheists or "pagan" Catholics who profaned the Sabbath. In 1809 an evangelical, Spencer Perceval, became prime minister. Three years later he was assassinated in the lobby of the House of Commons by a deranged bankrupt who had some grievance against the government.

In 1830 the young William Gladstone, who grew up in an evangelical household, decried the Parisian Sunday. "The city was indeed a painful sight: in England matters are bad enough, but by no means so far gone. . . . I believe there is no more exact criterion of the moral advancement of a people, than the sanctity which they accord to the Christian Sabbath."[82] In the view of Gladstone and others, if the English Sunday turned into the French Sunday England's political stability would be imperiled. In 1831 evangelicals founded the Lord's Day Observance Society (L.D.O.S.), which became the most powerful sabbatarian organization in England.

The L.D.O.S. and other sabbatarian organizations hoped to severely curtail or abolish Sunday trade and Sunday travel—especially train travel. They also wanted to stop the publication of Sunday newspapers, end Sunday mail delivery, restrict even further the hours that pubs could be open on Sunday, and make it illegal to play cricket on Sunday.[83] The first English-language Sunday newspaper was *The Observer,* which began publication on December 4, 1791. By the mid-nineteenth century there were several Sunday periodicals, including the popular *Sunday at Home*, which promoted "the sanctity of the Sabbath." It began in 1854 and folded in 1940.[84]

The sabbatarians did not get what they wanted. Their clamor for change provoked a backlash. Twice in June and July 1858 more than 150,000 people demonstrated in London against a bill that would curtail Sunday trade and further restrict the hours that pubs could be open on Sunday. Karl Marx, who was present at the first demonstration, was ecstatic. The "English Revolution" had begun, he said. There was no revolution, but the demonstration was effective: the sabbatarian bill did not pass.[85]

The sabbatarians fought back, and Sunday observance remained a contentious issue until the end of the century—occasioning many articles and pamphlets. In 1865 Robert Cox, an antisabbatarian writer and editor based in Edinburgh, published a two-volume work: *The Literature of the Sabbath Question*. The proliferation of sabbatarian and antisabbatarian organizations suggests how salient the issue had become. In 1884 Herbert Spencer noted that a dispute about opening a reading room on Sundays had split a workers' institute.[86]

Many writers satirized sabbatarianism. In George and Weedon Grossmith's *Diary of a Nobody* (1889), the comically stuffy Charles Pooter says: "I quite disapprove of driving on a Sunday." The most scathing attack on sabbatarianism in fiction is in Dickens' *Little Dorrit* (1857). (In the 1830s Dickens had covered parliamentary debates over sabbatarian legislation.) The sound of church bells reminds Arthur Clennam, the leading male character, of "a long train of miserable Sundays." After saying to himself, "How I have hated this day!" Clennam describes a variety of gloomy Sundays.

> There was the dreary Sunday of his childhood, when he sat with his hands before him, scared out of his senses by a horrible tract which commenced business with the poor child by asking him in its title, why he was going to Perdition? . . . There was the sleepy Sunday of his boyhood, when . . . he was marched to chapel by a picquet of teachers three times a day. . . . There was the interminable Sunday of his nonage; when his mother, stern of face and unrelenting of heart, would sit all day behind a Bible. . . . There was the resentful Sunday of a little later, when he sat down glowering and glooming through the tardy length of the day. . . . There was a legion of Sundays, all days of unserviceable bitterness and mortification, slowly passing before him.

In the second half of the century many antisabbatarian organizations were founded, including the National Sunday League in 1855, the Sunday Shakespeare Society in 1872, and the Sunday Tramps in 1879. The Sunday Tramps—an informal group led by Leslie Stephen, the father of Virginia Woolf—had sixty-odd members; only ten showed up on any given Sunday. Many were leading Victorian intellectuals. They usually walked for twenty miles along a route that

Stephen had charted. On the way home they would sometimes stop for dinner at the house of an acquaintance. One person they visited after a Sunday jaunt was Charles Darwin, whose ideas deeply influenced Stephen.[87]

Stephen not only walked on Sundays. He also spent many Sundays climbing mountains in Switzerland. He was a very experienced mountain climber—the president of Britain's Alpine Club from 1865 to 1868 and the editor of the *Alpine Journal* from 1868 to 1872. In "Sunset on Mont Blanc," Stephen sounds like Gray or Ruskin in his description of the mountain, but Stephen did not find God in the Alps. This "godless Victorian," as his biographer calls him, regarded all creeds, including pantheism, as unsatisfactory. For Stephen mountaineering was an end in itself. It was a game that required strength of character as well as skill. "The game is won," Stephen writes, "when a mountain-top is reached in spite of difficulties; it is lost when one is forced to retreat." Yet there may be some hint of worship in Stephen's hiking and mountaineering, for he insisted on doing both activities in silence. Noel Annan says that "he communed with Nature and Nature 'helped' him."[88]

Annan does not say if Stephen was a member of the Sunday Society (1875), the most influential antisabbatarian society, but many of Stephen's acquaintances were members. The society's membership list is impressive. It includes leading churchmen, academics, scientists, artists, and writers. John Stuart Mill, Herbert Spencer, Wilkie Collins, Charles Dickens, and Anthony Trollope were members. Its sole purpose was to lobby for the opening of libraries, museums, and art galleries on Sunday afternoons.[89]

Mill was strongly antisabbatarian. In *On Liberty* (1859) he argues that sabbatarian legislation is an "illegitimate interference with the rightful liberty of the individual." Mill compares sabbatarians to Christians who practiced religious persecution.

> The notion that it is one man's duty that another should be religious, was the foundation of all the religious persecutions ever perpetrated. . . . Though the feeling which breaks out in the repeated attempts to stop railway travelling on Sunday, in the resistance to the opening of Museums, and the like, has not the cruelty of the old persecutors, the state of mind indicated by it is fundamentally the same. It is a determination not to tolerate others in doing what is permitted by their religion, because it is not permitted by the persecutor's religion.[90]

Some sabbatarians agreed with Mill that sabbatarian legislation was wrong. In their view it was not the government's business to say how people should observe Sunday. But most sabbatarians supported such legislation, and in the 1850s and 1860s they formed new organizations to counter the growing strength of antisabbatarianism. They include the Working Men's Lord's Day Rest Association (1860), the Central Committee for Securing the Cessation of Sunday Excursion Trains (1860), and the Sunday Rest Association for Promoting the Voluntary Closing of Shops on Sundays (1871). When the Tay Bridge across the Firth of Forth collapsed one Sunday in 1879, sending seventy-five railway passengers to their death, many sabbatarians said the Lord had sent Britain a message.

By the end of the nineteenth century, the "notorious English Sunday," as innumerable visitors from Europe called it, was gradually becoming less sabbatarian. In 1885 the British Museum opened on Sunday afternoons. In March 1896 a motion to open the national museums and galleries on Sunday afternoons passed Parliament by a vote of 178 to 93. In 1905 an observer lamented that "the old religion . . . is . . . visibly dissolving. . . . The English Sunday of silence and spiritual exercises . . . belongs to a vanishing England."[91] Sabbatarian organizations continued to fight against the opening of other places of amusement on Sundays, including the cinema, but they failed. In 1932 the Sunday Entertainments Act was passed. It allowed cinemas to open on Sundays and it legalized many other cultural activities.

Though many sabbatarian laws were repealed, many remained on the books until the mid-twentieth century. In a short story by P. J. Wodehouse, written in 1935, the narrator says: "Maiden Eggesford, like so many of our rural hamlets, is not at its best and brightest on a Sunday. When you have walked down the main street and looked at the Jubilee Watering-Trough, there is nothing much to do except go home and then come out again and walk down the main street once more and take another look at the Jubilee Watering-Trough."

It is risky to generalize about the English Sunday in the 1930s. Though there were laws against playing sports on Sunday, there were many informal football (soccer) and cricket associations. In 1933 London allowed Sunday football in its parks. Boxing was legal. So was greyhound racing, which took place every day at more than sixty tracks, drawing some 6.5 million people. The term "going to the dogs" first referred to people who lost money betting on greyhound races.[92]

A major Sunday activity in twentieth-century Britain was checking on the results of bets one had made (usually on Thursday) on Saturday football matches. When mail-order football pools became legal after World War I, millions of Englishmen began to bet on football matches. On Saturday night or early Sunday morning, the betters learned how they had made out. "A sorrowful feature of the English Sunday," Randolph Churchill wrote, "is the sound of thousands of men cursing their luck as they check their football pools."[93]

In the 1950s the Lord's Day Observance Society still made its voice heard. Reporting from England for the *Baltimore Sun* in 1953, Russell Baker says that it was a "powerful lobby" that favored laws that "accounted for what was known as 'Gloomy Sunday' because they forbade dancing, billiards, sporting contests, and theater performances." When a member of Parliament wanted to repeal all these laws, "the fury of the gloom lobby was so intense that the House of Commons voted five-to-one against him."[94] The sabbatarian lobby was not as strong as Baker thought, for most Sunday laws have been repealed. In 1972 theaters were allowed to stage performances on Sundays. By 2000 most pubs in Britain were open for ten or eleven hours on Sunday. In 1953 pubs could only stay open for two and a half hours.

In the 1930s church attendance, which remained steady during the first two decades of the century, began to decline rapidly. Sunday still remained the Lord's Day for many Britons, but it was increasingly regarded as the second day of the weekend. In 1924 *The Week-End Book*, a handbook for weekend activities, was published. Revised and updated periodically, it is still in print and remains a popular book. In 1948 the Church of England issued a booklet, *Your Sunday in Danger*. Its warning went unheeded by most Britons. Writing in 1980, the author of *The Rise and Fall of the Victorian Sunday* concludes: "There are now few homes in which churchgoing is the accepted practice. . . . Only the Sunday dinner survives as a relic of an earlier age. Sunday afternoon is used more and more frequently for organised sport."[95]

According to Philip Jenkins, "between 1989 and 1998 alone, Sunday church attendance for all Christian denominations [in Britain] fell from 4.7 million to 3.7 million, a decline of 22 percent in just a decade."[96] The Lord's Day Observance Society still exists, but under a different name. It is now called Day One Christian Ministries. It says on its website that it "campaigns for Sunday to be a day of worship and rest; our day of rest is increasingly under threat as retail businesses, sports events and entertainment seek to make Sunday just another day to make money." Day One Christian Ministries also does "significant work in Christian publishing" and it supports the Daylight Christian Prison Trust. The organization realizes that if it wants to survive it cannot limit its concerns to the question of Sunday observance.

Chapter Seven

Four American Writers and Sunday

~ *Edwards, Emerson, Thoreau, Whitman*

*S*trict sabbatarianism was enforced in the Massachusetts Bay Colony, founded in 1629. According to its governor, John Winthrop, the colony was a new Israel that had a covenant with God, and the Lord "will expect a strict performance of the articles contained in it [the covenant]; but if wee shall neglect the observation of these articles . . . the Lord will surely breake out in wrathe against us." A "strict performance" meant a strict observance of the Sabbath. In seventeenth-century Massachusetts the courts spent "a remarkable amount of time" on Sabbath-breaking offenses.[1]

In seventeenth-century Connecticut the sabbatarian laws were similar to those in Massachusetts. In 1781 they were listed by Samuel Peters, a historian: "No one shall run on the Sabbath-day, or walk in his garden or elsewhere, except reverently to and from meeting [that is, going to church]. No one shall travel, cook victuals, make beds, sweep house, cut hair, or shave, on the Sabbath-day. No woman shall kiss her child on the Sabbath or fasting-day. . . . No one shall read Common-Prayer [the Anglican prayer book], . . . make minced pies, dance, play cards, or play on any instrument of music, except the drum, trumpet, and jews-harp."[2]

The importance of the Sabbath to colonial Puritans can be gauged from the confession of a James Morgan, who was sentenced to death in 1686 for a murder he committed in Boston during a drunken brawl. A few minutes before Morgan was executed, he was asked to name "which of all your sins you are now most sorry for—which lies most heavy." Morgan named Sabbath breaking. "On sabbath days I us'd to lie at home, or be ill employ'd elsewhere, when I should have been at church."[3]

Though the Congregationalist church became the established church in Massachusetts, Connecticut, and New Hampshire, many Puritans were Presbyterians and a dwindling number continued to be Anglicans. In 1691 a new royal charter for Massachusetts gave political rights to members of other churches and granted "liberty of Conscience . . . to all Christians (except Papists)." There now was more religious diversity, yet mandatory Sabbath attendance laws remained in effect. In 1708 Cotton Mather said New England had "the Best Sabbaths of any Countrey under the Cope of Heaven."[4]

Sixty years later mandatory church attendance was still enforced in Boston. An English midshipman was astonished that Boston selectmen paraded the streets on Sunday—obliging "everyone to go to Church or Meeting . . . on pain of being put in the Stocks or otherwise confined." A French army chaplain stationed in Boston during the Revolutionary War said the city was "a mere desert" on the Sabbath.[5]

In all the colonies commerce was severely restricted on Sunday and travel was banned except for churchgoing or in cases of life-threatening emergency, but the strict sabbatarianism of Massachusetts and Connecticut was not the norm in other colonies. Arriving in 1647 to become the Dutch governor of what was then New Amsterdam, Peter Stuyvesant issued orders against Sabbath breaking, but they were not enforced. Stuyvesant proclaimed the Dutch Reformed church the only legal church, yet a wide variety of religious sects flourished: Calvinists, Catholics, Puritans, Lutherans, Anabaptists. Edith Wharton says that "milder manners, a greater love of ease, and a franker interest in money-making and good food, certainly distinguished the colonial New Yorkers from the conscience-searching children of the 'Mayflower.'"[6] In Rhode Island, which allowed all sects to worship except those that threatened public order, there were no mandatory church attendance laws.

In Massachusetts sabbatarian laws could be strictly enforced because many people lived in or near a town (or the city of Boston), and there were many churches in a relatively small geographic area. (By 1750 Boston had eighteen churches.) In areas where the population was sparse and churches were few and far between, strict sabbatarianism was difficult to enforce. A law drawn up in 1611 in Virginia condemned to death anyone who repeatedly broke the Sabbath, but in rural Virginia one could break the Sabbath with impunity.[7]

Because roads in many parts of colonial America were poor, attending church on Sunday was not easy for many Americans. "Servants & Children, God help them, must remain at Home," a colonist from Maryland said. The diarist William Byrd, who lived in rural Virginia in the first half of the eighteenth century, says that he did not attend church when there was bad weather, but he also admits that sometimes domestic responsibilities or lassitude kept him from going. In some isolated rural areas, there was no Sunday observance of any kind. Byrd refers to North Carolinians who do not "know Sunday from any other day, any more than Robinson Crusoe did."[8]

Though Virginia received "a significant influx of Puritans," most Virginians were mainstream Anglicans who disliked sabbatarianism.

One Virginian said that on Sunday the church served as "a useful weekly resort to do business." Before and after Anglican worship news was exchanged about the going prices for tobacco and horse-flesh. George Washington went to church regularly (though not every Sunday), but his diary indicates that he did not strictly observe the Sabbath. He entertained guests, visited relatives and friends, or went fox hunting. After the Second Great Awakening, in the late eighteenth century, sabbatarianism became more commonplace in Virginia, as it did everywhere in the United States. James Madison shocked an Episcopalian woman "with his more lenient views about what activities were permissible on Sunday."[9]

There is no consensus among historians on the percentage of Americans who were regular churchgoers in colonial America. Patricia Bonomi says "recent estimates suggest that a majority of adults in the eighteenth-century colonies were regular church attenders." Craig Harline says that "at the founding of the republic not even two in ten Americans belonged to churches."[10] It may be that some Americans did not join a church but sampled different churches on Sunday, though this was impossible in sparsely settled areas that had few churches.

In colonial America, especially in the states that did not have an established church, many Americans switched churches. In 1750 a twenty-six-year-old Marylander wrote *Remarks on Religion*, in which he described his journey from Anglicanism to Presbyterianism and finally to Quakerism. The choice of a church to attend on Sunday depended on many factors, but the most important one for many Americans probably was convenience. In order to gain members, sometimes churches resorted to unusual tactics. An Anglican cleric complained that Presbyterians often provided wrong directions to Anglican worshipers. Or they hired ruffians to insult him—telling him they wanted no "Damned Black Gown Sons of Bitches" among them. Or they disrupted worship by surrounding the building with several dozen dogs and stirring up a fight among them.[11]

Though Presbyterian and Congregationalist ministers did not condone such tactics, they urged people not to join the Church of England. Like their Puritan forebears, they thought the Church of England was a corrupt institution—one that was too close in its theology and liturgy to the Church of Rome. Anti-Anglican sentiment was very strong in New England. At Yale's commencement ceremonies in 1722 the college's rector ended his remarks with seven words from the Anglican Book of Common Prayer: "and let all the people say, amen." The seven words shocked Congregationalists throughout New England. In Boston they were called the "thunder-claps" from Yale. Worried that a younger generation might be turning toward Anglicanism, Cotton Mather held a fast day at Old North Church for "the pouring out of God's Spirit on New England, especially the rising generation."[12] When the rector admitted that he was leaning toward Anglicanism, Yale's trustees fired him.

Jonathan Edwards

At the time of the rector's "apostasy" Jonathan Edwards, who would become the leading theologian in colonial America, was studying for a degree in divinity at Yale. The fired rector had been Edwards' teacher, but Edwards was not influenced by his views. Like most Congregationalists, Edwards was a strict sabbatarian. And, like most Calvinists, he was a providentialist; he believed that the handiwork of God could be seen in daily events. Providentialism was widespread in colonial America. Even Ben Franklin, a Deist, entertained the possibility that, as he said, God "sometimes interferes by His particular providence and sets aside the effects which would otherwise have been produced by . . . causes."[13]

Edwards often thought about the religious significance of events that took place on the Lord's Day. Six of his eleven children were born on that day, including his first four children. On a Sunday evening in October 1727 a strong earthquake hit New England, followed by nine days of aftershocks. New Englanders were rattled. In the view of many, God was angry. The governor of Massachusetts called for a fast day on December 21. Edwards, who eleven months earlier had become the assistant pastor of a Congregationalist church in Northampton, Massachusetts, thought God was angry because of the lax morals of many young people. In a sermon delivered on the fast day, he deplored the fact that on Sabbath-day night many young men and women would get together "for mirth and jollity, which they called frolics." According to Edwards, "'Tis the very probable opinion of some that the earthquake was sent as a token of God's anger against not only the wickedness of the land in general, but more especially the sin that is committed on a sabbath-day night."[14]

Ten years later, on a Sunday in March 1737, there was another unusual event on the Sabbath. Edwards was beginning his sermon when the gallery of the meeting-house collapsed, burying people below. At first it was thought that many worshipers had died, but it turned out that there were no deaths and no serious injuries. What did this mean? According to Edwards, it meant that God had rebuked the congregation "by so dangerous and surprising an accident," so that now they would "praise his name for so wonderful, and as it were miraculous, a preservation."[15]

Edwards hoped the miracle wrought by God would strengthen "vital piety" in his congregation. A few years earlier he had been hopeful about the future of Christianity because Northampton had experienced a Great Awakening. Yet in the late 1730s he was worried about the state of Christianity not only in Northampton but throughout colonial America. In 1739 he told his congregation that the only good news is that "the Pope is much diminished in power and influence." The bad news is that "the Reformed church is much diminished." (By "Reformed" he meant Calvinist Protestant churches: Congregationalist, Presbyterian, Baptist, and Dutch Reformed.) There was now "much less of the prevalency of the power of godliness" than at the beginning of the Reformation. Sounding apocalyptically gloomy, Edwards said that "history gives no account of any age wherein there was so great an apostasy of those that had been brought up under the light of the gospel to infidelity."[16]

When Edwards delivered his gloomy sermon about the state of religion in America, Christianity was gaining new vitality because of the First Great Awakening that was in large part the work of George Whitefield. In 1738 Whitefield preached with great success in Georgia. In the fall of 1739 he returned to the United States, preaching to large crowds in Philadelphia and New Jersey. Edwards rejoiced in Whitefield's success. He was astonished that an Anglican could be filled with "vital piety." He wrote Whitefield in February 1740: "It has been with refreshment of soul that I have heard of one raised up in the Church of England to revive the mysterious, spiritual, despised, and exploded doctrines of the gospel, and full of a spirit of zeal for the promotion of real vital piety. . . . I hope this is the dawning of a day of God's mighty power and glorious grace to the world of mankind."[17]

In October 1740 Whitefield preached twice on Sunday in Edwards' church after spending eleven days preaching in the Boston area in open-air and church settings. Whitefield noted in his journals that during the Sabbath morning service "good Mr. Edwards wept during the whole time of exercises. The people were equally affected." Whitefield stayed with Edwards and visited him again in 1745, yet Whitefield's closest American friend was Franklin, who rarely attended church.[18]

On Sunday, February 14, 1748, Edwards' daughter Jerusha died suddenly of an acute fever at the age of seventeen. Preaching to his congregation a week later, Edwards said that he was comforted by the fact that she had been a pious Christian. What if she had been "an eminent frolicker, much of a gallant, a jolly companion"? There would have been no comfort for him. He hoped his daughter's death, though it is "so bitter and afflictive to me," would promote "the beginning of a general awakening and reformation among you, the young people of my flock."[19] In Edwards' view the Great Awakening of a few years earlier had been but a temporary return to vital piety.

Edwards held his Northampton congregation to a very high standard of piety—chastising them Sunday after Sunday for lacking vital piety. On the Sunday after his uncle Colonel John Stoddard died, in June 1748, Edwards praised his uncle's godliness and implied that many people in the congregation lacked this quality. (Stoddard was a regional magistrate and an influential political figure in colonial Massachusetts.) His uncle, Edwards said, paid attention in church. "Who ever saw him irreverently and indecently lolling, and laying down his head to sleep, or gazing about the meeting house in time of divine worship?" Edwards also said that his uncle's death was "testimony of the divine displeasure, added to all the other dark clouds God has lately brought upon us, and his awful frowns upon us."[20] He was referring to Northampton's high death rate in 1748—more than 3 percent of its population.

In 1750 the Northampton congregation asked Edwards to resign. Edwards succeeded in obtaining a post in Stockbridge, forty miles to the West. Edwards' biographer bluntly sums up what happened: colonial America's "most powerful thinker . . . [was] run out of town and forced into exile in a frontier village." The members of Edwards' congregation probably disliked being told every Sunday that the only godly people in Northampton were the members of Edwards' family. Edwards told a friend: "It seems I am born to be a man of strife."[21]

In the last decade of his life Edwards concluded that the Great Awakening had been a failure. "Things are going downhill so fast," he wrote a friend in 1751. "Truth and religion, both of heart and practice, are departing by such swift steps that I think it must needs be, that a crisis is not very far off. And what will then appear, I will not pretend to determine." In his last major work, *Original Sin*, which appeared shortly after his death in 1758, Edwards said that Calvinist Protestantism was collapsing. "To what a pass are things come in Protestant countries at this day, and in our nation in particular. . . . To what a prodigious height has a deluge of infidelity, profaneness, luxury, debauchery and wickedness of every kind, arisen!"[22] By "profaneness" Edwards meant that the Lord's Day was not being observed in a sabbatarian manner.

Edwards was disturbed that many Congregationalists preferred Arminianism, which softened the harsh doctrine of predestination. Arminians argued that Christians could choose God's grace or resist it. In the last sermon Edwards preached in Northampton, he was referring mainly to Arminianism when he attacked "new, fashionable, lax schemes of divinity, which have so greatly prevailed in New England as of late."[23]

Edwards was wrong to think that Arminianism was undermining Christianity, but he was right to worry about the future of the Congregationalist church. Whitefield's emotional preaching alarmed many Congregationalists, who thought he was stirring up religious zealotry. The anti-Whitefield Congregationalists—called "Old Lights" Congregationalists, as opposed to "New Lights" Congregationalists like Edwards—became a strong force in Boston. Several decades later many Old Lights embraced Unitarianism, which became the religion of choice for New England's educated elites. In 1825 more than 120 Congregationalist churches in the Boston area came together to form the American Unitarian Association.[24] Unitarians rarely were sabbatarians.

Though many Congregationalist churches embraced Unitarianism, Calvinist Protestantism remained a strong force in the United States after the Second Great Awakening—and so did religion in general. "In 1776," a historian of the period writes, "about one in six Americans belonged to a church; by 1850, that number had risen to one in three."[25] Edwards continued to be read, in Scotland and England as well as the United States. His influential biography, *The Life of David Brainerd* (1749), has never gone out of print. Robert Louis Stevenson's strongly religious nurse, who thought Stevenson's parents had profaned the Sabbath because they played whist on Sunday evening, was reading it to the young Stevenson when Stevenson's mother (Stevenson says) "had the sense to forbid" further reading of it.[26]

After the Second Great Awakening, sabbatarianism became a stronger force in the United States, just as it had become a stronger force in England and Scotland. (Mandatory church attendance laws, though, no longer existed.) After 1810, when Congress required mail to be delivered seven days a week, several organizations were founded to lobby against the new law and promote sabbatarianism. They had the support of prominent clergy and laymen, including a former president, John Quincy Adams, who in 1843 told a convention of sabbatarians that he would work to propagate "opinions in favor of the sacred observance of the Sabbath."[27]

When Adams made his speech the antisabbatarians were becoming stronger, especially in eastern cities, where recent immigrants—mainly Catholics from Ireland and Lutherans from Germany—favored the so-called Continental Sunday. In 1830 a fire broke out in a Boston church. When the firemen, who mainly were Catholic immigrants, learned that it was the church of the Reverend Lyman Beecher, who was a leading sabbatarian, they let it burn down. In 1857 there were riots in New York City because it was rumored that beer would no longer be sold on Sunday.[28] In Edith Wharton's story "Bunner Sisters," which takes place in New York City in the 1880s, two sisters take the ferry to Hoboken on a Sunday afternoon, where they wait for a streetcar "near the door of a crowded beer-saloon."

Appalled that people would drink on the Sabbath, sabbatarians argued that strict Sunday observance was essential to the health of American society. In "Home Religion," a story by Harriet Beecher Stowe (Beecher's daughter), a sabbatarian says: "If the Sabbath of America is simply to be a universal loafing, picnicking, dining-out day, as it is now with all our foreign populations, we shall need what they have in Europe, the gendarmes at every turn." In an essay in *Harper's Weekly* entitled "The Foreign Movement and the Sunday Question," the author argues that the new immigrants are turning Sunday into "a day of pleasure, recreation, and enjoyment," whereas Sunday should be "a day of rest, of religious exercise, and of abstinence from labor and public diversions of every kind."[29]

Antisabbatarians defended the Continental Sunday. In "False Dawn," a story by Edith Wharton set in New York City in the 1840s, one character asks: "What is there to frighten a good Episcopalian in what we call the Continental Sunday?" He also thinks sabbatarians are wrong to attack Catholics. "Well, then, I say, what's all this flutter about the Papists? Far be it from me to approve of their heathenish doctrine—but, damn it, they go to church, don't they? And they have a real service as we do, don't they?"

Ralph Waldo Emerson

Emerson was not interested in the sabbatarian question. He wanted to redefine Christian worship. In March 1838, two months before he spoke to the graduating seniors of Harvard Divinity School, he wrote in his journal: "I ought to sit and think and then write a discourse to the American clergy showing the ugliness and unprofitableness of theology and churches at this present day." In his address to the Divinity School Emerson said that a church is not the best place to look for God. "In how many churches . . . is man made sensible that he is an infinite Soul; that the earth and heavens are passing into his mind; that he is drinking forever the soul of God?"[30]

Traditional worship, Emerson says, stifles the religious spirit. "I have heard a devout person, who prized the Sabbath, say in bitterness of heart, 'On Sundays, it seems wicked to go to church.'" He told the Harvard students that they should not go to church. "It is already beginning to indicate character and religion to withdraw from the religious meetings."[31]

"What greater calamity," Emerson asks, "can fall upon a nation, than the loss of worship?" Emerson believed in worship but not formal worship. "Let me admonish you, first of all, to go alone; to refuse the good models . . . and dare to love God without mediator or veil." He urges the divinity students to "cast behind you all conformity and acquaint men at first hand with Deity."[32]

Six years earlier Emerson had begun to disassociate himself from traditional Christian worship—resigning from his position as the junior pastor of a Unitarian church in Boston. In 1838 he asked to be relieved of his commitment to preach every Sunday at a Unitarian church in East Lexington. In January 1839 he preached his last sermon. For the rest of his life he was a lecturer, not a preacher.

Harvard was not amused by Emerson's view of traditional Christian worship, and for three decades it did not invite him back to speak. Emerson's disparaging remarks about "Historical Religion" provoked many counterattacks. He was accused of purveying impiety, nonsense, infidelity, blasphemy, and atheism. Andrews Norton, a leading Unitarian theologian who taught at Harvard, said that Emerson's Divinity School address was an "incoherent rhapsody" that was an "insult to religion." He added that "there can be no intuition, no direct perception of the truths of Christianity." Two professors of theology at Princeton said that there was not "a single truth or sentiment in the whole address that is borrowed from the Scriptures."[33]

Emerson was surprised by the strong criticism, but he should not have been. He offended many people when he said that traditional Christianity was dying—and that it should die. He continued to make the same point for the rest of his life. In the essay "Worship," published in 1860 as part of a collection called *The Conduct of Life*, he says: "God builds his temple in the heart on the ruins of churches and religions." In a lecture given in May 1867, he said churches no longer were useful and that "a technical theology no longer suits."[34]

What will replace the ruins of traditional religion? Emerson says "there will be a new church founded on moral science," but his description of the new church is vague in the extreme. "It will have heaven and earth for its beams and rafters; science for symbol and illustration; it will fast enough gather beauty, music, picture, poetry." Emerson's new church is an individual one that is constructed out of man's imagination. "Every man makes his own religion, his own God."[35]

Emerson's attack on Christianity is more radical than Ruskin's. Ruskin does not want to go to church on Sunday because he thinks Protestant Christianity has become narrow and insular—and Protestant ministers are tainted with "coarse lusts." He is not in principle against traditional worship, even though he often preferred to worship by himself in the Alps. By contrast, Emerson is against going to church in principle; he disapproves of organized religion. Is Emerson anti-Christian? His critics thought he was, but he says in his jour-

nals: "I believe the Christian religion to be profoundly true." He believes it to be true because Christianity "introduced the absolute authority of the spiritual law."[36] Emerson's idea of Christian worship
has nothing in common with the worship of the early Christians,
who broke bread every Sunday to celebrate the Resurrection.

Emerson's vague "spiritual" faith was described by a contemporary
as "egotheism." It has something in common with the Quaker notion of an "inner light." It is a benign form of enthusiasm. "Enthusiasm" still meant being possessed by God, but for Emerson the word
had lost its negative meaning. Enthusiasm is a good thing. It means
that "the highest revelation is that God is in every man." In the last
three chapters of *Germany*, which Emerson read in 1830, Madame
de Staël praises enthusiasm, saying that it is the engine of all great
achievements. In the last paragraph of "Circles," Emerson quotes
Coleridge's remark: "Nothing great was ever achieved without enthusiasm." Speaking at the founding of the Free Religious Association, Emerson said that enthusiasm is "the parent of everything good
in history."[37]

Emerson agreed with Madame de Staël about enthusiasm, and he
also agreed with her that religion is too important to be restricted to
Sunday. A person animated by enthusiasm, Emerson says, worships
every day. "I love the picturesque glitter of a summer's morning landscape. It kindles this burning admiration of nature and enthusiasm of
mind." Emerson talks a great deal about the sun. "The sun shines
today also. There is more wool and flax in the field. There are new
lands, new men, new thoughts. Let us demand our own work and
laws and worship." Discussing why it is not a good idea to think a
great deal about the past, he says: "An eye fastened on the past *unsuns nature* . . . [and] bereaves me of hope" (emphasis added). To
overcome despair, one must always look ahead.[38]

Far from becoming a pariah because of his attack on traditional religion, Emerson became a celebrity—giving 1,500 public lectures in the course of four decades. In 1849 an English visitor spoke of "Emerson mania." When Emerson died in 1882 Henry James wrote that people came "in wagons, on foot, in multitudes" to his funeral, which "was a popular manifestation, the most striking I have ever seen provoked by the death of a man of letters."[39]

Emerson's heyday coincided with the onset of the Third Great Awakening, which revitalized traditional religion in America. So why was he popular? There were many religious currents in mid-nineteenth-century America. If some Americans returned to traditional religion, others traveled in Emerson's direction. According to Orestes Bronson, Unitarianism had become "negative, cold, lifeless, and all advanced [Unitarian] minds . . . are dissatisfied with it, and are craving something higher, better, more living and life-giving."[40] Emerson gave dissatisfied Unitarians something "higher." Orestes Bronson himself was dissatisfied with Unitarianism, but eventually he also became dissatisfied with Emerson's "higher" religion, and he converted to Catholicism.

Emerson was also popular because he spent more time talking about the God in man than about the failure of traditional religion. He was a "spiritualist," as he called himself, though he was not a member of the spiritualist movement, which flourished in late nineteenth-century England and America—spawning Christian Science and theosophy. Henry James rightly noted that those who were shocked at Emerson's "ceasing to care for the prayer and the sermon . . . might have perceived that he *was* the prayer and the sermon: not in the least a seculariser, but in his own subtle insinuating way a sanctifier." Harold Bloom calls Emerson the theologian of "the American religion," whose essence is the belief that you can find God in yourself.[41]

James also notes that Emerson was a great speaker who had a "rare irresistible voice and a beautiful mild, modest authority." James drolly comments on the effect Emerson's lectures had on the audience: "We seem to see the people turning out into the snow after hearing them, glowing with a finer glow than the climate could give and fortified for a struggle with overshoes and the east wind."[42]

Emerson was a preacher who told people not to go to church on Sunday, yet many nonchurchgoers liked to do something communal on Sunday. In mid-nineteenth-century Boston, Sunday lectures often drew large crowds. One could hear a lecture at Amory Hall, where a group called the Society (an informal group of politically radical intellectuals) sponsored a lecture series on Sundays at 10:30 A.M. and 7:30 P.M. On a Sunday in March 1844 Emerson lectured on "New England Reformers."

In Boston the most popular Sunday speaker was Theodore Parker. Parker had been a Unitarian minister, but he lost his ministry because the Boston Association of Ministries decided that his views were not Christian. Impressed by Parker's sermons, a group of Bostonians formed a new independent church, the Twenty-Eighth Congregational Society, and asked him to become its minister. At first Parker was close to Emerson in his views, but in the mid-1840s he began to talk mainly about social issues, which Emerson generally avoided. He vilified slavery, attacked the Mexican War, and accused Bostonians of ignoring the poor. On a Sunday in February 1849 he gave "A Sermon on the Spiritual Condition of Boston." He berated Bostonians for their love of Mammon.

In 1845 Parker began to preach in a hall known as the Melodeon, which held a thousand people. His sermons were "electrifying," and on many Sundays the Melodeon was filled to capacity. "I want you to hear Parker preach now," Elizabeth Peabody, a leading Boston intellectual, said to a friend. "He has got on fire with the velocity of his spirit's speed—& the elements melt in the fervent heat of his word.

. . . He is a son of thunder."[43] Parker's sermons were great performances. Seven years later, Parker moved to a larger venue in Boston—the Music Hall, which had a capacity of 2,000.

In New York a decade later a disciple of Parker's gave sermons that also drew large crowds. Octavius Brooks Frothingham, the minister of the Independent Liberal Church, was such a popular speaker that his congregation leased a Masonic Temple for Sunday worship. Sunday services began at 10:45, but after an hour of hymns and readings from a collection of sacred texts from the world's major religions, the doors were reopened to admit people who came only for the sermon. Frothingham's religious views were similar to Emerson's. He argued that the historical Jesus was not the Christ. Jesus "glorified common qualities; he set the seal on principles that all share." He was the symbol "of that essential human nature which is the Messiah cradled in the bosom of every man."[44]

Henry David Thoreau

Thoreau's view of Christianity was more negative than Emerson's or Frothingham's. He was a self-declared pagan. Thoreau calls Christians infidels because they celebrate Sunday as the Lord's Day rather than the day of the sun. In *A Week on the Concord and the Merrimack Rivers* (1849), he says: "Really, there is no infidelity, now-a-days, so great as that which prays, and keeps the Sabbath, and rebuilds the churches." Thoreau's religion, his biographer says, "was more that of Olympian or Doric Greece than modern Christianity."[45]

In *A Week*, an account of a trip Thoreau took with his brother John in 1839, he says that his favorite god is Pan, the Greek god of nature. "In my Pantheon, Pan still reigns in his pristine glory; . . . for the great God Pan is not dead, as was rumored. No god ever dies. Perhaps of all the gods of New England and of ancient Greece, I am most constant at his shrine" (65).

Thoreau even dismisses the Judeo-Christian calendar. He argues that Sunday is the seventh day of the week—not the first day. He bases his view on two lines by Hesiod: "The seventh is a holy day, / for then Latona [Apollo's mother] brought forth golden-rayed Apollo" (63). In Thoreau's scheme of things, an ancient Greek writer's account of creation trumps Genesis' account. Thoreau cites Hesiod mainly to stress how important Apollo, the god of the sun, is to him.

In the chapter entitled "Sunday," Thoreau claims that he and his brother are "the truest observers of this sunny day" (63). Thoreau and his brother observe Sunday by observing the natural world. A contemporary of Thoreau's said that he was a man who had "experienced Nature as other men are said to have experienced religion." *A Week*, which Thoreau published at his own expense, was widely reviewed, but many readers found its paganism offensive. One spoke of Thoreau's "misplaced Pantheistic attack on the Christian Faith."[46] The book was not a financial success; 1,000 copies were printed, but only 219 were sold.

During the eight years it took Thoreau to complete *A Week*, he was reading Ruskin, who for roughly a decade called himself a pagan though he remained a Christian. Thoreau disapproved of Ruskin's Christianity, but he told a friend that Ruskin's works were "singularly good and encouraging"—with such themes as "Infinity, Beauty, Imagination, Love of Nature etc.—all treated in a very living manner." Like Ruskin, Thoreau loved mountaineering. He also agreed with Ruskin about the importance of being an accurate observer of the natural world. "How much virtue there is in simply seeing."[47]

In *A Week* Thoreau describes a Ruskinian experience he had early one morning when on a mountaintop in northwestern Massachusetts. "All around beneath me was spread for a hundred miles on every side, as far as the eye could reach, an undulating country of clouds, answering in the varied swell of its surface to the terrestrial world it veiled. It was such a country as we might see in dreams, with all the delights of paradise." Thoreau doesn't say that he found God on the mountaintop. He says he found purity. "There was not the substance of impurity, no spot nor stain" (188). Thoreau is a new kind of Puritan. He worships a natural world uncontaminated by humankind.

Sun worship is central to Thoreau's paganism. He associates sun worship with the ancient Greeks, especially Homer. "Homer," he says, "does not allow us to forget that the sun shone" (157). The chapter entitled "Sunday" begins with a Homeric description of the sunrise and ends with a Homeric description of the sunset. "The Scene-shifter [Apollo] saw fit here to close the drama of this day. . . . This Sunday ended by the going down of the sun, leaving us still on the waves" (114).

For Thoreau, who venerates Apollo and Pan, every day is a sun day—or what he calls "a natural Sabbath." Canoeing on the river on a Sunday morning, he says that "the stillness was intense, and almost conscious, as if it were a natural Sabbath, and we fancied that the morning was the evening of a celestial day" (46). Thoreau dislikes Christianity because it makes a radical distinction between Sunday and other days of the week. He also dislikes it because it frowns on idleness. "Men are as busy as the brooks or bees and postpone every thing to their busy-ness" (218). Christianity, he says, turns people into neurotic souls who worry that an angry God will punish them for being idle, or for not observing the Sabbath.

Thoreau once was "reproved by a minister" because he went mountain climbing on Sunday. After telling Thoreau that he was breaking the Fourth Commandment, the minister "proceeded to enumerate, in a sepulchral tone, the disasters which had befallen him whenever he had done any ordinary work on the Sabbath" (76). Thoreau thinks the views of the minister are absurd. "He really thought that a god was on the watch to trip up those men who followed any secular work on this day, and did not see that it was the evil conscience of the workers that did it" (76).

By "evil conscience" Thoreau means a conscience that, as Samuel Johnson might have put it, is overly burdened with scruples. Johnson thought some Christians had too many scruples; Thoreau thinks all Christians have too many scruples. In "Conscience," a poem that appears in *A Week*, Thoreau says:

> Conscience is instinct bred in the house,
> Feeling and Thinking propagate the sin
> By an unnatural breeding in and in.
> I say, Turn it out doors,
> Into the moors.
> I love a life whose plot is simple,
> And does not thicken with every pimple,
> A soul so sound no sickly conscience binds it. (74)

Like Nietzsche, Thoreau thinks Christianity breeds sickly consciences. He tells his readers that they should be content with the life we have and not worry about an afterlife. "We need pray for no higher heaven than the pure senses can furnish, a *purely* sensuous life" (382).

Christianity, Thoreau says, is a religion for the unhealthy. "A healthy man . . . will not be a good subject for Christianity. The New Testament may be a choice book to him on some, but not on all or most of his days. He will rather go a fishing in his leisure hours" (74). Fishing is a kind of worship. Describing an old man who fishes regularly, Thoreau says: "His fishing was not a sport, nor solely a means of subsistence, but a sort of solemn sacrament and withdrawal from the world" (25).

In addition to telling his readers to take their consciences "out doors," Thoreau urges them to change their reading habits. They should spend less time reading the Bible and more time reading sacred texts from China, India, and Iran. Thoreau's favorite Hindu work is the *Laws of Menu* (or Manu), an ancient Sanskrit text that was first translated into English in the late eighteenth century. His references to the New Testament are slighting. "The New Testament treats of man and man's so-called spiritual affairs too exclusively" (73). He does acknowledge, though, that the New Testament "is an invaluable book," but he adds: "I confess to having been slightly prejudiced against it in my very early days by the church and the Sabbath school" (71).

Were the Sundays of Thoreau's childhood gloomy? Probably not, for his parents were not sabbatarians. His mother "was a lively, talkative, hospitable person active in all the town charities and in the antislavery society."[48] She was a member of a local Congregationalist church. When it became Unitarian she left to become one of the founders of a Trinitarian Congregational church, but later she returned to the Unitarian church.

Aside from sacred Asian texts, Thoreau, an accomplished classicist, praises Greek and Roman writers. Homer, whom he quotes extensively, is his favorite. He always calls Homer a "natural" poet. In "Friday," the last essay in *A Week*, Thoreau says: "The Iliad is not Sabbath but morning reading, and men cling to this old song, because they still have moments of unbaptized and uncommitted life, which give them an appetite for more" (369). The *Iliad* is morning reading because in Homer's world every day is a day of the sun. In *Walden* (1854) Thoreau says: "I have been as sincere a worshipper of Aurora as the Greeks. I got up early and bathed in the pond; that was a religious exercise."[49]

The *Iliad* is also important because it "represents no creed nor opinion, and we read it with a rare sense of freedom and irresponsibility, as if we trod on native ground, and were autochthones of the soil" (369). "Autochthone" means "sprung from the land." Reading the *Iliad*, we become more rooted to the natural world. Reading the *Iliad*, we become "unbaptised," more like an American Indian. "By the wary independence and aloofness of his dim forest life he preserves his intercourse with his native gods" (55).

There is another "natural" writer whom Thoreau admires: Ossian. "The genuine remains of Ossian, or those ancient poems which bear his name, . . . are, in many respects, of the same stamp with the *Iliad* itself. . . . In his poetry, as in Homer's, only the simplest and most enduring features of humanity are seen" (343–344). In his lengthy analysis of Ossian—which quotes roughly 100 lines of Ossian's poetry—Thoreau never alludes to the controversy about the authenticity of the poems.

"The wisest man," Thoreau says, "preaches no doctrines" (70). Yet in *A Week* Thoreau preaches. He exhorts his readers to become pagans who venerate Pan and Apollo—to become sun day observers instead of observers of the Sabbath. Pagans, he suggests, get more joy out of life. Though James Russell Lowell admired *A Week*, he also complained: "We were bid to a river-party, not to be preached at."[50]

How do we practice paganism? We practice it, Thoreau says, by cultivating idleness and by going canoeing, hiking, or fishing on Sunday instead of going to church. We practice it by reading Homer and Ossian as well as sacred Asian texts. Like Hugh Blair, Thoreau thinks the ancient heroes of Homer and Ossian have much to teach modern man. So do Native Americans—or, as Thoreau said, Indians. "If we could listen but for an instant to the chaunt of the Indian muse, we should understand why he will not exchange his savageness for civilization" (56). Thoreau compiled eleven notebooks for a book he hoped to write about Native Americans. One wonders what

Thoreau made of Joe Polis, a Penobscot Indian who served as his guide on his trip to the Maine woods in 1856, for Polis was a Christian who prayed regularly and worried about breaking the Sabbath.[51]

Was Thoreau as pagan as he claimed to be? In one passage he tells Christians to widen their intellectual horizons rather than reject Christianity. "It would be worthy of the age to print together the collected Scriptures or Sacred Writings of the several nations, the Chinese, the Hindoos, the Persians, the Hebrews, and others, as the Scripture of mankind. . . . Such a juxtaposition and comparison might help to liberalize the faith of men" (143–144). In this passage he is not preaching against Christianity. He is accusing Christians of being intellectually complacent and narrow-minded.

Whatever we make of Thoreau's paganism, he was more of a pagan than Ruskin was. Yet, like Ruskin, he praises George Herbert. "How rarely in our English tongue do we find expressed any affection for God. Certainly, there is no sentiment so rare as the love of God. Herbert almost alone expresses it" (373). Thoreau, it seems, had not completely distanced himself from his Christian upbringing. His letters and journal entries for March 1842, his biographer says, "are unusually full of uncharacteristic references to God . . . [and] they are also marked by plaintive and despairing outpourings: 'Why God did you include me in your great scheme?'"[52] It does not seem as if Thoreau achieved perpetual joy by being a sun day observer.

Cape Cod, written in the 1850s but published posthumously, is less of a sermon than *A Week.*[53] (Between 1849 and 1857 Thoreau made four trips to Cape Cod.) Quoting Homer while describing sunrises and sunsets, Thoreau still calls himself a pagan, yet he is more playful than he is in *A Week*—more inclined to make fun of the bewildering variety of Christian sects than solemnly talk about ancient sacred texts. A man Thoreau meets "said that he had been to hear thirteen kinds of preaching in one month, when he was young, but

he did not join any of them,—he stuck to his Bible. There was nothing like any of them in his Bible." When the man asks Thoreau's
companion which sect he belongs to, the companion replies (tongue
in cheek): "O, I belong to the Universal Brotherhood." Assuming
that Thoreau's companion was referring to a real sect, the man asks:
"What's that? Sons o'Temperance?" (78).

In *Cape Cod* the natural world is a darker force than it is in *A
Week*. The sea is "a wild, rank place" that brings death as well as life.
Thoreau says to an old man "who was sitting on the edge of the bank
smoking a pipe," that he must like to hear the sound of the surf. The
man replies: "No, I do not like to hear the sound of the surf." He had
lost a son at sea "and could tell many a tale of the shipwrecks which
he had witnessed there" (126).

Thoreau's reflections on Sunday, however, are the same in *Cape
Cod* as they are in *A Week*. In *A Week* he says: "There are few things
more disheartening and disgusting than when you are walking the
streets of a strange village on the Sabbath, to hear a preacher shouting like a boatswain in a gale of wind, and thus harshly profaning the
quiet atmosphere of the day" (76). It is the preacher who is profaning the Sabbath. In *Cape Cod* Thoreau makes the same point in a
lengthy anecdote.

On a Sunday morning in Provincetown (Thoreau says) "I had
joined a party of men who were smoking and lolling over a pile of
boards on one of the wharves . . . when our landlord, who was a sort
of tithing-man [i.e., an observant Christian], went off to stop some
sailors who were engaged in painting their vessel." Thoreau doesn't
agree with the tithing-man. "I remarked that . . . they might as well
let the man [*sic*] paint. . . . It was not noisy work, and would not dis-
turb our devotions." By "our devotions" Thoreau means "smoking
and lolling." Another man agrees with the "tithing-man," saying (in
Thoreau's paraphrase) that "it was a plain contradiction of the law of

God, which he quoted, and if they did not have some such regulation, vessels would run in there to tar, and rig, and paint, and they would have no Sabbath at all" (198–199). Allow some people to work on the Sabbath, and soon many people will be working.

"This was a good argument enough," Thoreau says, "if he had not put it in the name of religion" (199). How else could the argument be put if not in the name of religion? Thoreau's point is that if we consider the Sabbath to be a day of rest—removing its Christian dimension—both painters and preachers are profaning the Sabbath because both are working. But the painters are silent, so they are not disturbing anyone, whereas the preachers are shouting, so they are disturbing people.

Thoreau drives home his point by throwing in a second anecdote. "The next summer, as I sat on a hill there one sultry Sunday afternoon, the meeting-house windows being open, my meditations were interrupted by the noise of a preacher who shouted like a boatswain, *profaning the quiet atmosphere*" (emphasis added). Thoreau remarks: "Few things could have been more disgusting or disheartening. I wished the tithing-man [the man from the previous anecdote] would stop him" (199).

In an earlier passage in *Cape Cod*, Thoreau shows his distaste for Sunday preaching. Referring to a law passed in 1665 by the town of Eastham, to the effect that "all persons who should stand out of the meeting-house during the time of divine service, should be set in the stocks," he sarcastically says: "It behoved such a town to see that sitting in the meeting-house was nothing akin to sitting in the stocks, lest the penalty of obedience to the law might be greater than that of disobedience" (36). In other words, listening to some preachers may be more painful than sitting in the stocks.

In the last decade of his life Thoreau remained firmly in the pagan camp. In "Walking," an essay that appeared a month after he died

(1862) though it was written ten years earlier, Thoreau celebrates wildness. "I wish to speak a word for Nature, for absolute freedom and wildness. . . . I wish to make an extreme statement . . . for there are enough champions of civilization: the minister and the school committee and everyone of you will take care of that."[54] Thoreau assumes the reader ("everyone of you"), like the minister and the school committee, will disagree with him and take the side of civilization.

In "Walking" Thoreau offers his own version of the Apostle's Creed. "I believe in the forest, and in the meadow, and in the night in which the corn grows." After describing a sunset—"so pure and bright a light"—he ends the essay with a vision of the future. "So we saunter toward the Holy Land, till one day the sun shall shine more brightly than ever he has done, shall perchance shine into our minds and hearts, and light up our whole lives with a great awakening light."[55] Thoreau hopes there will be a new great awakening in America when Americans will regard Sunday as the day of the sun, not the Lord's Day.

Few Americans heeded Thoreau's call for a pagan great awakening. Though his death in 1862 was widely reported, he was not well known during his lifetime. Thoreau, who knew that his paganism would anger most Americans, had mixed feelings about being a successful writer. In his journal he worries about the cost of success. "After lecturing twice this winter [1854] I feel that I am in danger of cheapening myself." Thoreau worried that he was trying too hard to please his audiences. "Those services which the community will most readily pay for it is most disagreeable to render." Thoreau thought financial success was proof positive that a writer lacked integrity.

Dismissing Christians as narrow-minded, busy, dogmatic, sick, joyless, superstitious, and unnatural, Thoreau would seem to be a writer who is *not* in the American grain. Yet *A Week* was described by Bronson Alcott, a contemporary, as an "American book," and *Walden* has been called "one of the classic works of American literature." Thoreau, a contemporary critic says, is now "considered the first major interpreter of nature in American literary history, and the first American environmentalist saint."[56] The Thoreau Society is "the largest and longest-lived organization of its kind devoted to an American author."[57]

What is American about Thoreau is not his celebration of nature. It is his do-it-yourself view of life. He is a self-made man who not only builds his own cabin in the woods, but also constructs his own religion. He is a radical individualist. In *Walden* he says: "I desire that there may be as many different persons in the world as possible; but I would have each one be very careful to find out and pursue *his own* way, and not his father's or his mother's or his neighbor's instead."[58]

Thoreau says to his readers that he will observe Sunday his own way. Yet, like Emerson, he hopes Americans will spend their Sundays outdoors rather than in church. He wishes they would observe the "natural Sabbath" by hiking, canoeing, or fishing (I don't think Thoreau would praise team sports). While canoeing on Sunday, he jokingly (in *A Week*) notes the behavior of frogs: "the frogs sat meditating, all sabbath thoughts, summing up their week, with one eye out on the golden sun, and one toe upon a reed, eyeing the wondrous universe in which they act their part" (49).

Walt Whitman

Whitman has a lot in common with Thoreau. He too is a pantheist who celebrates every day as a day of the sun. "I too have sought, and ever seek, the brilliant sun, and make my songs according." On the wall in Whitman's room were prints of Hercules, Bacchus, and a sa-tyr. Bronson Alcott, Thoreau's friend, said Whitman struck him as "the very God Pan." Whitman admired Thoreau, whom he met briefly. According to Alcott, Whitman saw in Thoreau "a sagacity [as] potent, penetrating, and peerless as his own."[59]

The Sundays of Walt Whitman's childhood were not gloomy. Whitman's parents were of Quaker descent. Walt's father was irreli-gious; he admired the anti-Christian Thomas Paine, whom he once met, and he also admired Frances Wright, a Scottish-born free-thinker. Whitman's mother attended church occasionally. Accord-ing to his brother George, "she pretended to be a Baptist . . . [but] went almost anywhere." Walt's parents sent him to Sunday school at a local Episcopal church, but for educational rather than religious reasons. The school was free and it would give Walt a good knowl-edge of the Bible. Walt, his biographer says, "grew up unscathed by the conviction of sin and damnation that oppressed so many of his contemporaries and made the Sabbath a day of gloom and horror for them."[60]

Walt also admired Paine, but he was not as anti-Christian as his father was; he took an interest in Christian worship and he cele-brated religious sentiment. He told an admirer that "I had perfect faith in all sects, and was not inclined to reject one single one." Whitman, an acquaintance said, "is a born *exalté.* . . . His *religious sentiment* . . . pervades and dominates his life." Whitman contem-plated becoming a Quaker but decided against it: "I was never made to live inside a fence."[61]

Whitman regarded himself as a prophet whose "main life work [is] . . . the Great Construction of the New Bible"—his verse collection *Leaves of Grass.* But Whitman did not reject the "old" Bible, the book that—according to a friend—"he knew best."[62] Whitman's sense of himself as a prophet owes a lot to the Quaker notion of an "inner light." According to Whitman, a prophet is someone "whose mind bubbles up and pours forth as a fountain, from inner, divine spontaneities revealing God. Prediction is a very minor part of prophecy. The great matter is to reveal and outpour the God-like suggestions pressing for birth in the soul. This is briefly the doctrine of the Friends or Quakers" (887–888). He is writing about Thomas Carlyle, but the remarks apply to himself as well.

When Whitman was a young man, he occasionally attended church on Sunday. Working as an apprentice printer, Whitman went with his boss "to a great old rough, fortress-looking stone church . . . near where the Brooklyn city hall now is" (699). In 1880 Whitman attended a Sunday service in Toronto, but it was not in a church. It was in an asylum for the mentally ill. "Went over to the religious services (Episcopal) [of the] main Insane asylum. . . . Some three hundred persons present, mostly patients" (878).

Whitman is moved by the experience. "Everything, the prayers, a short sermon, the firm, orotund voice of the minister, and most of all . . . *that audience*, deeply impress'd me." During the service, the patients are transformed. They are "now temporarily so calm, like still waters . . . [and] all the woes and sad happenings of life and death" can no longer be seen on their "crazed faces" because "now from every one the devotional element [is] radiating." During the service he and the patients are part of "common humanity, mine and yours, everywhere" (878).

Whitman asks himself: What does this experience mean? "Was it not, indeed, *the peace of God that passeth all understanding*, strange as it may sound?" (878–879). He is not sure what it means. "I can only say I took long and searching eye-sweeps as I sat there, and it seem'd so, rousing [in himself] unprecedented thoughts, problems unanswerable" (879). He leaves off speculation, returning to description. "A very fair choir, and melodeon accompaniment. They sang 'Lead, kindly light,' after the sermon. Many join'd in the beautiful hymn" (879). Whitman inserts the first two stanzas of the famous hymn that John Henry Newman composed.

The description of the Sunday service in the insane asylum is from Whitman's *Specimen Days* (1882), which Whitman called "the most wayward, spontaneous, fragmentary book ever printed."[63] The book comprises 248 short essays that he wrote during two periods in his life: the decade (from 1862 to 1872) when he lived mainly in Washington, working at several jobs and also serving as a volunteer male nurse in Civil War hospitals, and the ensuing decade (from 1873 to 1882), when he lived in Camden, New Jersey, with his brother George after suffering a paralytic stroke in January 1873.

Whitman considered *Leaves of Grass* his major work, yet *Specimen Days* is a great work in its own right. In *Leaves of Grass* Whitman is a prophet who wants his readers to become pantheists. In *Specimen Days* he is occasionally a prophet but for the most part he does not preach; he describes a wide variety of experiences and ponders their meaning. Whitman calls *Specimen Days* "a mélange of loafing, looking, hobbling, sitting, traveling—a little thinking thrown in for salt, but very little" (884).

Many essays in *Specimen Days* talk about spirituality or spiritual experiences. "Spirituality" for Whitman means an acute sensitivity to the sights and sounds of the natural world. "I guess I am mainly sensitive to the wonderfulness & perhaps spirituality of things in their physical & concrete expressions—& have celebrated all that."[64] In "Full-Starred Nights" he looks at the stars and asks himself: "Where would be any food for spirituality without night and the stars?" (804). Whitman also thinks of spirituality as a certain quality that some people radiate. In "Spiritual Characters among the Soldiers," he says that "every now and then, in hospital or camp, there are beings I meet—specimens of unworldliness, disinterestedness, and animal purity and heroism." Such people, Whitman says, have a "strange spiritual sweetness" (738).

Whitman finds spiritual experiences on every day of the week, but some of the most moving occur on a Sunday. On a Sunday evening in May 1880, while sitting outside a friend's house, he hears "the church-choir and organ on the corner opposite" play Bach's famous cantata: *Ein feste Burg ist unser Gott.* (Whitman calls it "Luther's hymn.") "The air was borne by a rich contralto. For nearly half an hour there in the dark . . . came the music, firm and unhurried, with long pauses. The full silver star-beams of Lyra rose silently over the church's dim roof-ridge. Varicolor'd lights from the stain'd glass windows broke through the tree-shadows. And under all—under the Northern Crown up there, and in the fresh breeze below, and the *chiaroscuro* of the night, that liquid-full contralto" (876). Listening to religious music under the stars is for Whitman a spiritual experience.

On a Sunday afternoon in December 1865 Whitman describes a different spiritual experience. He is walking to Harewood Hospital for Civil War veterans, which is in a wooded area on the outskirts of Washington. "Again spending a good part of the day at Harewood. I write this about an hour before sundown. I have walk'd out for a few minutes to the edge of the woods to soothe myself with the hour and scene. It is a glorious, warm, golden-sunny, still afternoon. The only noise is from a crowd of cawing crows. . . . Clusters of gnats swimming and dancing in the air in all directions. The oak leaves are thick under the bare trees, and give a strong and delicious perfume." Then he enters the hospital and the spiritual moment turns into a vision of darkness. "Inside the ward everything is gloomy. Death is there. As I enter'd, I was confronted by . . . a corpse of a poor soldier, just dead, of typhoid fever. The attendants had just straighten'd the limbs, put coppers on the eyes, and were laying it out" (774).

Another Sunday spiritual experience occurred at "a secluded little dell off one side by my creek." (It took place five years after Whitman left Washington.) Whitman goes there "every hot day" in order to get "close to Nature" by going naked for several hours—walking about and bathing in the creek. "As I walk'd slowly over the grass, the sun shone out enough to show the shadow moving with me." During those moments he feels one with nature. "Somehow I seem'd to get identity with each and every thing around me, in its condition. Nature was naked, and I was also" (807).

This spiritual moment, Whitman says, "was too lazy, soothing and joyous-equable to speculate about" (807). Yet he does speculate about it—giving a new twist to the notion of purity. "Perhaps indeed he or she to whom the free exhilarating extasy [*sic*] of nakedness in Nature has never been eligible . . . has not really known what purity is—nor what faith or art or health really is." In a parenthetical remark, Whitman then talks about the importance of nakedness to the ancient Greeks. "Probably the whole curriculum of first-class philosophy, beauty, heroism, form, illustrated by the Hellenic race . . . came from their natural and religious idea of Nakedness." According to Whitman, going naked in nature is a form of worship, but he realizes that his notion of worship is one that many people would find odd. "Some good people may think it a feeble or half-crack'd way of spending one's time and thinking. May-be it is" (808).

Though Whitman describes many spiritual experiences he had on Sundays, he is not saying that Sunday is a special day in a Christian sense. Sunday is a special day because most people do not have to go to work. Like Thoreau, he thinks it is a day that should be spent outdoors. Introducing the second half of *Specimen Days*, he says: "I restore my book to the bracing and buoyant equilibrium of concrete outdoor Nature, the only permanent reliance for sanity of book or human life" (780).

Whitman ends *Specimen Days* with a prescription: "I conceive of no flourishing and heroic elements of Democracy in the United States . . . without the Nature-element forming a main part" (926). Is Whitman urging Americans to become pantheists? In *Leaves of Grass* he seems to be preaching pantheism, which is why Thoreau praised the book. Yet Whitman did not preach pantheism when he visited wounded soldiers in Washington hospitals. He sums up what he did on those visits, which usually took place on Sundays: "not only . . . cheering talk and little gifts—not only washing and dressing wounds . . . but [reading] passages from the Bible, expounding them, prayer at the bedside, explanations of doctrine, & c. (I think I see my friends smiling at this confession, but I was never more in earnest in my life.)" (743).

What does Whitman mean by saying that "I think I see my friends smiling at this confession"? He means that his friends know that he is not a Christian even though he reads Scripture and explains Christian doctrine to wounded soldiers. Appointed a delegate of the Christian Commission (a wartime agency of the YMCAs), Whitman thinks it is appropriate for him to tell the wounded soldiers what they want to hear. He celebrates all forms of worship, so he doesn't see why he should undermine a wounded soldier's faith. In serving as a "Soldiers' Missionary," which is what he calls himself, he is lifting the spirits of wounded and dying soldiers. He is also lifting his own spirits by relieving misery. "I have seen all the horrors of [a] soldier's life," he says, "& not been kept up by its excitement—it is awful to see so much, & not be able to relieve it."[65]

In another Civil War vignette a dying soldier asks Whitman to read from the New Testament. Whitman obliges—reading passages about the Crucifixion and the Resurrection. "It pleased him [the soldier] very much, yet the tears were in his eyes. He ask'd me if I enjoy'd religion. I said, 'Perhaps not, my dear, in the way you mean, and yet, may-be, it is the same thing'" (731). What does Whitman mean by "may-be, it is the same thing"? He means that though he does not believe in Christianity in the way the dying soldier does, he believes, so to speak, in belief. He celebrates the religious sentiment.

Some people did not approve of Whitman's presence in the Civil War hospitals. A nurse wrote her husband: "There comes that odious Walt Whitman to talk evil and unbelief to my boys. I think I would rather see the Evil One himself." The nurse probably knew about the anti-Christian passages in *Leaves of Grass*, but it is unlikely that Whitman read these passages to soldiers, for most would have found them shocking. A soldier wrote Whitman in 1871: "Please send me some of your Poems . . . for I always enjoyed them so much when you read them to me in old Ward A. I shall never forget what pains you took to pass away our weary hours. Our Heavenly Father will reward you for it."[66] If Whitman had preached pantheism, would the soldier have spoken of "our Heavenly Father"?

In *Specimen Days* Whitman does at times preach pantheism, but he also celebrates all aspects of America's predominantly Christian culture. In a crowded hospital he hears nurses and patients sing hymns. "They sang very well, mostly quaint old songs and declamatory hymns, to fitting tunes" (732). In 1860, when Whitman spent some time in Boston, he went to Sunday morning services at the Seamen's Bethel, a Methodist chapel by the harbor, to hear the sermons of a certain Father Taylor. Whitman thought he was the best public speaker he had ever heard. "When Father Taylor preach'd or pray'd, the rhetoric and art, the mere words . . . seem'd altogether to disappear, and the *live feeling* advanced upon you and seiz'd you with a power before unknown."[67]

Whitman also admired the preaching of Henry Ward Beecher, the minister of the Plymouth Congregationalist Church in Brooklyn.

Beecher's church had become a leading tourist attraction; the Brooklyn ferries that took people on Sunday to hear him preach were called "Beecher boats." When Whitman first heard Beecher speak in 1849, "he hit me so hard, fascinated me to such a degree, that I was afterward willing to go far out of my way to hear him talk."[68]

Beecher had come a long way from his Calvinist Presbyterian childhood. His father, Lyman Beecher, was the sabbatarian minister whose church had burned down. "Sunday," Henry Ward Beecher recalled, "was the dreadful day of the week for me." On Sunday, as a boy, he had not been allowed to play or read anything but the Bible or religious literature. Laughing had been forbidden. On Sunday he had always been impatient for the sun to go down. "It seemed to me that there was nothing so lazy as the sun on Sunday." He and his brother would watch it sink "and the moment it was down, we would give utterance to an outcry of joy." Beecher preached against the God-fearing religion of his childhood. God, he said, is love; and God does not want us to be solemn. "To be mirthful is part of our constitution and I believe God never gave us that which it is sin to exercise."[69]

Beecher's Gospel of Love was not very different from Whitman's Gospel of Nature. Whitman thought Beecher "stole terrifically" from *Leaves of Grass*. A friend of Whitman's agreed: "I heard Henry Ward Beecher last night . . . and his whole sermon was you, you, you, from top to toe." In September 1858 Whitman wondered (in an article published in the *Brooklyn Times*) whether Beecher's rapt listeners were becoming Beecherites rather than Christians. Beecher, he said, is "teaching them to worship him instead of that Creator whom he so eccentrically defines as 'a dim and shadowy effluence.'"[70] Whitman was not defending Christianity; he was attacking the cult of Beecher.

The preacher who influenced Whitman the most was Elias Hicks, a famous American Quaker. The leader of the liberal wing of Quakers, Hicks thought there should be no creedal basis to Quakerism whereas the Orthodox wing of Quakers subscribed—broadly speaking—to traditional Christian doctrine. Whitman has nothing but praise for Hicks. "His whole life was a long religious missionary life of method, practicality, sincerity, earnestness, and pure piety" (1231). In Whitman's house in Philadelphia—he moved there in 1884—there was a large plaster bust of Hicks, which Whitman said was "one of my treasures."[71]

It was not until the last decade of Whitman's life that he wrote about Hicks. At the time Whitman was plagued by ill health and general feebleness, which may explain why his portrait of Hicks, published in *November Boughs* (1888), is rambling and disjointed. Yet the short essay tells us why Hicks was so important to Whitman. One night Whitman's father came home from work and said: "Come, mother, Elias preaches to-night." Hicks was a family acquaintance; he had grown up with Whitman's great-grandfather in Central Long Island, and he knew Whitman's grandfather and father. Hicks was eighty years old, so this might be the last chance Whitman's father would get to hear him. The ten-year-old Walt was allowed to go "as I had been behaving well that day" (1232).

In the "handsome ball-room" in Brooklyn Heights where Hicks preached that night, there were "many fashionables [who came] out of curiosity." They included "all the principal dignitaries of the town" (1233). Hicks's preaching made a great impression on the young Whitman. He remembers how Hicks looked when he began to talk.

> At length after a pause and stillness becoming almost painful, Elias rises and stands for a moment or two without a word. A tall straight figure . . . dress'd in drab cloth, clean-shaved face, fore-

head of great expanse, and large and clear black eyes, long or mid-dling-long white hair; he was at this time between 80 and 81 years of age, his head still wearing the broad-brim. [Quakers did not take their hats off indoors. Whitman says in *Leaves of Grass:* "I wear my hat as I please indoors and out."] A moment looking around the audience with those piercing eyes, amid the perfect stillness. (I can almost see him and the whole scene now.) Then the words come from his lips, very emphatically and slowly pronounc'd, in a resonant, grave, melodious voice, *"What is the chief end of man?* I was told in my early youth, *it was to glorify God, and seek and enjoy him forever."* (1233)

Whitman then says: "I cannot follow the discourse. It presently becomes very fervid, and in the midst of its fervor he takes the broad-brim hat from his head, and almost dashing it down with violence on the seat behind, continues with uninterrupted earnestness. But, I say, I cannot repeat, [or] hardly suggest his sermon" (1234). Hicks's sermon is too difficult for the ten-year-old Walt, yet he remembers that Hicks was "a magnetic stream of natural eloquence, before which all minds and natures, all emotions, high or low, gentle or simple, yielded entirely without exception. . . . Many, very many were in tears" (1234).

In the remainder of the essay Whitman tries to explain Hicks's religious views. Hicks "had much to say of 'the light within'" (1234). What does Hicks mean by this phrase? Whitman is not sure. Perhaps it is "only another name for the religious conscience" (1235). After noting that Emerson and Omar Khayyam have similar ideas, Whit-man acknowledges that it is difficult to clarify the term. "Indeed, of this important element of the theory and practice of Quakerism, the difficult-to-describe 'Light within' . . . I will not undertake where so many have fail'd—the task of making the statement of it for the average comprehension" (1236). Preferring to let Hicks speak for himself, he cites passages from a sermon by Hicks and from one of Hicks's letters.

Whitman, though, does clarify Hicks's religious views—in a footnote. "The true Christian religion, (such was the teaching of Elias Hicks,) consists *neither in rites or Bibles or sermons or Sundays*—but in noiseless secret ecstasy and unremitted aspiration, in purity, in a good practical life, in charity to the poor and toleration to all" (1234; emphasis added). Then he quotes Hicks: "A man may keep the Sabbath, may belong to a church and attend all the observances, have regular family prayer . . . and yet not be a truly religious person at all" (1234).

Hicks—Whitman says—is not criticizing Christians for being superficially observant; he is attacking Christian institutions. Hicks "believ'd little in a church as organiz'd—even his own—with houses, ministers, or with salaries, creeds, Sundays, saints, Bibles, holy festivals, &c." What did Hicks believe in? "He believ'd always in the universal church, in the soul of man, invisibly rapt, ever-waiting, ever-responding to universal truths" (1234).

Whitman surely exaggerated Hicks's anti-institutional views. After all, Hicks was a member of the Quakers. In these passages Whitman is describing his own views rather than Hicks's. Whitman, a friend said, disapproved of "institutional, official, teleological goodness." Whitman did not think highly of the ministers who visited the wounded soldiers in Washington hospitals. "You ought to see the way the men as they lie helpless in bed turn away their faces from the sight of these Agents . . . [and] Chaplains."[72]

In a note appended to his portrait of Hicks, Whitman sounds like Emerson when he says: "I consider that the churches, sects, pulpits, of the present day, in the United States, exist not by any solid convictions, but by a sort of tacit, supercilious scornful sufferance. . . .

Who is not aware that any such living fountains of belief in them are now utterly ceas'd and departed from the minds of men?" (1242–1243). Whitman's claim that religious institutions in the United States "exist not by any solid convictions" cannot be taken seriously. Writing in the late 1880s, James Bryce noted that religion was alive and well in the United States. "The relaxation of the old strictness of orthodoxy has not diminished the zeal of the various churches, nor their hold upon their adherents, nor their attachment to the fundamental doctrines of Christianity."[73]

Whitman criticizes Thoreau for "an inability to appreciate the average [American] life," yet he too looks down at "average" Christian worship. Whitman seems to like Christian worship only when it is unusual—when it takes place in an insane asylum in Toronto. Or he likes Christian worship when the minister is a great performer, such as Father Taylor or Henry Ward Beecher or Elias Hicks. Harold Bloom calls Whitman "the national religious poet," yet Whitman's preference for private spiritual experiences puts him at odds with most American Christians, who prefer communal worship on Sunday.[74]

Some observant Christians argue that those who call themselves "spiritual"—people who prefer private worship to traditional Christian worship—tend to be narcissists who continually search for self-fulfillment. Whitman was narcissistic: "I dote on myself" he says in *Song of Myself.* Yet he was remarkably generous with his time—visiting thousands of wounded and dying soldiers. On many Sundays during the 1860s Whitman did what sabbatarians said a good Christian should do on the Lord's Day—visit those in need of succor.

Twenty-five years after Whitman met Thoreau, he visited Thoreau's grave in Concord, Massachusetts, on a Sunday morning. He also visited Hawthorne's grave, since the two graves were near each other. "I got out [of the carriage] and went up of course on foot, and stood a long while and ponder'd. They lie close together in a pleasant wooded spot." Then he went to Walden pond—"that beautifully embower'd sheet of water, and spent over an hour there. On the spot in the woods where Thoreau had his solitary house is now quite a cairn of stones, to mark the place; I too carried one and deposited [it] on the heap" (914).

Thus Whitman paid homage to two very different writers whom he admired: Thoreau, a self-declared pagan sun worshiper, and Hawthorne, a lapsed Christian who said that "the spirit of my Puritan ancestors was mighty in me."[75] Hawthorne occasionally expressed pantheistic sentiments, but he was not a nature worshiper. *The Marble Faun* ends with the sarcastic remark: "Hilda had a hopeful soul, and saw sunlight on the mountain-tops." Whitman had far more in common with Thoreau than with Hawthorne, yet all three writers felt that Sunday, as Wallace Stevens would put it, had a "peculiar life."

Chapter Eight

Sunday Nostalgia, Sunday Despair

~ *Wallace Stevens and Robert Lowell*

*I*n the 1920s a biographer of Jonathan Edwards said: "It is hardly a hyperbole to say that, if Edwards had never lived, there would be to-day no blue laws." If Edwards had never existed, blue laws still would have been widespread because Calvinist Protestantism, which was strongly sabbatarian, was a powerful current in nineteenth-century America. Yet by the late nineteenth century sabbatarianism gradually was becoming a weaker force. In many states sabbatarian laws remained on the books but they were laxly enforced. In 1888 James Bryce noted that South Carolina had many laws promoting "piety and true religion," but he added: "It need hardly be said that these laws are practically obsolete, except so far as they forbid ordinary and unnecessary traffic and labour."[1]

In *Little House in the Big Woods* (1932), Laura Ingalls Wilder's account of the time she lived in the Wisconsin woods in the late 1870s, the young Laura learns that her grandfather's parents observed Sunday far more strictly than her parents do. After a solemn Saturday night supper, "Grandpa's father read a chapter of the Bible, while everyone sat straight and still in his chair." After a long prayer, "they must go straight to bed, with no playing or laughing, or even talking." Breakfast on Sunday morning was served cold, because cooking was not allowed. Then they walked to church because "hitching up the horses was work, and no work could be done on Sunday." Church service was long. They were required to "sit perfectly motionless, and never for one instant take their eyes from the preacher." When church service was over, they walked home. They could talk, but not laugh or smile. "At home they ate a cold dinner which had been cooked the day before. Then all the long afternoon they must sit in a row on a bench and study their catechism, until at last the sun went down and Sunday was over."

Laura's Sundays as well as the Sundays of Laura's future husband, Almanzo, were less rigorous. In *Farmer Boy* (1933), Almanzo's family celebrates Sunday as a holiday as well as a holy day—a day for cooking as well as worship. There is an elaborate Sunday breakfast and a hearty Sunday dinner. The family drives to church in a sleigh. Church service, however, had not changed. During the two-hour sermon, the boy "must sit perfectly still and never take his eyes from the preacher's solemn face and wagging beard." The hours after Sunday dinner also went slowly. "Almanzo just sat. He had to. He was not allowed to do anything else, for Sunday was not a day for working or playing. It was a day for going to church and for sitting still."

Wallace Stevens

Wallace Stevens, the author of "Sunday Morning," which has been called "one of the greatest contemplative poems in English," grew up in the 1880s and 1890s in a Presbyterian household that was mildly sabbatarian.[2] In a letter to his future wife, Elsie Moll, whom he married in 1909, Stevens talks about the Sundays of his childhood in Reading, Pennsylvania. "On Sundays, in those days, I used to wear patent leather pumps with silver buckles on 'em—and go to Sunday school and listen to old Mrs. Keeley, who had wept with joy over every pap in the Bible. . . . The First Presbyterian church was very important: oyster suppers, picnics, festivals." Stevens sang in the church choir for two years. Stevens' mother was more devout than his father. "She would play hymns on Sunday evenings, and sing."[3]

Stevens usually describes his religious upbringing in a neutral or positive way. In June 1912, when his mother was dying, he writes in his journal: "I remember how she always read a chapter of the Bible to all of us when we were ready for bed" (173). A year later he writes Elsie: "How thrilling it was to go to the old church last Sunday! [He means the church in Reading.] I had no idea I was so susceptible" (181). Stevens was a lapsed Christian, but he still enjoyed going to church occasionally.

Stevens' biographer says that "the month of rainy Sundays during his first year in New York had contributed to the early stage of Stevens's crisis of faith."[4] Yet before Stevens moved to New York in 1900 he said he had embraced a new faith: paganism. In 1899 he makes an entry in his journal that sounds like Thoreau: "Last evening I lay in a field on the other side of the creek to the S.E. of the house and watched the sunset. . . . I remember thinking that this must have been an old, Greek day, escaped, somehow, from the past" (29).

On a Sunday evening in March 1907 he sounds like Thoreau again: "I am not in the least religious. The sun clears my spirit, if I may say that, and an occasional sight of the sea, and thinking of blue valleys and the odor of the earth, and many things" (96). One month later he rhapsodizes about ancient Greece. "The impression of Greece is one of the purest things in the world. It is not a thing, however, that you get from any one book, but from fragments of poetry that have been preserved, and from statues and ruins, and a thousand things, all building up in the mind a noble conception of a pagan world of passion and love of beauty and life" (101).

Stevens did not come to paganism easily. In several essays and many letters he talks about his loss of faith. In 1951 he writes: "It left us feeling dispossessed and alone in a solitude, like children without parents, in a home that seemed deserted."[5] By "us" Stevens presumably means one or all of his siblings; he had an older brother, a younger brother, and two younger sisters.

Though Stevens never regained his faith, he always defended the church as an institution. He asks Elsie: "Was this the day you joined [the] church—or is it next Sunday? . . . You have kept so quiet about it. Well, if it was, I salute you no longer as a Pagan but as just what you ought to be" (98). He is happy that Elsie has joined a church. In 1940 he wrote to a literary critic who admired his work: "No one believes in the church as an institution more than I do" (348).

When Stevens was working in New York City in his twenties and early thirties, he enjoyed sitting in churches. "Last night [Saturday] I spent an hour in the dark transept of St. Patrick's Cathedral where I go now and then in my more lonely moods" (58). On another Saturday evening he went to a different church in Manhattan. "In the evening went to Christ Church. Full litany—sweet and melodious and welcome" (86). Stevens, though, rarely attended a service. "I dropped into St. John's chapel an hour before the service and sat in the last pew and looked around" (139). After leaving the chapel, he went for a long walk and eventually went into another church. "I dropped into a church for five minutes, merely to see it, you understand. I am not pious. But churches are beautiful to see" (140).

The young Stevens also took long walks on Sunday. "I walked from Van Cortlandt Park . . . to Greenwich, Connecticut—say, by my route, and judging from the time it took, roughly, thirty miles. It makes me feel proud of myself" (177). A few years earlier he walked forty-two miles one Sunday—getting up at 4 A.M. On a Sunday in August 1911, he went to church before going on a walk. "There's the sexton announcing morning services with his bell. After an hour at church, I am going out into the country somewhere—haven't had any fresh air for a long time. I may go to Yonkers, cross the river and walk down the Palisades among the locusts" (170). Unlike Leslie Stephen, who walked with his Sunday Tramps, Stevens went on these jaunts by himself.

On many Sundays Stevens also ruminated about Christianity. One Sunday he says that the night before he had read a life of Jesus. Then he reflects on Christianity in general. "The church should be more than a moral institution, if it is to have the influence that it should have. The space, the gloom, the quiet mystify and entrance the spirit. But that is not enough" (140). In Stevens' view Christianity is becoming a diminished force in many people's lives because few people believe in the Trinity. Yet many lapsed Christians believe in God even if they do not believe in Jesus. "People doubt the existence of Jesus—at least, they doubt incidents of his life, such as, say, the Ascension into Heaven after his death. But I do not understand that they deny God. I think everyone admits that in some form or other.—The thought makes the world sweeter—even if God be no more than the mystery of Life" (140).

Stevens occasionally worries that he talks too much about religion. He tells Elsie: "Yet if I prattle so much of religious subjects, . . . my girl will think me a bother; and so, no more, as we used to say when we had stumbled across something unpleasant" (141). Nevertheless, he continued to talk about religion. And though he was a lapsed Christian, he continued to pray. "I say my prayers every night—not that I need them now, or that they are anything more than a habit, half-unconscious" (96). He tells Elsie that he has thrown away his Sunday school Bible—"I'm glad the silly thing is gone"—yet two years later he writes her: "I have been digging into the Psalms—anything at all, so long as it is full of praise—and rejoicing. I am sick of dreariness" (102, 141).

Sunday was often a dreary day for Stevens because his Sunday ruminations left him dissatisfied. "I am in an odd state of mind to-day," he writes in his journal in April 1905. "It is Sunday. I feel a loathing . . . for things as they are; and this is the result of a pretty thorough disillusionment. Yet this is an ordinary mood with me in town [New York City] in the Spring time. I say to myself that there is nothing good in the world except physical well-being. All the rest is philosophical compromise" (82). This Sunday he is annoyed with himself because on the previous Sunday he went to church. "Last Sunday, at home, I took communion," in the church of his childhood. He regards his church attendance as a moral and intellectual failure. "It was from the worn, the sentimental, the diseased, the priggish, and the ignorant that 'Gloria in excelsis!' came" (82).

In his twenties Stevens thought a great deal about religion, but he also thought about what kind of profession he should choose. After completing a three-year program at Harvard, he worked as a journalist for roughly a year before deciding to go to law school. He worked for several law firms before landing a job in 1908 with the American Bonding Company, where he specialized in legal matters connected with insurance. In 1916 he joined the Hartford Accident and Indemnity Company—moving from New York to Hartford, Connecticut. In his new job he traveled a lot, and occasionally he worked on Sundays.

Writing from Erie, Pennsylvania, in May 1920, Stevens says to Elsie: "I should like to go to a pleasant little Episcopalian Church not far from the hotel but my Irish friends will no doubt be here in a short time and might object to my worshipping the principle of things instead of the stuff that makes the mare go round" (219). On a business trip to Florida in February 1923 he found time for a brief excursion to Cuba, where he visited several churches in Havana:

"During my walk this [Sunday] morning I dropped into every big church that I passed so that I can honestly say that I went to church most assiduously. They are all Catholic, gorgeous and shabby" (235).

In his later years Stevens rarely mentions visiting a church, yet he continued to think about faith while insisting that he was not an observant Christian. Two years before he died at the age of seventy-five, he wrote a literary critic: "I am afraid that you expect a monumental explanation of my religion. But I dismiss your question by saying that I am a dried-up Presbyterian, and let it go at that because my activities are not religious" (792).

Stevens seems annoyed that the critic asked him about his religious beliefs, yet in a letter to Hi Simons, a critic he admired, he talks at length about religion. "I ought to say that it is a habit of mind with me to be thinking of some substitute for religion. I don't necessarily mean some substitute for the church. . . . My trouble, and the trouble of a great many people, is the loss of belief in the sort of God in Whom we were all brought up to believe. Humanism would be the natural substitute, but the more I see of humanism the less I like it" (348). By "humanism" Stevens means a completely secular outlook.

Stevens continually asked himself: What kind of belief is possible for himself—or anyone? "To my way of thinking, the idea of God is an instance of benign illusion" (402). Did he subscribe to a benign illusion? In December 1951 he writes Sister M. Bernetta Quinn, a literary critic: "I am not an atheist although I do not believe to-day in the same God in whom I believed when I was a boy" (735). In a lecture given the same year, he says: "In an age of disbelief, or, what is the same thing, in a time that is largely humanistic, in one sense or another, it is for the poet to supply the satisfactions of belief."[6]

How can a poet supply the satisfactions of belief? It is a question that Stevens thought about for fifty years without arriving at a conclusion. In October 1952 he writes: "At my age it would be nice to be able to . . . make up my mind about God, say, before it is too late, or at least before he makes up his mind about me" (763). It did not bother Stevens that he could not make up his mind about God. "I have no wish to arrive at a conclusion. Sometimes I believe most in the imagination for a long time and then, without reasoning about it, turn to reality and believe in that and that alone. But both of these things project themselves endlessly and I want them to do just that" (710). He is a poet, not a philosopher. "I have never studied systematic philosophy and should be bored to death at the mere thought of doing so" (636).

Since Stevens spent so many Sundays thinking about faith, it is not surprising that he wrote "Sunday Morning," which is a meditation about faith by a lapsed Christian. The main speaker in the poem is a woman, though at times it seems to be Stevens who is talking. In the first four lines the woman is drinking coffee, eating oranges, and gazing at a rug. She seems to be a figure in a Matisse painting—Stevens admired Matisse—but after four lines the mood changes. She begins to think about the Christian faith that she has lost.

> She dreams a little, and she feels the dark
> Encroachment of that old catastrophe,
> As a calm darkens among water-lights.
> The pungent oranges and bright, green wings
> Seem things in some procession of the dead,
> Winding across wide water, without sound.
> The day is like wide water, without sound,
> Stilled for the passing of her dreaming feet
> Over the seas, to silent Palestine,
> Dominion of the blood and sepulchre.[7]

The woman is half-thinking, half-dreaming. She thinks about the "old catastrophe," but she also thinks about the oranges and the rug with a cockatoo. At first her secular Sunday and the Christian past are mixed, but in the last three lines her thoughts—her "dreaming feet"—move to "silent Palestine."

In the second stanza the woman tries to persuade herself that her loss of faith is a good thing. Stevens describes the woman's thoughts in the third person—writing in the free indirect style.

> Why should she give her bounty to the dead?
> What is divinity if it can come
> Only in silent shadows and in dreams?
> Shall she not find in comforts of the sun,
> In pungent fruit and bright green wings, or else
> In any balm or beauty of the earth,
> Things to be cherished like the thought of heaven?
> Divinity must live within herself.

Asking questions rather than making declarative statements, the woman has not yet persuaded herself that she will be content with "comforts of the sun." The phrase "must live" (rather than "lives") suggests that she wants to believe that divinity lives within herself but she is not sure that it does.

In the third stanza the woman continues to raise questions. She is still pondering the new faith that she has not fully accepted. "And shall the earth / Seem all of paradise that we shall know?"

In the fourth stanza Stevens has the woman speak directly. She begins with a declarative statement, which suggests that now she is confident about her new faith, but the sentence ends with a question.

> She says, "I am content when wakened birds,
> Before they fly, test the reality of
> Of misty fields, by their sweet questionings;

But when the birds are gone, and their warm fields
Return no more, where, then, is paradise?"

The woman says she is content, but she still has questions. Her mind is not at ease. In the fifth stanza she rephrases the question. "She says, 'But in contentment I still feel / The need of some imperishable bliss.'" Her answer, given in the third person, is that an imperishable bliss is not something desirable. "Death is the mother of beauty." The remainder of the stanza is an elaborate metaphorical argument in favor of this proposition.

Stanza six repeats the point that beauty comes from transience, but it does so by asking questions rather than making statements.

Is there no change of death in paradise?
Does ripe fruit never fall? . . .

. . . . .

Death is the mother of beauty, mystical,
Within whose burning bosom we devise
Our earthly mothers waiting, sleeplessly.

The lines are difficult to interpret because it is not clear who is speaking.[8] If the woman is saying again that death is the mother of beauty, then the lines are a kind of whistling in the dark—an attempt to persuade herself that her new faith is better than her old faith. But the lines seem more authoritative, as if Stevens himself is saying that death is the mother of beauty and that he is describing a world in which there is only the cycle of birth and death, of "our earthly mothers waiting, sleeplessly." The adverb "sleeplessly" suggests a permanent restlessness, yet the stanza implies that the waiting and sleepless state is better than the traditional paradise, where "the boughs / Hang always heavy in that perfect sky."

Whoever is speaking, it seems that the woman's doubts about her new faith have been allayed, for in the next stanza there is a confident assertion of paganism.

> Supple and turbulent, a ring of men
> Shall chant in orgy on a summer morn
> Their boisterous devotion to the sun.

This stanza recalls Matisse's famous painting of orange nudes dancing in a blue landscape. Is the woman having this vision? It would seem so, since the next stanza begins with "She hears," as if the pagan vision is suddenly dispelled by the intrusion of a voice.

In the concluding stanza, the mood changes dramatically. Instead of hearing a pagan chant, the woman hears a mysterious cry.

> She hears, upon that water without sound,
> A voice that cries, "The tomb in Palestine
> Is not the porch of spirits lingering.
> It is the grave of Jesus, where he lay."

What does the woman make of this voice, which seems to lament the loss of Christian belief, since Jesus has not been resurrected? Should the word "cries" be taken in a negative sense, as if we should lament the loss of Christian faith? Or is "cries" meant neutrally—signifying that a loud voice has interrupted the woman's reverie?

The poem shifts abruptly again. In the next four lines it seems to be Stevens who is speaking, not the woman.

> We live in an old chaos of the sun,
> Or old dependency of day and night,
> Or island solitude, unsponsored, free,
> Of that wide water, inescapable.

In these lines Stevens doesn't chant a "boisterous devotion to the sun." The mood is grave, though not necessarily gloomy: "We live in an old chaos of the sun." Each "or" is an attempt to clarify "the age of disbelief" that Stevens refers to in his essay, "Two or Three Ideas."[9] We live in an "island solitude"—a world where we cannot worship communally. We live in an "unsponsored" world—a world without transcendence. And our situation is "inescapable"; there is no going back to faith.

The widely admired last seven lines of the poem are mysterious.

> Deer walk upon our mountains, and the quail
> Whistle about us their spontaneous cries;
> Sweet berries ripen in the wilderness;
> And, in the isolation of the sky,
> At evening, casual flocks of pigeons make
> Ambiguous undulations as they sink,
> Downward to darkness, on extended wings.

The first three lines describe a dreamlike landscape—one that we might see in a Renaissance painting. In the last four lines a specific action is described, but what does it mean?

"Poetry," Stevens once said, "is essentially romantic," but it is not "romantic" in the conventional sense of the term. It is an austere romanticism that is in search of transcendence. "Without this new romantic, one gets nowhere; with it, the most casual things take on transcendence" (277). Are the "casual flocks of pigeons" a "casual thing" that takes on transcendence? A journal entry Stevens made in 1902, a decade before he wrote "Sunday Morning," may clarify its concluding stanza: "The true religious force in the world is not the church but the world itself: the mysterious callings of Nature and our responses" (58).

Stevens often said that he disliked discussing the meaning of his poems. "I have the greatest dislike for explanations. As soon as people are perfectly sure of a poem they are just as likely as not to have no further interest in it" (294). Yet thirteen years after he wrote "Sunday Morning" he offered a paraphrase of the poem. "This is not essentially a woman's meditation on religion and the meaning of life. It is anybody's meditation. . . . The poem is simply an expression of paganism, although, of course, I did not think that I was expressing paganism when I wrote it" (250). But the poem is less an expression of paganism than an exploration of paganism in the hope that it will fill the void left by the loss of Christian faith.

"Poetry," Stevens says in *Adagia*, a collection of aphorisms, "is an effort of a dissatisfied man to find satisfaction through words, occasionally of the dissatisfied thinker to find satisfaction through his emotions."[10] The woman in "Sunday Morning" is Stevens' dissatisfied man and dissatisfied thinker.

"Sunday Morning" appeared in *Harmonium* (1923), Stevens' first volume of verse. A different version of "Sunday Morning" was published eight years earlier in *Poetry* magazine (November 1915). Then the poem had five rather than eight stanzas. They were chosen by Harriet Monroe, the editor, but the arrangement of the stanzas was made by Stevens. What is now the last stanza was then the second stanza of the poem. And the penultimate stanza, with its pagan chant, was the last stanza. The new version of the poem—the version of the poem we now read—ends on a note of elegiac resignation to an "unsponsored" world, whereas the old version ends with a celebration of paganism. Stevens, Helen Vendler says, "never was a poet formed to chant in orgy to the summer sun."[11]

Did Stevens regret his loss of faith? At times he seems to regret it, but he always suggests that there is no going back. In "Notes toward a Supreme Fiction," he says: "To sing jubilas at exact, accustomed times . . . this is a facile exercise." Stevens, Frank Kermode writes, "agrees with Freud *(The Future of an Illusion)* that we must come to terms with 'the cruelty of reality,' and cast off the 'religious illusion.'" But it is misguided to say, as Stevens' biographer does, that Stevens "struck blows at religion" or "struck hard at religion." Stevens was not hostile to Christianity in the way Thoreau sometimes appears to be. Stevens speaks of "abandoning" Christian belief, not unmasking it. "After one has abandoned a belief in god, poetry is that essence which takes its place as life's redemption."[12]

In *Adagia* Stevens says that "loss of faith is growth."[13] Many of Stevens' poems are exuberantly pagan. In "Ploughing on Sunday" Stevens describes a pagan Sunday—a day of the sun.

> Remus, blow your horn!
> I'm ploughing on Sunday,
> Ploughing North America.
> Blow your horn!
>
> Tum-ti-tum,
> Ti-tum-tum-tum!
> The turkey-cock's tail
> Spreads to the sun.

He prefers to be silly rather than solemn on Sunday.

"The Sense of the Sleight-of-Hand Man," which can be called a Sunday meditation because it refers to Sunday baths, is an elaborate celebration of Sunday as sun day. The poem begins:

> One's grand flights, one's Sunday baths,
> One's tootings at the weddings of the soul
> Occur as they occur.

Sunday, the day when one traditionally toots at the weddings of the soul, is a day like any other day—a day for celebrating nature. If in "Sunday Morning" Stevens describes the "ambiguous undulations" of pigeons, in this poem he describes a swooping bluejay. The second stanza begins:

> Could you have said the bluejay suddenly
> Would swoop to earth? It is a wheel, the rays
> Around the sun. The wheel survives the myths.

The speaker, who is a sleight-of-hand man—someone with a fertile imagination—imagines that the rays of the sun are a wheel. The imagination is energized by its encounter with the swooping bluejay—another example of a "casual thing" that takes on transcendence. And the rays of the sun are a force—a wheel that "runs" the imagination. The result is a new reality, this poem, which is a new sun. In a late poem, "The Planet on the Table," Stevens says:

> His self and the sun were one
> And his poems, although makings of his self,
> Were no less makings of the sun.

Poems are the product of two suns: the sun of reality and the sun of the imagination.

When Stevens celebrates the imagination in its encounter with the natural world, he sounds like Emerson. In 1898 Stevens' mother gave him a twelve-volume set of Emerson's works, which he kept for the rest of his life. He reread Emerson frequently. The following aphorism in *Adagia* could have been written by Emerson: "It is the belief and not the god that counts."[14]

Stevens, though, is not completely in Emerson's camp. He also is a descendant of "good Puritans," which is how he describes his Dutch ancestors.[15] "Sometimes I am terribly jangled, full of clashing things" (131). He writes his future wife about his mixed feelings: "The priest in me worshipped one God at one shrine; the poet another God at another shrine. . . . As I sat dreaming with the Congregation I felt how the glittering altar worked on my senses stimulating and consoling them; and as I went tramping through the fields and woods I beheld every leaf and blade of grass revealing or rather betokening the Invisible" (59).

"The Sun This March" is not a celebration of the imagination. In this poem the sun's "exceeding brightness" makes Stevens aware of his own dark imagination. "The exceeding brightness of this early sun / Makes me conceive how dark I have become." In the penultimate stanza, the poet says: "Cold is our element and winter's air / Brings voices as of lions coming down." What is the element that is cold? It is the poet's imagination, which takes him to an earlier self where "voices" roar to him "as of lions coming down." The earlier self is a dark and angry self. Stevens, Vendler says, had a "wintry temperament."[16]

The poem concludes with a plea: "Oh! Rabbi, rabbi, fend my soul for me / And true savant of this dark nature be." In using the word "rabbi," Stevens is not making a comment about Judaism. Stevens wrote his Italian translator that "the rabbi is a rhetorical rabbi. Frankly, the figure of the rabbi has always been an exceedingly attractive one to me because it is the figure of a man devoted in the extreme to scholarship and at the same time to making some use of it for human purposes" (786). The key word in the two lines is "fend," which means "defend"—protect his soul from harm. "Fend" also means (according to the *OED*) "provide substance for, support." Stevens sees his "dark nature" as a danger to his soul. The plea, cast in the imperative, is more an expression of melancholy than a call for help. He knows the "rabbi" cannot help him. He once wrote Elsie on a Sunday evening: "No one loathes melancholy more than I, yet there are times when no one is more melancholy" (129).

Toward the end of his life Stevens began to write poems in which Emersonian enthusiasm triumphs over Puritan melancholy. Cold is no longer his element. In "The World as Meditation," he calls the imagination mankind's "barbarous strength." In "Final Soliloquy of the Interior Paramour," he says:

> We say God and the imagination are one . . .
> How high that highest candle lights the dark.
>
> Out of this same light, out of the central mind,
> We make a dwelling in the evening air,
> In which being there together is enough.

Is Stevens endorsing the notion that divinity lives within ourselves? He said so in an aphorism, but in the poem he distances himself from this statement by using the construction "We say" and also by ending the remark with an ellipsis. We say many things about God, and they may or may not be true. According to one critic, "Stevens pointedly declares that everything we believe is a fiction, that reality is an invention of the mind."[17] Stevens doesn't pointedly declare anything except that the mind is never satisfied. The last line of "The Well Dressed Man with a Beard" is: "It can never be satisfied, the mind, never."

On a Sunday morning walk in July 1950 Stevens gave himself a mental exercise: "I tried to pretend that everything in nature is artificial and that everything artificial is natural, as, for example, that the roses in Elizabeth Park [in Hartford] are placed there daily by some lover of mankind and that Paris is an eruption of nature"

(684). Stevens is always thinking—here somewhat whimsically—about his relation to nature.

Stevens prefers to think about things by himself. "Poetry is like prayer in that it is most effective in solitude and in the times of solitude as, for example, in the earliest morning." He did not wish to be accompanied on his Sunday walks. In April 1906 he writes in his journal: "Took my customary [Sunday] ramble yesterday—with three, for company. I detest 'company' and do not fear any protest of selfishness for saying so" (89). A year later he writes Elsie: "The fact is, most people are a great nuisance, and my own disposition is not remarkably lenient in such things" (107). There is no reason to think that when Stevens was in his seventies he felt any differently. In September 1954 he told the *New York Herald-Tribune Book Review*: "A great deal of my poetry has been written while I have been out walking. Walking helps me to concentrate."[18] Stevens doesn't say "walking by myself," but that is what he means.

Stevens' love of solitude makes him seem more like Thoreau than Emerson, but he differs from Thoreau—and Emerson as well—in that he liked churches and defended the church as an institution. He never lost his emotional attachment to Christian culture. In April 1955, four months before he died, he wrote a literary critic: "How good of you to think of me for Easter! I return your greetings most sincerely. In spite of its solemnity, Easter is the most sparkling of all fêtes since it brings back not only the sun but all the works of the sun, including those works of the spirit that are specifically what might be called Spring-works: the renewed force of the desire to live and to be part of life" (879). Stevens thinks of Easter in pagan terms as the renewal of the sun, but he says that Easter is about renewal in general, including the renewal of spiritual life.

A Roman Catholic priest testified that shortly before Stevens died he was baptized in the Catholic church, but Holly Stevens, his daughter, said that her father complained he was being bothered by visits from a priest.[19] Even if Stevens did have a deathbed conversion, it has no bearing on his poems, which are the ruminations of a lapsed Christian. "Modern reality," Stevens wrote, "is a reality of decreation, in which our revelations are not the revelations of belief, but the precious portents of our own powers."[20]

Robert Lowell

In 1967 Robert Lowell, who is regarded by many as the major American poet of the last half of the twentieth century, published "Waking Early Sunday Morning" in a collection of poems entitled *Near the Ocean*. Writing to his Japanese translator, Lowell said: "I think I meant to pay Stevens some sort of little compliment with my title." Lowell of course was referring to Stevens' "Sunday Morning," which he admired. "I'd be happy," he added, "to have someone sometime read our two poems together for their contrasts."[21] Lowell is right to speak of contrasts. "Waking Early Sunday Morning" is very different from "Sunday Morning," yet the poems have one thing in common: they are what might be called Sunday ruminations by lapsed Christians.

Lowell, unlike Stevens, had a superficial religious upbringing. On Sunday Robert and his mother usually attended Trinity Episcopal Church in Boston, but the main event of the day was Sunday dinner. In "91 Revere Street," a memoir included in *Life Studies* (1959), Lowell says: "Sunday mornings are long. Ours were often made tedious by preparations for dinner guests." Lowell's mother worried that her husband might not carve the roast properly. "Father, faced with this opinion, pored over his book of instructions or read the section on table carving in the Encyclopedia Britannica. Eventually he discovered among the innumerable small, specialized Boston 'colleges' an establishment known as a carving school. Each Sunday from then on he would sit silent and erudite before his roast [before starting to carve it]." Lowell's father did not go to church. A graduate of the Naval Academy, he "believed that churchgoing was undignified for a naval man; his Sunday mornings were given to useful acts such as lettering his three new galvanized garbage cans: R. T. S. Lowell—U.S.N."[22]

In the memoir Lowell's only extended reference to religion is a sarcastic paragraph about a Christian Scientist who occasionally came to Sunday dinner. (She is the wife of a cousin.) "She wouldn't hear of my mother's distress from neuralgia, dismissed my asthma as 'growing-pains,' and sought to rally us by gossiping about healers. . . . In a discourse which lasted from her first helping of roast beef through her second demitasse, Mrs. Atkinson held us spellbound by telling how her healer had 'surprised and evaporated a cyst inside a sac' inside her 'major intestine.'"[23]

Thus, Sunday was an ordeal for the young Lowell, but not for religious reasons. He had to sit through a long Sunday dinner, during which his parents often embarrassed him, and the guests (mostly naval officers) irritated him. "I used to sit through the Sunday dinners absorbing cold and anxiety from the table. . . . Waiting for dinner to end and for the guests to leave, I used to lean forward on my elbows, support each cheekbone with a thumb, and make my fingers meet in a clumsy Gothic arch across my forehead. I would stare through this arch and try to make life stop."[24]

Lowell also disliked Sunday because he had to be with his parents for most of the day. In a poem that refers to Sunday dinner, Lowell says that he preferred to be with his grandfather (his mother's father), whom he admired. In another poem about his grandfather, he says: "He was my Father. I was his son." Lowell admits that he was a difficult child. "I bored my parents, they bored me."[25]

Boredom is only one of many emotions Lowell felt when he thought about his parents. He regarded his father with a mixture of pity and contempt; his father was a weak man who allowed himself to be dominated by his mother. He regarded his mother with irritation and anger; she was a snob who thought few people were worthy of her company. "Very few people *were* her sort in those days. . . . She did not have the self-assurance for wide human experience. She needed to feel liked, admired, surrounded by the approved and familiar. Her haughtiness and chilliness came from apprehension." Lowell was close to an older cousin, Harriet Winslow. In a poem he says that she "was more to me than my mother."[26]

Though the young Lowell's Sundays were different from the young Stevens' Sundays, Lowell too became a pagan. In a letter to Ezra Pound, the nineteen-year-old Lowell says: "I had always chafed against what I thought was Christianity, the immortality of the soul, the idealistic unreal morality and the insipid blackness of the Episcopalian church. Homer's world contained a God higher than anything I had ever known. . . . Your *Cantos* have re-created what I have imagined to be the blood of Homer" (4). Lowell, who began to write poetry when he was in prep school, wanted to study with Pound, but Pound declined to take him on as a pupil.

Lowell's paganism, unlike Stevens', was short-lived. Five years after he wrote Pound, Lowell converted to Catholicism. In 1946, after publishing his first book of poems (*Lord Weary's Castle*), Lowell was considered by many, including Stevens, to be a leading Catholic writer. Lowell took his Catholicism seriously. The novelist Jean Stafford, whom Lowell married in 1940, said: "Cal [Lowell's nickname] is becoming a Catholic. A real one with all the trimmings, all the fish on Friday and the observance of fasts, and confessions and grace before meals and prayers before bed."[27] Lowell attended Mass on Sunday and on other days of the week as well. During the winter of 1942–43, when Lowell and Stafford were living in Tennessee, they took a bus several times a week to a church in a town twelve miles away. One Sunday morning, after Stafford described a goofy religious dream she had, Lowell thought she was being flippant and he ordered her to spend the rest of the day reading the Gospel.

In February 1944, when Lowell was serving a prison sentence because he was a conscientious objector (he was not a pacifist, but he opposed the Allied fire-bombing of Hamburg and other German cities), he told Stafford that he wanted to be an itinerant outdoor preacher for a Catholic organization. When she asked him how they would manage financially, he said that God would provide. Stafford thought Lowell was becoming "more Catholic than the church."[28] A Jesuit priest who edited a Catholic weekly agreed with her.

Why did Lowell become a Catholic when a few years earlier he had scoffed at Christianity? Lowell's biographer says that two people shaped Lowell's thinking about religion when he was a graduate student at Louisiana State University: the college chaplain for Catholics and a philosophy student. There may also have been a less edifying reason—a desire to shock his mother, who thought Catholics were the wrong sort. In her view, Catholicism was the religion of Irish servant girls.[29]

Lowell's zealous Catholicism may have been a harbinger of the mental illness that would plague him for most of his life. The first major attack of acute mania occurred in 1949, but five years earlier Stafford had worried that her husband's religiosity might be a sign of incipient mental illness. She wrote Peter Taylor—Lowell's college roommate and close friend—that Lowell had become "so fanatical, so insanely illogical that our conversations and his letters could be written into a case history of religious mania."[30] In 1946 Lowell lost interest in Catholicism—and lost interest in Stafford as well. He left the church and separated from her. He wrote an acquaintance: "Now I'm filled to the gills with theology and churches" (96).

A few years later Lowell briefly returned to Catholicism. On a

Sunday in February 1949 he went with Flannery O'Connor (a devout Catholic) to Mass for the first time in a year. He and O'Connor were both at Yaddo, a writers' colony in Upstate New York. The next day Lowell announced that he was going back to the church, and he told friends that he had received "an incredible outpouring of grace" and felt that God was speaking through him. Two months later, when he was visiting Peter Taylor, who was teaching at Indiana University, he sniffed the air and said: "Do you smell that?" When Taylor said he couldn't smell anything, Lowell told him it was the smell of brimstone. In the throes of an acute manic episode, Lowell had to be hospitalized.[31]

For the next eighteen years the manic episodes recurred frequently. During them Lowell was fervently religious or fervently in love. He often would propose marriage to an attractive young woman he had recently met. After 1967, when he began to take lithium, the attacks became less frequent, yet in 1975 and 1976 he had four manic episodes that required hospitalization. Lowell called his manic episodes "enthusiasm"—putting "enthusiasm" in quotation marks to stress that he was referring to the old meaning of the word: religious zealotry. If in Emerson "enthusiasm" stands for the creative imagination, in Lowell "enthusiasm" stands for the imagination gone haywire. In November 1954 he tells his close friend Elizabeth Bishop: "These things [his attacks of mania] come on with a gruesome, vulgar, blasting surge of 'enthusiasm'" (242). A decade later he writes T. S. Eliot about how he feels "when the 'enthusiasm' is coming on me" (444).

For most of Lowell's adult life, Sundays brought back memories of his childhood Sundays and stirred up fears about his mental health. Yet Lowell also liked to think about the religious dimension of Sunday. In October 1954 he writes from Boston to his cousin Harriet Winslow: "This has been a very traditional Sunday—this morning we strolled down to King's Chapel (very white, sparsely attended and Unitarian)" (241). He told William Empson, the English literary critic: "I rather enjoy Church, hymns, communion and all" (294). He wrote in his will that he wanted a solemn funeral Mass at the Episcopal Church of the Advent in Boston.

Lowell's interest in religion should be taken at face value—not explained away as a consequence of his neuroses and occasional psychosis. Lowell admired George Santayana, a religious skeptic who defended the Catholic tradition. In "For George Santayana," Lowell calls him a "free-thinking Catholic infidel." In 1947 Lowell sent Santayana his first book of poetry. Lowell says that Santayana, who was living in a convent in Rome, "took a fancy to my craggy, dark, apocalyptic poetry because I was both an old Bostonian and an apostate Catholic." A few months later Lowell told Santayana that he would send him a book of Stevens' poetry. He found an anthology that included a selection from Stevens' work, and he particularly recommended "Sunday Morning." In the fall of 1950, when Lowell and Elizabeth Hardwick, his second wife, were in Rome, Lowell paid a daily visit to Santayana, who wrote to an Italian acquaintance that Lowell is "sensitive in religious matters."[32]

In May 1955 Lowell became an Episcopalian—returning to the religion of his parents. "About two months ago after much irresolution," he writes Elizabeth Bishop, "I became an Episcopalian again (a high one). I used to think one had to be a Catholic or nothing. . . . I don't know what to say of my new faith; on the surface I feel eccentric, antiquarian, a superstitious, sceptical fussy old woman, but down under I feel something that makes sober sense and lets my eyes open."[33]

Did Lowell join the Episcopalian church because he had become a believer? Lowell himself didn't know the answer to this question. Trying to explain to Bishop (an ex-Baptist) why he became an Episcopalian, Lowell writes: "I think most people who are Christians find profession and practice something commonsensical, cow-like, customary. I'd like to take it that way. Doing much more seems extravagant" (248). Becoming a cow-like Episcopalian was not possible for Lowell, who was not cow-like or commonsensical about anything.

Lowell told John Berryman that his "feelings about Christianity are confused" (400). Lowell's feelings about Christianity continually changed. The year before Lowell became an Episcopalian, he wrote Flannery O'Connor that "Henry Adams called himself a conservative, Catholic anarchist; I would take this for myself, only adding agnostic" (226). Fourteen years later he said he was "an aristocratic, Christian atheist." A student of Lowell's once said: "Can you imagine how hard it is to live as Robert Lowell, with that inner life?"[34]

Lowell was often driven by what he called "squabbling uncontrollable desires," so he hoped that if he became an observant Christian his mental turmoil would subside.[35] He told Santayana that when he became Catholic "what I was after was a way of life" (167). Yet he also told Santayana that he feared going back to Catholicism because he thought it might trigger an acute manic episode. "Often I long to walk in the great house of the Church, but the candles would set my clothes on fire long before I reached the altar" (153).

Lowell never became a regular churchgoer. In letters and poems he says that on Sunday he reads, listens to music, goes fishing, or takes his daughter Harriet for a walk. In a sonnet called "Familiar Quotations," he quotes his daughter, who asks: "Who made God? Did God the Father take Baby/Jesus to Central Park on Sunday?" On one Sunday in October 1960 Lowell spent twelve hours at the Bronx Zoo with Harriet and a friend. In June 1971 he writes the poet Adrienne Rich: "Our weekends are much like yours—sun, grass, children. Sometimes I go trout fishing and fail to land them" (575). In May 1977, four months before he died, Lowell writes Caroline Blackwood (his third wife): "Sunday I sat by the Charles River watching the strollers, the joggers, the sunners—and the river" (668).

On a Sunday in October 1970 Lowell spent several hours reading Emerson's poetry for a class he was teaching in England at the University of Essex. Lowell admired Emerson, whom he taught on a number of occasions. Emerson, he says, "not only spoke America's mind; he emerged like a whale[,] adding something that wasn't there, and [that] never would have even been if Emerson had never lived" (225). Lowell does not say what it was that Emerson added to America's mind.

Like Stevens, Lowell was influenced by Emerson, but the writer who haunted Lowell's imagination is Jonathan Edwards. A direct descendant on his mother's side of the *Mayflower* pilgrims, Lowell told Santayana that "Jonathan Edwards was one of my ancestors" (79). When Lowell was a Catholic, he began to write a biography of Edwards. He never completed it, but in the next two decades he wrote two poems about Edwards. The second poem, "Jonathan Edwards in Western Massachusetts," is in effect a short biography of Edwards. Describing the highlights of Edwards' life, the poem ends with a long quotation from a letter Edwards wrote to the board of trustees of the College of New Jersey (now Princeton), in which he outlined the reasons he didn't think he was suitable for the job of president of the university.

Lowell's first poem about Edwards, "Mr. Edwards and Spider," takes passages from Edwards' sermon "Sinners in the Hands of an Angry God" and from a work Edwards wrote when he was eleven: *Of Insects*. The poem is an elegant and powerful sermon that describes what happens to sinners in the hands of an angry God. Just as the spider sizzles and dies when thrown on a burning brick, so the sinful soul will burn forever in the fires of hell.

How long would it seem burning! Let there pass

A minute, ten, ten trillion; but the blaze

Is infinite, eternal: this is death,

To die and know it. This is the Black Widow, death.

Another poem in *Lord Weary's Castle*—"After the Surprising Conversions"—is based on the conclusion of Edwards' "Narrative of the Surprising Conversions," which describes the religious revival that began in Northampton in 1736.

A critic has described Lowell's early poetry as "a head-on collision between the Catholic tradition and an Apocalyptic Protestant sensibility."[36] The poems in Lowell's first book are more Puritan than Catholic. One poem, "Dea Roma" (The Goddess of Rome), is implicitly anti-Catholic, since it regards Rome as a corrupt city. Like so many poems in *Lord Weary's Castle*, "Dea Roma" is a public poem—a sermon by an angry Puritan. "I am modern and angry and puritanical," Lowell said in 1940, a year before he became a Catholic (25). It is not clear what Lowell means by "puritanical," but from the context it seems that he is aligning himself with the Puritan literary tradition, which includes Edwards and Hawthorne. In June 1971 Lowell wrote Elizabeth Hardwick: "I learned all I know about the Puritans from Hawthorne" (574).

"Waking Early Sunday Morning," which begins as an anxious reverie and ends as an apocalyptic sermon, is not the first poem Lowell wrote about Sunday morning. Two decades earlier he had published "Falling Asleep over the Aeneid," which is a monologue—to quote the epigraph—by *"an old man in Concord [who] forgets to go to [Sunday] morning service. He falls asleep, while reading Vergil, and dreams that he is Aeneas at the funeral of Pallas, an Italian prince."* The poem is a clever yet somewhat labored antiwar poem.

In the first stanza of "Waking Early Sunday Morning" the speaker wakes before he wants to—wakes with the sense that he must change

his life. Lowell said that "the waking is meant to be simply insomnia" and the poem is "a mosaic of partly true and partly fictional autobiography" (487). The speaker is not thinking about faith or the
loss of faith. He is thinking about himself. He feels he is stuck in a
rut; he desperately wants to change his life.

> O to break loose, like the chinook
> salmon jumping and falling back,
> nosing up to the impossible
> stone and bone-crushing waterfall—
> raw-jawed, weak-fleshed there, stopped by ten
> steps of the roaring ladder and then
> to clear the top on the last try,
> alive enough to spawn and die.

The tetrameter couplets and the arresting description of a salmon
making its way upstream convey a sense of urgency—even panic.

The second stanza of Lowell's poem begins with an abrupt command: "Stop, back off." The speaker orders himself to refrain from
panicking. He realizes that on Sunday morning he is not burdened
by the constraints of weekday time. The time is his—to use as he
pleases. Sunday is a day he can do anything—a day fraught with possibility.

In the third stanza the mood changes abruptly again. Now the
speaker does not talk about himself. Rather, he thinks about busy
nocturnal animals.

> Vermin run for their unstopped holes;
> in some dark nook a fieldmouse rolls
> a marble, hours on end, then stops;
> the termite in the woodwork sleeps—
> listen, the creatures of the night

> obsessive, casual, sure of foot,
> go on grinding, while the sun's
> daily remorseful blackout dawns.

Why is night "the sun's . . . remorseful blackout"? Is the sun filled with remorse at the human condition? In any case, the dawn brings a renewed awareness on the speaker's part that he has not yet broken loose. The creatures of the night were busy, but he cannot get out of bed.

In an earlier version of the poem, which appeared in the *New York Review of Books* in April 1965, the third stanza is different. There is nothing about "creatures of the night." Instead, Lowell thinks of Sunday morning as a time for pruning his work and also for reviewing his own conduct.

> Time to grub up and junk the year's
> output, a dead wood of dry verse:
> dim confession, coy revelation,
> liftings, listless self-imitation,
> whole days when I could hardly speak,
> came pluming home unshaven, weak
> and willing to read anyone
> things done before and better done.

Why did Lowell get rid of this powerful stanza? Lowell always worried about being too personal in his poetry. In the "Introduction" to Lowell's *Collected Poems* Frank Bidart says: "The question that hung over his work was, what does this have to do with other people?"[37] By junking both this stanza and six lines in stanza nine, Lowell makes the speaker stand for every depressed and anxious person on a Sunday morning.

In the fourth stanza the sun has risen, so the speaker can now look around. He looks out the window and sees pleasure boats on the water:

> Fierce, fireless mind, running downhill.
> Look up and see the harbor fill:
> business as usual in eclipse
> Goes down to the sea in ships.

His mind is fierce and fireless because it is filled with thoughts that do not kindle. His imagination unnerves him rather than strengthens him. His mind is running downhill.

In the fifth stanza the speaker looks at a glass of water in his room.

> I watch a glass of water wet
> with a fine fuzz of icy sweat,
> silvery colors touched with sky,
> serene in their neutrality—
> yet if I shift, or change my mood,
> I see some object made of wood,
> background behind it of brown grain,
> to darken it, but not to stain.

The speaker is a prisoner of his moods, which have the effect of making him incapable of doing anything. Everything he thinks about and sees increases his despondency. The freedom of a Sunday morning is a terrible burden.

In the sixth stanza the speaker thinks of other things he could do on a Sunday morning. He could go stack firewood or he could go to church. The speaker wants to go to church, but not because he is a man of faith. He wants to get out of the room, where he is a prisoner of his gloomy thoughts. He says: "anywhere, but somewhere else!" He hears church bells chiming, but he still cannot get out of bed.

In the seventh stanza the speaker thinks about a church service, but he finds it unappealing. He dislikes the hymns that are sung, which lack subtlety. He calls them "stiff quatrains shoveled out four-square," yet he acknowledges that "they gave darkness some control,/ and left a loophole for the soul." Christian hymns—and Sunday worship in general—might help control his unruly psyche. And the hymns implicitly acknowledge the existence of a soul.

In the eighth stanza the speaker abruptly decides that he will not go to church. Instead, he will do household chores.

> No, put old clothes on, and explore
> the corners of the woodshed for
> its dreg and dreck.

The jumble of half-broken items he finds in the shed calls to mind fragments of passages from the Bible. And the jumble is also a representation of his cluttered mind—a mind that lacks purpose. Lowell said: "I suppose one should think of the speaker in 'Waking Early,' as someone in a sort of rambling dramatic monologue. He begins in the dark with the rambling gloomy thoughts of insomnia, and never leaves his bed. . . . Humor and temperament, and also the Sunday morning[,] made me load the poem with half pious half blasphemous Biblical allusions" (488).

The speaker cannot stop thinking about religion. In the ninth stanza he asks:

> When will we see Him face to face?
> Each day, He shines through darker glass.
> In this small town where everything

is known, I see His vanishing
emblems, His white spire and flag-
pole sticking out above the fog,
like old white china doorknobs, sad,
slight useless things to calm the mad.

In the first line of this stanza, the speaker raises a question that never comes up in Stevens' "Sunday Morning": "When will we see Him face to face?" The speaker has a strong religious hunger, yet he belittles his own feelings: the emblems of religion are useful only to "calm the mad."

In the tenth stanza the speaker shifts from religion to war: "Hammering military splendor, / top-heavy Goliath in full armor." Does a hammer in the woodshed lead him to think of "hammering"? It is hard to say. These are rambling thoughts by a speaker who is filled with anxiety and despair. To remind himself to be calm, the speaker opens the eleventh stanza with a command to himself: "Sing softer!" But he continues to feel despondent; he is not breaking loose. The stanza ends with the repetition of a line in stanza six: "anywhere, but somewhere else!"

In the twelfth stanza the speaker repeats the phrase he began the poem with: "O to break loose." The repetition is an act of desperation. He must do something now, but he cannot. He would also like to break loose from oppressive thoughts. He tries to summon up positive thoughts, daydreaming about a summer romance which elated him, but he ends up thinking of an elated Lyndon B. Johnson:

elated as the President
girdled by his establishment
this Sunday morning, free to chaff
his own thoughts with his bear-cuffed staff,

swimming nude, unbuttoned, sick
of his ghost-written rhetoric!

The president is not a man who lies in bed on Sunday morning. He is an energetic man, a leader who can joke with his staff even though he is "sick/of his ghost-written rhetoric." By "rhetoric" Lowell probably means the president's speeches about the war in Vietnam.

When Lowell was writing "Waking Early Sunday Morning," he was a political activist—an opponent of the Vietnam War. In August 1965 he flew to Washington to address a huge crowd of students who were protesting the war. Lowell said he wrote "the poem directly after my White House business" (488). Lowell wrote a letter to President Johnson saying that he would not accept the White House's invitation to read at a White House festival for the arts. In the letter to the president, he says: "I . . . follow our present foreign policy with the greatest dismay and distrust. . . . We are in danger of imperceptibly becoming an explosive and suddenly chauvinistic nation, and may even be drifting on our way to the last nuclear ruin" (459). Just how the war in Vietnam could lead to "the last nuclear ruin" is not clarified.

In the thirteenth stanza Lowell goes from thoughts about President Johnson to thoughts about endless war.

No weekends for the gods now. Wars
flicker, earth licks its open sores,
fresh breakage, fresh promotions, chance
assassinations, no advance.
Only man thinning out his kind
sounds through the Sabbath noon.

The stanza is a Puritan jeremiad against man's violent ways. The Sabbath is not a day of rest; it is another day for war, when man is "thinning out his kind."

The last stanza begins with the imperative: "Pity the planet, all joy gone." The speaker is no longer brooding about himself. He is praying for everyone:

> peace to our children when they fall
> in small war on the heels of small
> war—until the end of time
> to police the earth, a ghost
> orbiting forever lost
> in our monotonous sublime.

The editors of the *Collected Poems* gloss the line about policing the earth with a remark Walter Lippmann made in May 1965: "Our official doctrine is that we must be prepared to police the world."[38] But the last stanza does not refer only to American foreign policy. "Our children" are children everywhere. Does Lowell mean "sublime" in a sarcastic sense—the sublime rhetoric of an American president, whose speeches are monotonous?

"Waking Early Sunday Morning" is not an easy poem to paraphrase. One critic said it was about a poet's hangover and other physical ailments. Lowell disagreed. "The speaker," Lowell said, "has no bowel trouble, or erection trouble. He never leaves his bedroom. The poem is about energy (Too much and too little, both dangerous, a sort of non-clinical manic-depressive state, resembling the world and the American national character[,] mine too . . .[)]—then about the pathos and impotence of the old religion, belief in the state etc. Then, of course about American imperialism, Viet Nam etc." (487).

The poem is about many subjects, but the subjects are less important than the speaker's psyche. The speaker is gloomy on a Sunday morning because he is disturbed by his own passive life, disturbed by his lack of faith, disturbed by Lyndon Johnson's foreign policy, and disturbed by the state of the world.

In this reader's view the last five stanzas of "Walking Early Sunday Morning" lack the elegance, clarity, and power of the first nine stanzas, which contain some of Lowell's best writing. Lowell wrote many poems about politics and political figures, but they are not his best work. One wonders how well Lowell understood politics, for in 1977 he remarked: "We live in the sunset of Capitalism. We have thundered nobly against its bad record all our years, yet we cling to its vestiges, not just out of greed and nostalgia, but for our intelligible survival. Is this what makes our art so contradictory, muddled and troubled?"[39] This was written at a time when most observers talked about the sunset of socialism and communism.

Lowell thought more deeply about religion than politics. He took a great interest in the English religious poets, especially Gerard Manley Hopkins and George Herbert. When Lowell was a graduate student, he considered publishing an edition of George Herbert's poems. In August 1957 he gave Elizabeth Bishop a two-volume edition of Herbert that had been in his family for a century. But Lowell did not think poetry could be a substitute for religion. He wrote the poet and critic Allen Tate that "art and religion per se have nothing to do with each other, but . . . in this imperfect world they are always colliding . . . and . . . this is as it should be" (197).

What Hawthorne says of Melville applies to Lowell: "He can neither believe, nor be comfortable in his unbelief."[40] In August 1965 Lowell wrote the poet Stanley Kunitz: "At our age, it would be consoling to believe in repentance, reformation and eternal life, like the Catholics" (461). Six months before he died, Lowell wrote the Catholic priest who played an important role in his religious awakening. "I remember well your long patient explanations to me of catechism. The books we discussed, I still have. You were a road over a dark stream" (664). In the final stanza of a poem Lowell was working on the week before his death, he prays to Christ that he may die "with a semblance of my faculties."

Lowell lost his faith, but he wished he could be a man of faith. He never would have said what Stevens said—that "loss of faith is growth." He never was an Emersonian pagan. He was a gloomy man, a Puritan, and Sundays were often his gloomiest days. Writing about "Waking Early Sunday Morning," he says that the speaker is "trying to escape the graceless tedium of Sunday" (488). A sonnet entitled "Dawn," which appears in the volume *History* (1973), ends with the following lines:

> Nothing more established, pure and lonely,
> than the early Sunday morning in New York—
> the sun on high burning, and most cars dead.

Chapter Nine

Sunday Now

∼ Sacred and Profane

*I*n Edith Wharton's story "False Dawn," which is set in New York City in the 1840s, a Mr. Raycie asks: "The Sundays—the Sundays? Well, what of the Sundays?" He is not pondering the meaning of the Lord's Day. He is annoyed by the remarks of a Mr. Kent, who thinks the Continental Sunday undermines religion and morality. In the 1840s most Americans were either sabbatarians like Mr. Kent or antisabbatarians like Mr. Raycie, but as sabbatarianism waned a new religious division was becoming apparent—between observant Christians and lapsed Christians. On Sunday the former went to church. On Sunday the latter looked for God (or transcendence) in nature. Lapsed Christians often said they were spiritual rather than religious. Emerson, who wrote an influential essay entitled "Spiritual Laws," was the patron saint of many lapsed Christians. A recent collection of Emerson's work, which appeared on the bicentenary of his birth, is called *The Spiritual Emerson*.[1]

"Spiritual" is a fuzzy word. Reviewing a biography of Melville in which the novelist is called "a deeply spiritual man," James Woods asks: "And what, exactly, is 'a deeply spiritual man'?" And what ex-

248

actly is the difference between "religious" and "spiritual" in the sentence, "[Emerson] remained a deeply religious man with a thoroughly spiritual view of human life and the world"? A reviewer of the *Encyclopedia of New Religions* puts the word "spirituality" in quotation marks, as if to imply that he is not sure what it means. The encyclopedia, he says, includes such topics as "creation spirituality," "Postmodern Spirituality," and "Feminist and Eco-Feminist Spirituality." Martin Marty, a leading historian of American religion, decries the solipsistic world of "religionless spirituality."[2]

A spiritual person is generally understood to be a believer who is not affiliated with an organized religion but is looking for God or transcendence (as Stevens did) in the "casual things" of the natural world. A religious person is someone who participates in communal worship in an established religion. But the boundary line between "spiritual" and "religious" is not clear, and some writers use the words interchangeably. Fifty-five percent of the respondents to a survey conducted by *Newsweek* in 2005 described themselves as religious and spiritual. The article is called "In Search of the Spiritual," which implies that the term "spiritual" is more inclusive than the term "religious."[3]

In the second half of the nineteenth century, spiritual Americans were a small but growing minority. Their view of Sunday was similar to Emily Dickinson's, who wrote (in 1860):

> Some keep the Sabbath going to Church—
> I keep it, staying at Home—
> With a Bobolink for a Chorister—
> And an Orchard, for a Dome—

Edith Wharton also rarely went to church. When she returned from a visit to England in 1903, she wrote: "And in England I like it *all*—

institutions, traditions, mannerisms, conservatisms, everything but the women's clothes and the having to go to Church every Sunday." Her biographer notes that in her late sixties she began to take an interest in the Church of Rome. One of the entries in her commonplace book is: "I don't believe in God but I do believe in His saints—and then?" She never did join a church.[4]

Wharton, who admired Emerson, enjoyed spending Sunday outdoors. Describing the Sunday rambles of her childhood, she remembers "my secret sensitiveness to the landscape—something in me quite incommunicable to others, that was tremblingly and inarticulately awake to every detail of wind-warped fern and wide-eyed briar rose, yet more profoundly alive to a unifying magic beneath the diversities of the visible scene—a power with which I was in deep and solitary communion whenever I was alone with nature."[5]

William James also admired Emerson. James told an acquaintance that "reading the whole of him over again continuously has made me feel his real greatness as I never did before." One of the most annotated essays in James's collection of Emerson is "Spiritual Laws." In a speech delivered in Concord on the centenary of Emerson's birth, James speaks of Emerson's "spiritual voice" and "spiritual seeing." James was also interested in the spiritualist movement, which was popular in late nineteenth-century America. He attended séances because he wanted to investigate all psychological phenomena, but he regarded the claims of mediums with skepticism.[6]

In *The Varieties of Religious Experience* (1902), James makes no distinction between the religious and the spiritual. Speaking of "religious opinions," he says that "their value can only be ascertained by spiritual judgments." James also says that he is not interested in institutional religion. He is studying "personal religion." He defines religion as *"the feelings, acts, and experiences of individual men in their solitude, so far as they apprehend themselves to stand in relation to whatever they may consider the divine."*[7]

According to James, it is good to think about religious questions, but it is important to have faith. "Every sort of energy and endurance, of courage and capacity for handling life's evils, is set free in those who have religious faith." Faith in what? James rarely mentions God; he speaks of the "Ideal," or the "unseen order above us," or the "Absolute," or the "divine," or a "larger power." He speaks of "the actual inflow of energy in the faith-state and the prayer-state." In other words, people should have faith in faith. They should not unduly worry about what it is they have faith in. James was fond of quoting his friend Benjamin Paul Blood's remark: "Simply, *we do not know*. But when we say we do not know, we are not to say it weakly and meekly, but with confidence and content."[8]

Faith, James says, "creates its own verification." James's notion of faith is similar to Emerson's notion of enthusiasm. If people have faith they will have energy. James continually battled against depression by willing himself to have faith—thereby tapping into "transmundane energies, God, if you will."[9]

James said he was not a Christian. "I am more interested in religion than in anything else, but with a strange shyness of closing my hand on any definite symbols that might be too restrictive. So I cannot call myself a Christian." He agrees with Emerson's critique of Christianity. "Historic Christianity, with its ecclesiasticism and whatnot, stands between me and the imperishable strength and freshness of the original books." (He is referring to the Bible.) In James's view most forms of institutional Christianity stifle spirituality. The exception is Quakerism, which he calls "a religion of veracity rooted in spiritual inwardness."[10]

James does not tell Americans to stay away from church on Sunday, yet he looks down on traditional worship, suggesting that it is a "dull habit." He praises his father, Henry James Sr., for attacking institutional Christianity and for trying "to prevent religion from becoming a fossil conventionalism—and to keep it forever alive." One observer has called James an "obsessively religious man . . . who was committed to devising a philosophy that would provide a foundation for spiritual experience."[11] In James's scheme of things, spiritual beings like himself—beings who have faith in faith, people who will themselves to believe—are keeping religion alive.

In the twentieth century the "spiritual movement" continued to grow, though "movement" is a misleading term because there is no organization of spiritual persons. Alan Wolfe, the director of the Boisi Center for Religion and American Public Life at Boston College, says that "many Americans consider themselves spiritual more than they do religious. . . . Some writers believe that the 'spiritual but not religious category' is in fact America's largest religion, claiming more adherents than Catholics or Baptists." According to a 2005 *Newsweek* survey, Americans, especially those under sixty, are more likely to consider themselves spiritual rather than religious.[12]

In *The Varieties of Religion Today* (2002), Charles Taylor speaks of the "free-floating not very exigent spirituality" that is widespread in the United States, and he says that our age "tends to multiply somewhat shallow and undemanding spiritual options." In 1963 Lionel Trilling worried about "the disgust and rage which are essential to the state of modern spirituality."[13] Trilling, though, was not referring to Emersonian spirituality; he was talking about the spirituality of a number of modernist writers who were hostile to bourgeois culture. It would be wrong to assume that most Americans who call themselves spiritual are political or social radicals, though undoubtedly there are more spiritual people on the left than on the right.

In addition to religious Americans and spiritual Americans, there are also secularist Americans. A secularist, a *Wall Street Journal* columnist says, is someone who does not "hold religious beliefs or engage in religious practices." (The writer does not clarify what she means by "religious belief.") Some observers would lump spiritualists into the secularist category, but this would be a mistake, for secular Americans are not interested in seeking transcendence. Secularists are generally far more hostile to traditional religion than spiritualists. Secularists argue that all religious beliefs are foolish, and some religious beliefs are dangerous. David Brooks offers another category: the quasi-religious. "Quasi-religious people attend services, but they're bored much of the time. They read the Bible, but find large parts of it odd and irrelevant." But the quasi-religious surely belong to the religious category.[14]

Secularism has always been a weak force in the United States. When Thomas Paine attacked Christianity in *The Age of Reason*, he was vilified as an atheist and shunned by his friends, including the aged Samuel Adams, who lamented that Paine was trying to "unchristianize the mass of our citizens." Secularists often are atheists, but only five million Americans call themselves atheists. According to a USA Today/Gallop poll taken in 2007, only 49 percent of Americans would vote for an atheist candidate for president. A 2007 poll by the Pew Forum on Religion and Public Life found a small increase in the number of people who identify themselves as secular— from 8 percent in 1987 to 12 percent in 2007—but a 2007 poll by the Barna Group says that the number of atheists has not changed in recent years: five million Americans.[15]

The big change in the American religious landscape is in the number of people who say they do not belong to any religious faith. According to a report by the Pew Forum in February 2008, 16 percent of Americans are unaffiliated with a religion. Are these people spiritual or secular? The report says that 6.3 percent of the unaffiliated are "secular unaffiliated," and 5.8 percent are "religious unaffiliated." Does the phrase "religious unaffiliated" mean "spiritual"? The report makes it clear that it would be wrong to jump to the conclusion that unaffiliated Americans are secularists. After all, Wallace

Stevens was unaffiliated, but he cannot be called a secularist. In fact, he disliked secularism.[16]

Many American writers have not been observant Christians, but no major American writer has been a secularist. Robert Frost said he was "safely secular till the last go down," and he also remarked that his religious progress was "Presbyterian, Unitarian, Swedenborgian, Nothing." Yet Jay Parini points out that Frost's correspondence, conversation, and poems "are saturated with religious feeling, with questing after God." Parini also notes that Emerson became "a crucial influence on his thought."[17]

Many American writers are lapsed Christians like Stevens who on Sundays feel the weight of the Christian tradition they have abandoned. In Hawthorne's story "Sunday at Home," the narrator looks at the local church from a window in his house. "It must suffice, that, though my form be absent, my inner man goes constantly to church." The contemporary American poet Charles Wright calls himself "a God-fearing agnostic."

(The contemporary English philosopher Anthony Kenny goes to church on Sunday even though he is not a believer. Kenny, who calls himself a "devout agnostic," thanks the "Christian communities" that have allowed him "to join in their worship without acknowledging their authority." He says that "prayer to a God about whose existence one is doubtful is no more irrational than crying out for help in an emergency without knowing whether there is anyone within earshot.")[18]

How different are churchgoing Americans from spiritualists and secularists? Most Americans—the religious, the spiritual, and the secular—subscribe to Emerson's gospel of enthusiasm. Most Americans are radical individualists who believe, as Emerson says, that "each man is a jet of flame." Most Americans think they should look forward because an "eye fastened on the past unsuns nature." Most

Americans believe—or want to believe—in "the power of positive thinking," which is the title of a book that has sold millions of copies. The pastor of a megachurch in Connecticut sounds like Emerson when he says: "Sundays are about real life, inspiration, and hope."[19]

According to Alan Wolfe, American churchgoers have no interest in the kind of Calvinism Jonathan Edwards promoted. "More Americans than ever proclaim themselves born again in Christ, but the lord to whom they return rarely gets angry and frequently strengthens self-esteem. . . . If Jonathan Edwards were alive and well, he would likely be appalled; far from living in a world elsewhere, the faithful in the United States are remarkably like everyone else."[20]

Churchgoing Americans are different from their spiritualist and secularist counterparts in one respect; they make a commitment to a religious community, which often entails other commitments. Their Sunday mornings are taken—and sometimes weekday evenings or Saturdays are taken as well.

Americans, then, spend Sunday morning in different ways. The observant Christian attends church, the spiritualist may go for a long walk, and the secularist probably reads the Sunday papers. Non-Christians—Jews, Muslims, Buddhists, Hindus—do whatever they please. But on Sunday afternoon and Sunday evening religious, spiritual, and secular Americans do the same things. They go shopping, enjoy an outdoor barbecue, attend a sports event, watch sports on television, play golf, go hunting or fishing, or eat out with friends. Sunday is a holy day for 80 percent of Americans, but it is a holiday for all Americans—all, that is, but a very small number of Christians who remain resolutely sabbatarian. And for an increasing number of Americans it is also a working day.

By contrast, in mid-nineteenth-century America what one was allowed to do on Sunday varied according to where one lived—and varied according to one's religious affiliation. A Sunday in a large northeastern city was different from a Sunday in a small midwestern town—and a Catholic's Sunday was different from a Methodist's Sunday.

Varieties of Sunday Worship

If the way people spend their Sunday afternoons and evenings has become more uniform, the way people worship on Sunday morning has become less uniform because the American religious marketplace has expanded dramatically in the past century. "In 1900 there were 330 different religious groups [in the United States]; now there are over 2,000." The United States, a leading historian of religion said in 2005, is "a nation growing ever more diverse in belief and practice."[21]

In seventeenth-century England and eighteenth-century colonial America, there was a great diversity of religious beliefs and practice, but in contemporary America the diversity is much greater. (Peter Berger, a leading sociologist of religion, says that "modernity is not intrinsically secularizing—it is necessarily *pluralizing*.") There are forty-seven major religious groups in the United States that call themselves Christian. Jews constitute 1.8 percent of the population. Owing to increasing immigration from Asia, Muslims, Hindus, and Buddhists now constitute almost 2 percent of the population. Some mosques offer Sunday services, as do some Buddhist temples, though neither Buddhists nor Hindus have a weekly holy day. Sunday, though, is the day of rest for Hindus.[22]

Since there are so many religious "products" to chose from, many Americans are religious shoppers who change their faiths. In October 2001 a survey conducted by the City University of New York Graduate Center reported that 20 percent of Americans have changed their faith since childhood. In February 2008 the Pew Forum reported that the nation's religious landscape is in a state of flux. Forty-four percent of adults have switched religious affiliations, moved from being unaffiliated with any faith tradition to affiliated, or abandoned any ties to a specific religion altogether. However, the percentage of people who call themselves Christian has remained constant at 80 percent. Given this religious restlessness, it is not surprising that religious denominations in America grow or decline. Rarely do they remain stable in their membership. In one hundred years the Church of God in Christ, the nation's largest Pentecostal church, grew from a congregation of nineteen persons who met under a tent to a denomination with 6.5 million members.[23]

The CUNY study also reported that 15 percent of Americans belong to a religious group that is completely different or mostly different from the religious group of their spouse or partner. Attending a "Roundtable for Religious Leaders," Supreme Court Justice Stephen Breyer noted that he is Jewish, his wife is Anglican, and his daughter is an Episcopal priest. (Hawthorne said he was a pantheist. His daughter Rose became a nun, establishing a charitable organization to care for indigent cancer patients. In 1899 she received the Holy Habit of the Third Order of St. Dominic.) At the roundtable attended by Justice Breyer were a rabbi, two Episcopalian priests, a practitioner of voodoo, an imam, a Buddhist monk, two Baptist ministers, and representatives of the Sikh, Hindu, and Native American communities. The author of the article half-jokingly adds that there were no "Wiccans, Mormons or Scientologists on hand."[24]

Stephen Prothero says that survey takers miss the dynamic nature of American religion. "Sociologists herd Americans into religions and then denominations, but they do not inquire into how our spiritual lives measure out certainty and confusion." A woman who now considers herself a pagan told the *New York Times* that after she was raised a Roman Catholic she became a Jehovah's Witness for fifteen years. Then she became a Baptist before turning to paganism. The *Washington Post* interviewed a Wiccan who wanted to become the Army's first Wiccan chaplain (he was turned down). He said that after being raised as a Catholic, he became a born-again Christian and a Baptist preacher. Then he served as the pastor of two messianic congregations, which blend Jewish traditions with a belief in the divinity of Jesus. While he was a pastor, he read books about other religions, especially Buddhism, and eventually he became a Wiccan.[25]

An acquaintance of this writer was raised as a Baptist but at the age of twenty she converted to Catholicism. Twenty years later she explored Buddhist as well as Hindu meditation. She also practiced Judaism, since her second husband was Jewish, though she did not convert to Judaism. Now she is an Episcopalian. Her three children have widely different religious views and practices. One is an Episcopalian, another is an Emersonian spiritualist (though she occasionally attends Catholic Mass), and the third is an agnostic.

Many Americans learn about religions on the Internet. Beliefnet. com, the largest religious website, offers a vast amount of information on different religious groups. The director of teenage programs for a conservative Christian foundation says that young people "gravitate to where they feel a connection. They're more pragmatic than their parents' generation. They look at what works for them." These young Americans, the headline says, "seek [a] faith that fits."[26]

In August 2005 Pope Benedict XVI voiced his disapproval of those who look for a faith that fits. Attacking what he called "D-I-Y" (do-it-yourself) religion, he said: "If it is pushed too far, religion becomes almost a consumer product. People choose what they like, and some are even able to make a profit from it. But religion constructed on a do-it-yourself basis cannot ultimately help us."[27]

Where there is religious liberty, religion inevitably is a consumer product. American Protestantism has always been entrepreneurial. Even in colonial times Protestant sects employed salesmanship to gain adherents. "Evangelism," the author of an article on Billy Graham says, "is measured in won souls, and Graham's productivity at the altar call was unmatched." Before Graham became a minister, he spent a summer as a door-to-door Fuller Brush salesman, and "outsold every other Fuller man in two states."[28]

Worship in America, except perhaps for worship by Quakers, has always had its theatrical side. Itinerant preachers were performers who kept their audiences spellbound. Philip Kevin Goff, the director of the Center for the Study of Religion and American Culture at Indiana University, Indianapolis, says that "a visit to your local megachurch—including Starbuck's coffee, entertaining music and drama, and a short talk that seems less like a sermon than an inspiring self-help lesson—will not seem much different than a trip to the mall." Religion in America, he says, "is increasingly tied to secular culture in its presentation." In his view, this is not necessarily a bad thing. It is a sign of Christianity's ability to find new ways to attract worshipers. James Twitchell calls American religion "a wonderful free-for-all that has been studiously overlooked by all except for a few die-hard economists and marketing scholars."[29]

Even the Catholic church is responsive to the concerns of lay Catholics. In recent years the church has reinstituted the traditional Latin Mass because an increasing number of Catholics say they prefer it.[30] And the church has always found ways to respect the pagan traditions of some worshipers without endorsing paganism. Willa Cather's *Death Comes for the Archbishop* (1927) contains the following description of a church: "The church was clean and the doors were open: a small white church, painted above and about the altar with gods of wind and rain and thunder, sun and moon." In this church in New Mexico, Native American gods decorate the walls.

If Boswell were alive today, he would need a year to sample the different forms of Christian worship available to him on any given Sunday in the United States. If he also wanted to sample non-Christian forms of worship, he would probably need two years.

Boswell could begin by going to one of forty-two parks in Pennsylvania that hold outdoor nondenominational Christian services on Sunday mornings. In 2005, 18,000 people attended such services. Or he could attend a Sunday service at a megachurch. There are more than 1,200 Protestant churches that attract at least 2,000 worshipers every Sunday. Five percent can seat more than 3,000; two or three of them can seat 10,000.[31]

Boswell could also go to an informal Sunday service in someone's house. A growing number of Christians are moving to home churches "both as a way to create personal connections in the age of the mega-church and as a return to the blueprint for the Christian church spelled out in the New Testament, which describes Jesus and the apostles teaching small groups in people's homes." In the Washington suburb of Rockville a dozen or so people of different Christian "faith backgrounds" meet without an ordained pastor.[32] They meet on Sunday evenings.

Boswell could also watch a religious service on his cell phone or computer. A minister in Alexandria, Virginia, has started what he calls "Godcasting"—making his Sunday services available on the Internet. The hour-long podcasts of his weekly services have brought new parishioners to his church. "I can't possibly have a conversation with everyone each Sunday," the minister says. "But this builds toward a digital discipleship. We're orthodox in belief but unorthodox in practice."[33]

Boswell could participate in a virtual service by creating an avatar—that is, a graphic or iconic representation of himself—in Second Life, the online virtual universe that is growing rapidly. Second Life enables members of a religious group to engage in discussion or even practice a religious ritual. Some religious institutions, especially evangelical churches, have become interested in Second Life. A megachurch in Oklahoma broadcasts its weekly sermon to twelve locations—eleven to its satellite campuses across the country and one to its virtual church in Second Life.[34]

Boswell, a sociable man, would probably be dissatisfied with virtual worship. He might want to go to a church where dancing is a major part of worship. In New York City there is the Praise Dance School and Ministry. Praise dance "is a form of worship that seeks to articulate the word and spirit of god through the body." In recent years, praise dance has been added to the services of many Pentecostal churches. According to Doug Adams, a professor of Christianity and the arts at the Pacific School of Religion, praise dance is popular because of its visual appeal. "Most churches now greet you with a video screen, and dance is a visual art."[35]

If Boswell wanted to sample non-Christian worship, he might attend Sunday services at the New York Buddhist church or at a Buddhist temple in Anaheim, California. Or he might worship with pagans who revere Sunna, a Germanic sun goddess. Or worship with pagans who call themselves Christo-Pagans because they use some Christian rituals.[36]

Sunday is not a holy day for most contemporary pagans, who often celebrate seasonal festivals. Paganism, Barbara Berger says, "includes a number of different religious expressions that fall under the category of earth-based spirituality." According to Berger, pagans "take things from a number of different sources, like Eastern religions, Celtic practices. You are the ultimate authority of your own experience." Some pagans practice communal worship; many do not. Wicca, a pagan religion, is the country's fastest-growing religion, with 134,000 adherents in 2001 compared with 8,000 in 1990. But the number of pagan Americans is less than one-half of 1 percent of the population: between 200,000 and 700,000.[37]

Boswell might also join Paul and Patricia Churchland, who go to

the beach every Sunday at dawn. The Churchlands, who are professors of philosophy at the University of California at San Diego, probably do not consider themselves to be Emersonian spiritualists, since
they think mental states are functions of brain processes. Material-
ists are not immune to the pleasures of nature, though they are not
likely to worship nature. Lucretius, the Roman philosopher-poet,
was a materialist, yet in his epic poem, *The Way Things Are*, he is
awed by the sunrise.

> When dawn bathes earth with morning light, and birds,
> All kinds of them, flying through pathless woods,
> Fill all the delicate air with liquid song,
> How suddenly at such a time the sun
> Clothes everything with light!

The Churchlands, like Lucretius, enjoy observing the sunrise. Do
they seek transcendence in "casual things"? Perhaps, but the main
thing is: their Sunday mornings are different from other mornings of
the week.[38]

Many Americans do something special on Sunday. A man in
Anne Tyler's *Digging to America* (2006) enjoys taking his adopted
Korean daughter out on Sunday mornings. "Sunday mornings, Jin-
Ho and I go out for croissants and the *New York Times*. . . . It's my
favorite thing of the week. I love it! Just me and my kid together."
A young woman in Zadie Smith's novel *On Beauty* (2005) says:
"I'm going to make toast and scrambled. I can have scrambled once
on a Sunday—I feel like I earned it." In the same novel a young
man offers a laconic account of what he does on Sunday: "Go to
church, Sunday lunch. Family stuff." His Sunday is more traditional
than hers.

The notion that Sunday is a special day remains widespread.

Barnes and Noble recently began selling two compact discs called *Sunday Music*. Pasted on the disc is the following blurb: "Discover the world of Sunday Music. Great Artists. Extraordinary Songs. Quiet Times." Sunday, according to Barnes and Noble, "is a day when your personal soundtrack takes a more reflective turn." A reviewer says that *Sunday Music* "features fifteen genre-leaping tracks that revel in the reflective nature and recuperative powers of the most gentle (for some) day of the week."

Whether we call Sunday the Lord's Day, the day of the sun, the second day of the weekend, or the most gentle day of the week, it is a special day for many Americans. In Los Angeles civic groups have begun a project called Big Sunday, which enlists the help of 50,000 volunteers to work on a wide variety of civic projects—from refurbishing a women's shelter to organizing an animal-adoption fair at a local pound.[39] Sunday is even a special day for some atheists. The Humanist Community Center in Palo Alto, California, runs a Sunday school for atheists. There are similar schools in several western states.[40]

The Future of the Sabbath

On a Sunday afternoon in February 1909 Wallace Stevens wrote his fiancée a rambling letter in which he talked about "the peculiar life of Sundays." In 1909 Sunday was becoming less peculiar because Americans were turning away from sabbatarianism. The Continental Sabbath had triumphed in many parts of the country, especially in the major cities of the North and Midwest, where there were many immigrants.

The antisabbatarians were aided by Mark Twain, one of many writers who disliked sabbatarian Sundays. In Twain's satirical *Extracts from Adam's Diary, Translated from the Original MS* (1903), which purports to be the diary Adam wrote in the Garden of Eden, there is the following entry: "SUNDAY—Pulled through. This day is getting to be more and more trying. It was selected and set apart last November as a day of rest. I already had six of them per week before. This is another of those unaccountable things." Twain clearly disliked the amount of attention Congress paid to sabbatarian questions, for Adam adds: "There seems to be too much legislation; too much fussing, and fixing, and tidying up, and not enough of the better-let-well-enough-alone policy." In an entry for Monday, Adam says: "I believe I see what the week is for: it is to give time to rest up from the weariness of Sunday."[41]

In 1909 Sunday was still the Sabbath in New York, since most retail businesses were closed, but it was not a day most New Yorkers spent in a sabbatarian fashion. Many began the day by reading the Sunday paper. By 1890 there were 660 Sunday papers in the United States.[42] Though observant Christians went to church on Sunday morning, on a Sunday afternoon most strolled or picnicked in Central Park (or other parks) or drank beer in a beer garden, or went to a museum, a concert, a movie, a play, or a baseball game.

Outraged that Sunday was becoming a holiday as well as a holy day, the New York Sabbath Committee issued regular bulletins in which they warned that "liberty's only secure foundation is the Holy Sabbath." The bulletin quotes Justice John McLean, who served as Associate Justice of the U.S. Supreme Court from 1830 to 1861: "Where there is no Christian Sabbath, there is no Christian morality; and without this free institutions can not long be sustained."[43] The New York Sabbath Committee occasionally succeeded in closing a theater when the entertainment was considered inappropriate for Sunday, but in the next three decades the Continental Sabbath triumphed in most parts of the country.

A half-century after the Continental Sabbath became widespread, Sunday was transformed in another way: retail stores began to open on Sunday. "The day of rest," Russell Baker says, "vanished in mid-century, and the country hasn't paused since." With the opening of most businesses on Sunday, the debate about the Continental Sabbath was now superseded by a debate about whether commerce on Sunday should be different from commerce on other days of the week.[44]

In recent years those favoring no restrictions of commerce on Sunday have continued to win victories in state legislatures, so that now only a handful of states have restrictions on the sale of liquor on Sundays. In November 2003 Governor Mitt Romney of Massachusetts signed laws allowing liquor stores to be open on Sundays. A Bostonian who runs a wine store said: "Everything else is open on Sundays. Why can't this be, too?"[45]

In June 2007 those favoring restrictions on commerce had a minor victory in South Carolina. A bill was introduced to repeal a blue law that prevents most retailers in forty counties from opening before 1:30 P.M. on Sunday. The bill passed, but the governor vetoed it, saying that a change in the law would make it difficult for employees who work on Sunday to attend church services. (The veto was upheld.) Many supporters of the bill argued that the blue law favors businesses in the six counties in South Carolina where there are no restrictions on commerce on Sunday. They also pointed out that Michelin, a major employer in South Carolina, operates around the clock seven days a week.[46]

South Carolina's blue law will have only a marginal effect on the way Sunday is observed in the state. In South Carolina (and in the South in general) stock-car racing, which holds its major races on Sunday, is popular. Sponsored by NASCAR, an acronym for Na-

tional Association for Stock Car Auto Racing, stock-car racing is
the second most popular sport on television. (A recent book on the
subject is called *Sunday Money*.) Many of the drivers, crews, and
spectators are descended from sabbatarian households, but they do
not think they are profaning the Sabbath by racing on Sunday.
NASCAR advertises itself as a Christian sport suitable for the whole
family. Its leading figures often talk about their religious faith, and
there are pit-stop church services on Sunday for the crews.[47]

The commercialization of Sunday disturbs some Americans. In
December 2004, Daniel Avila, an official with the Massachusetts
Catholic Conference, decried Massachusetts' decision to repeal its
long-standing ban on Sunday liquor sales. "This is one step in the
process of making the Sabbath into just another day, and it is hap-
pening in many other states as well. We think that is wrong." In
Chicago a minister asked his congregation to turn off their cell
phones on Sunday in order to observe the Sabbath.[48]

Some Christians were upset that in 2004 Family Christian Stores,
the country's largest chain of Christian bookstores, decided to open
on Sunday afternoons. A petition was placed on the Internet to
gather support to reverse the new policy. "We understand that your
business (Family Christian Stores) has added Sunday hours, which
have been slowly phasing in around the country. We believe, as a
Christian bookstore, you should feel especially obligated to close
your stores on Sunday. . . . By opening your stores [on Sunday],
you are contributing to the decay of our society and the lowering of
moral standards." The petition was launched in 2004, but as of 2008
it had garnered only 285 signatures.[49]

It is not only observant Christians who are in favor of having a
day of rest. In 1901 the American psychologist G. Stanley Hall said:
"Sunday is a psychological institution which modern hygiene of the
soul would have to invent if religion had not provided it." A decade

later a congressional committee that recommended the end of Sunday mail delivery said a day of rest elevated "the moral condition of society" and made Americans "better citizens and better men."[50]

Hawthorne and Twain disliked sabbatarianism, but both approved of a day of rest. The narrator of Hawthorne's "Sunday at Home" says that "on the Sabbath I watch the earliest sunshine, and fancy that a holier brightness marks the day, when there shall be no buzz of voices on the Exchange, nor traffic in the shops, nor crowd, nor business, anywhere but at church." In Twain's *Extracts from Adam's Diary*, Adam says: "I have come to like Sunday myself. Superintending all the week tires a body so. There ought to be more Sundays. In the old days they were tough, but now they come [in] handy."[51]

The jacket of a recent book promoting the Sabbath (not only the Christian Sabbath but the Jewish and Muslim Sabbath as well) says that "in today's frantic 24/7 world, the Sabbath—a day devoted to rest and contemplation—has never been more necessary." A popular rock group called Taking Back Sunday says that the name for the band was chosen "because Sunday's when you should hang [out] with your family and friends . . . like the Bible says, a day to kick back." A website called BlueLaws.net is a clearinghouse for those who are opposed to the commercialization of Sunday. The statement on its site says: "Sunday closing laws are compassionate legislation . . . pro-family, pro-environment and pro-labor." BlueLaws intends to "promote family and national observance of Sunday."[52]

Those who want to preserve the Sabbath are swimming against the current. Any attempt to restore blue laws would encounter objections from retailers—and probably from many shoppers. It would also stir up religious discord, for some people would see it as a maneuver by Christians to make their holy day the holy day of the week—thereby bringing religion into the public square.

Chick-fil-A, which has more than 1,100 restaurants in the United

States, does not open on Sundays. Its website gives a nonreligious reason for this practice. "Admittedly, closing all of our restaurants every Sunday makes us a rarity in this day and age. But it's a little habit that has always served us well, so we're planning to stick with it. Our founder, Truett Cathy, wanted to ensure that every Chick-fil-A employee and restaurant operator had an opportunity to worship, spend time with family and friends or just plain rest from the work week. Made sense then, still makes sense now."

It is unlikely that other restaurants or retail businesses will adopt Chick-fil-A's policy. An article in *Custom Retailer*, a business magazine, is headlined: "Sunday Shopping Gaining Steam." A moving company in Northern Virginia calls itself Sunday Movers. A new bank in the same area advertises that it is open on Sundays. A chain of eyeglass stores tells customers that it now has Sunday hours. A writer in the *Wall Street Journal* says that many Christian-owned businesses remain dark on Sundays, but he only lists Chick-fil-A and Hobby Lobby Stores Inc., which has more than 300 shops nationwide.[53]

In 2004 an independent Christian bookstore in Iowa decided to open on Sunday for the Christmas season. Its owner said: "It's important to take a day of rest, yes. But what does keeping the Sabbath day holy really mean? When we go out to eat on Sundays, we go to a business that's open—how is that right or wrong? Besides, we are very concerned with paying the bills."[54]

Even if Americans do not go to an office or a store on Sunday, they may find it difficult to resist the temptation to work and shop at home. The Internet is open twenty-four hours a day, seven days a week. A writer in the *New York Times* speaks of his attempt to have what he calls a "secular Sabbath"—a day when he does not use his computer or cell phone—but he finds it difficult to maintain the new regimen. He looks back with nostalgia to the time "when we had no choice but to reduce activity on Sundays; stores and offices—even restaurants—were closed, [and] there were certainly no electronics."[55]

Finally, globalization has made it imperative for an increasing number of people to work on Sundays. Companies have clients who are a day ahead of them—or a day behind them. It may be Sunday for a business's headquarters, but it is Monday where the client lives, and the client's concerns may be urgent. (An acquaintance of mine in the international shipping business has to be on call seven days a week to fill orders.) In international finance Sunday often turns out to be a working day. The *Wall Street Journal* describes the "manic Sunday" of a high-powered lawyer who spent one Sunday (in September 2006) dealing with the affairs of two major corporations. On a Sunday in November 2007 Citigroup, the global banking giant, held an emergency meeting of its directors to discuss what to do about major losses in various credit markets.[56]

To be sure, the currents of religious thought are unpredictable, and there may be a backlash against the commercialization of Sunday. In June 2007 the *Washington Post* reported that the Dutch defense minister Eimert van Middlekoop, who is a member of the Christian Union party, refuses to work Sundays and that he declined an invitation to participate in the U.S. Embassy's Memorial Day commemoration "because it was held on the Sabbath."[57] There have been no reports of other politicians taking a similar stand.

The transformation of Sunday seems to have had no effect on churchgoing in the United States, though different observers have different opinions about the state of Christianity in America. It is clear that the number of people who do not have a religious affiliation is increasing, but church attendance has remained steady in recent years.

Americans under thirty have never lived during a time when Sunday was a day when most stores were closed, so they may not be disturbed by the transformation of Sunday. Do older Americans look back in nostalgia to the Sundays of their childhood? Wendell Berry, born in 1934, is an American poet who farms for a living. His book *A Timbered Choir* comprises a series of "Sabbath poems" that were written from 1979 to 1997.[58] Berry refers to the Resurrection, so he seems to be an observant Christian, yet he prefers to spend Sundays outdoors.

> The bell calls in the town
> Where forebears cleared the shaded land
> . . . . .
> I hear, but understand
> Contrarily, and walk into the woods.

Berry writes about his encounters with nature, but he often reflects on what the day of rest means to him. In one poem he thinks about the negative effects of the loss of a Sabbath.

> Six days of work are spent
> To make a Sunday quiet
> That Sabbath may return.
> . . . . .
> Suppose rest is not sent
> Or comes and goes unknown.

Berry describes a Sabbathless world that is "lost in loss/Of patience." He ends with an apocalyptic vision:

> In hopeless fret and fuss,
> In rage at worldly plight
> Creation is defied,

All order is unpropped,
All light and singing stopped.

The loss of a day of rest, Berry suggests, damages our psyche, so we become impatient and angry. We need a sabbath to keep order in our soul.

Many observers have said that there is a lot of anger in America, but most blame it on the rise of the so-called blogosphere or the popularity of talk radio. Whether the transformation of Sunday has contributed to anger in America is anyone's guess. Sunday will continue to remain the Lord's Day for Christian Americans, and it will continue to remain a vaguely special day for spiritual and even secular Americans, but the loss of a sabbath is—to quote a key word in "Sunday Morning"—inescapable.

Notes

One. Sunday Gladness, Sunday Gloom

1. Information about "Gloomy Sunday" can be found at www.phespirit.info/gloomysunday (accessed May 12, 2008). Lewis' English lyrics are not based on Seress' lyrics; they are a translation of lyrics by László Javór.
2. George M. Marsden, *Jonathan Edwards: A Life* (New Haven: Yale University Press, 2003), 163; Alexis McCrossen, *Holy Day, Holiday: The American Sunday* (Ithaca, N.Y.: Cornell University Press, 2000), 41.
3. E-mail communication from the American Association of Suicidology, May 16, 2007. The data on American suicides are for 2004. The British information is from www.statistics.gov.uk/articles/hsq (accessed May 10, 2007).
4. McCrossen, *Holy Day*, 185; John Updike, *Still Looking: Essays on American Art* (New York: Knopf, 2006), 195.
5. Carol Troyen, "'The Sacredness of Everyday Fact': Hopper's Pictures of the City," in Troyen et al., *Edward Hopper* (Boston: MFA Publications, 2007), 117.
6. Witold Rybczynski, *Waiting for the Weekend* (New York: Penguin, 1991), 210–211; Ellen McCarthy, "The Sunday Slump," *Washington Post*, Weekend Section, October 12, 2007, 26.
7. Emily Dickinson, *Final Harvest: Emily Dickinson's Poems*, ed. Thomas H. Johnson (Boston: Little, Brown, 1971), 97; Howard Nemerov, *Collected Poems of Howard Nemerov* (Chicago: University of Chicago Press, 1977), 367.
8. John Keats, *Selected Letters of John Keats*, ed. Grant F. Scott, rev. ed. (Cambridge, Mass.: Harvard University Press, 2002), 23.

9. John Keats, *John Keats: The Complete Poems*, ed. John Barnard (London: Penguin, 1973), 93–94.

10. Louis MacNeice, *Collected Poems of Louis MacNeice*, ed. E. R. Dodds (New York: Oxford University Press, 1967), 23.

11. Robert Dessaix, *Twilight of Love: Travels with Turgenev* (Washington, D.C.: Shoemaker and Hoard, 2005), 59, 263.

12. George Herbert, *George Herbert: The Complete English Works*, ed. Ann Pasternak Slater (New York: Everyman's Library, 1995), 72–74.

13. James B. Twitchell, *Shopping for God: How Christianity Went from in Your Heart to in Your Face* (New York: Simon and Schuster, 2007), 183.

14. Wallace Stevens, *Letters of Wallace Stevens*, ed. Holly Stevens (Berkeley: University of California Press, 1996), 117. On Churchill see Craig Harline, *Sunday: A History of the First Day from Babylonia to the Super Bowl* (New York: Doubleday, 2007), 276–277.

15. All biblical quotations are from the *New Oxford Annotated Bible: Third Edition*, ed. Michael D. Coogan (Oxford: Oxford University Press, 2001).

16. *New Yorker*, April 23, 2007, 57.

17. The International Organization for Standardization is a nongovernmental organization headquartered in Geneva. Its alternate name, ISO, derives from the Greek word *isos*, meaning "equal." It is composed of representatives of national standards organizations.

18. Aelfric cited in Bonnie Blackburn and Leofranc Holford, eds., *Oxford Companion to the Year* (Oxford: Oxford University Press, 1999), 568. In Hungarian, *hétvö*, the word for Monday, means "head of seven," so Monday is the first day of the week.

19. McCrossen, *Holy Day*, 120.

20. Alexandra Starr, "Tokyo Diarist," *New Republic*, November 14, 2005, 34.

21. Alan Wolfe, *The Transformation of American Religion: How We Actually Live Our Faith* (Chicago: University of Chicago Press, 2003), 228.

22. Stevens, *Letters*, 133.

23. James Boswell, *Life of Johnson*, ed. G. B. Hill, rev. L. F. Powell, 6 vols. (Oxford: Oxford University Press, 1934–1950), 1: 67.

24. McCrossen, *Holy Day*, 34.

25. Benjamin Franklin, *A Benjamin Franklin Reader*, ed. Walter Isaacson (New York: Simon and Schuster, 2003), 199.

26. Alexis de Tocqueville, *Democracy in America*, ed. J. P. Mayer (New York: Doubleday, 1969), 712–714; letter quoted in McCrossen, *Holy Day*, 28.

27. On French soldiers in America, see Stacey Schiff, *A Great Improvisation: Franklin, France, and the Birth of America* (New York: Henry Holt, 2005), 169. Lord Melbourne is quoted in John Wigley, *The Rise and Fall of*

the *Victorian Sunday* (Manchester, U.K.: Manchester University Press, 1980), 41.

28. James Bryce, *The American Commonwealth*, 2 vols. (Indianapolis: Liberty Fund, 1995; orig. pub. 1888), 2: 1387.

29. McCrossen, *Holy Day*, 29, 32; see also Bryce, *American Commonwealth*, 2: 1388n2.

30. Bryce, *American Commonwealth*, 2: 1387n1.

31. McCrossen, *Holy Day*, 73–74.

32. Ibid., 109.

33. Russell Baker, *Growing Up* (New York: Penguin, 1982), 26.

34. Ibid., 120.

35. Ibid., 176, 248.

36. Ibid., 95.

37. Frances (Fanny) Trollope, *Domestic Manners of the Americans*, ed. Pamela Neville-Sington (London: Penguin, 1997), 84; Alistair Cooke, *The American Home Front, 1941–1942* (New York: Atlantic Monthly Press, 2006), 224–225.

38. Cooke, *American Home Front*, 225.

39. See Harline, *Sunday*, ix; Christine Rosen, *My Fundamentalist Education: A Memoir of a Divine Girlhood* (New York: Public Affairs, 2005), 174, 215.

40. Claire Harman, *Myself and the Other Fellow: A Life of Robert Louis Stevenson* (New York: HarperCollins, 2005), 32. Edith Wharton, *A Backward Glance: An Autobiography* (New York: Simon and Schuster, 1998), 216. On sabbatarianism in Scotland, see T. M. Devine, *The Scottish Nation: A History, 1700–2000* (London: Penguin, 1999), 364.

41. I thank Barton Swaim for this information.

42. Quoted in John Ross, "After a Year of Service, Sunday Ferry to Harris Is Still Controversial," *The Scotsman*, April 7, 2007 (accessed at thescotsman.scotsman.com, May 21, 2007).

43. "When Malls Stay Open on Sundays, the Pious Party," *Washington Post*, September 14, 2006, A2; Nancy Gibbs, "And on the Seventh Day We Rested?" *Time*, July 25, 2004 (accessed at Time.com, May 21, 2007). The headline writer assumes that Sunday is the seventh day of the week, not the first day.

44. McLennan's sermon is available at www.stanford.edu/group/religiouslife/docs (accessed April 12, 2006).

45. Pope John Paul's apostolic letter is available at www.vatican.va/holy_father/john_paul_ii/apost_letters (accessed November 1, 2005).

46. Pope Benedict XVI, quoted in *Los Angeles Times*, September 10, 2007 (accessed at LATimes.com, September 11, 2007).

47. Judith Shulevitz, "Bring Back the Sabbath," *New York Times Magazine,* March 2, 2003, 50–53.

48. *Washington Post,* July 3, 2005, C12; ibid., September 12, 2006, A12.

49. Harline, *Sunday,* 285; *Wall Street Journal,* June 3, 2006, A14.

50. *Washington Post,* September 14, 2006, A2.

51. Wigley, *Victorian Sunday,* 204–208.

52. Harline, *Sunday,* 281; McCrossen, *Holy Day,* 50.

53. *New York Times Book Review,* December 25, 2005, 10.

54. William James, *The Varieties of Religious Experience: A Study in Human Nature* (New York: Modern Library, 1929), xvii.

55. Andrew Delbanco, *Melville: His World and Work* (New York: Vintage, 2006), 21.

56. Frederick W. Dillistone, "The Holy Hush of Sunday Morning," *Theology Today,* 33, no. 1 (April 1976), 15–23.

Two. Sunday in Antiquity

1. In Greek the "Lord's Day" is *kyriake hemera*—usually shortened by ancient writers to *kyriake.*

2. Lesley Adkins and Roy A. Adkins, *Handbook to Life in Ancient Rome* (Oxford: Oxford University Press, 1998), 338.

3. Ovid, *Fasti,* ed. and trans. A. J. Boyle and R. D. Woodard (London: Penguin, 2000).

4. See C. Claiborne Ray, "Sunday All Over the World," *New York Times,* May 2, 2006, D2. Sanskrit also calls the days of the week according to the planetary calendar—i.e., day of the sun, day of the moon, day of Mars, day of Mercury, day of Jupiter, day of Venus, day of Saturn.

5. Denis Feeney, *Caesar's Calendar: Ancient Time and the Beginnings of History* (Berkeley: University of California Press, 2007), 9, 209. Feeney points out that there is no Greek or Roman word for "date." An ancient date is "a relationship between two or more events." See ibid., 15.

6. Jerome Carcopino, *Daily Life in Ancient Rome* (New Haven: Yale University Press, 2003), 205–206.

7. On Constantine's decree, see Michael Grant, *Constantine the Great: The Man and His Times* (New York: Barnes and Noble, 1993), 184.

8. Edward Gibbon, *The History of the Decline and Fall of the Roman Empire,* ed. David Womersley, 3 vols. (London: Penguin, 1994), 1: 728; Augustine, *The City of God against the Pagans,* ed. and trans. R. W. Dyson (Cambridge: Cambridge University Press, 1998), 287. Subsequent page references to *The City of God* will appear in parentheses in the text.

9. Gibbon, *Decline,* 1: 727n8; Grant, *Constantine,* 134. On Constantine's sun worship, see also Peter Brown, *The Rise of Western Christendom: Tri-*

ctrine and Discipline from the Reformation to the Civil War* (Cambridge: mbridge University Press, 1988), 115.

ee. Sunday in Elizabethan and Jacobean England

s not clear if the title of the pamphlet is Herbert's. See Cristina Mal-mson, *George Herbert: A Literary Life* (New York: Palgrave Macmillan, ɔ4), xii.

ɪnk Kermode, *The Age of Shakespeare* (New York: Modern Library, ɔ5), 16.

mon Duffy, *The Stripping of the Altars: Traditional Religion in England, 1400–c. 1580*, 2nd ed. (New Haven: Yale University Press, 2005; orig. b. 1992), 422, 432–433.

d., 464, 463.

d., 480. In some countries Calvinists were not as hostile to traditional urches. In Transylvania, Hungarian Calvinist churches were often "a t of newly painted colour" and often contained "figure decoration that uld alarm censorious western European Calvinists." See Diarmaid ɪcCulloch, *Reformation: Europe's House Divided, 1490–1700* (London: ɪnguin, 2004), 460.

trick Collinson, *The Religion of Protestants: The Church in English ciety, 1559–1625* (Oxford: Oxford University Press, 1984), 207–208, ɔn17.

ɪffy, *Stripping of the Altars*, 582, 585.

ɪnes Shapiro, *A Year in the Life of William Shakespeare, 1599* (New York: ɪrperCollins, 2005), 145–146.

ɪnneth L. Parker, *The English Sabbath: A Study of Doctrine and Discipline m the Reformation to the Civil War* (Cambridge: Cambridge University ɛss, 1988), 48.

d., 72, 121.

ɪ the controversy over the term "Puritan" see MacCulloch, *Reforma-ɪn*, 382–383; Drayton quoted in the *Oxford English Dictionary*.

ɪam Nicholson, *God's Secretaries: The Making of the King James Bible ɛw York: HarperCollins, 2003), 86–92.

ɔllinson, *Religion of Protestants*, 200, 202n48; see also Parker, *English bbath*, 84.

ɪker, *English Sabbath*, 83–84.

ɪn Northbrooke, *A Treatise against Dicing, Dancing, Plays, and Inter-les with Other Idle Pastimes, from the Earliest Edition, about* A.D. *1577 oston: Adamant Media, Elibron Classics, 2005; reprint of 1843 ed.). bsequent page references to this work will appear in parentheses in e text.

umph and Diversity*, A.D. *200–1000*, 2nd ed. (Oxford: Blackwell, 2003), 60; Ramsay MacMullen, *Christianity and Paganism in the Fourth to Eighth Centuries* (New Haven: Yale University Press, 1997), 34.

10. Eusebius quoted in Grant, *Constantine*, 139–140.

11. Gibbon, *Decline*, 1: 743.

12. Grant, *Constantine*, 107.

13. Henry Chadwick, "The Early Christian Community," in John McManners, ed., *The Oxford Illustrated History of Christianity* (Oxford: Oxford University Press, 1990), 58.

14. Gibbon, *Decline*, 1: 730–731.

15. Manfred Clauss, *The Roman Cult of Mithras: The God and His Mysteries*, trans. Richard Gordon (New York: Routledge, 2001), 3. Arnaldo Momigliano, *On Pagans, Jews, and Christians* (Middletown, Conn.: Wesleyan University Press, 1985), 183.

16. Patrick Leigh Fermor, *Between the Woods and the Water* (New York: Viking Penguin, 1986), 38; Ramsay MacMullen and Eugene N. Lane, eds., *Paganism and Christianity, 100–425* C.E.: *A Sourcebook* (Minneapolis: Fortress Press, 1992), 72–73.

17. Maarten Vermaseren quoted in David Ulansey, *The Origins of the Mithraic Mysteries: Cosmology and Salvation in the Ancient World* (Oxford: Oxford University Press, 1989), 44.

18. Clauss, *Cult of Mithras*, 16, 170–172.

19. On Akhenaton, see Melvin Konner, *Unsettled: An Anthropology of the Jews* (New York: Penguin, 2003), 34–35; Hesiod, *Theogony and Works and Days*, trans. M. L. West (Oxford: Oxford University Press, 1988), 58; for Eusebius on Cleanthes, see Ulansey, *Mithraic Mysteries*, 107–108; Plotinus cited in Peter Brown, *Augustine of Hippo: A Biography*, new ed. with epilogue (Berkeley: University of California Press, 2000), 45.

20. Konner, *Unsettled*, 84.

21. Julian cited in Gibbon, *Decline*, 1: 871; Gibbon, 1: 877.

22. MacMullen, *Christianity and Paganism*, 130; Paul Johnson, *A History of Christianity* (New York: Atheneum, 1968), 67–68; Grant, *Constantine*, 135.

23. Grant, *Constantine*, 136; MacMullen, *Christianity and Paganism*, 157, 39, 181n19.

24. Grant, *Constantine*, 135. In the Hebrew Bible the prophet Malachi says: "But for you who revere my name the sun of righteousness shall rise, with healings in its wings" (Malachi 4:2).

25. Boethius, *The Consolation of Philosophy*, trans. Richard Green (Indianapolis: Bobbs-Merrill, 1962), 104.

26. Corippus cited in Averil Cameron, "Remaking the Past," in G. W. Bowersock, Peter Brown, and Oleg Grabar, eds., *Interpreting Late Antiquity: Essays on the Postclassical World* (Cambridge, Mass.: Harvard University Press, 2001), 12.

27. James Kugel, *How to Read the Bible: A Guide to Scripture, Then and Now* (New York: Free Press, 2007), 48, 54.

28. Philipp Vielhauer, "On the 'Paulism' of Acts," in Wayne Meeks, ed., *The Writings of Saint Paul* (New York: Norton, 1972), 171.

29. Wayne Meeks, "Paul as Satan's Apostle: Jewish-Christian Opponents," in Meeks, *Writings of Saint Paul*, 176.

30. Abraham Joshua Heschel, *The Sabbath* (New York: Farrar, Straus and Giroux, 1975), 19–20.

31. Oxford Bible, 237nn35–36; Robert Louis Wilken, *The Spirit of Early Christian Thought: Seeking the Face of God* (New Haven: Yale University Press, 2003), 36.

32. Quoted in Wilken, *Early Christian Thought*, 28–29.

33. The first-century Jewish writer Philo, who wrote in Greek, also noted that many nations have adopted the Jewish Sabbath.

34. Brown, *Augustine of Hippo*, 450; Gerhard von Rad, *The Message of the Prophets*, trans. D. M. G. Stalker (New York: Harper and Row, 1967), 282.

35. Kugel, *How to Read the Bible*, 261. On the debate about the Sabbath in early Judaism, see Herold Weiss, *A Day of Gladness: The Sabbath among Jews and Christians in Antiquity* (Columbia: University of South Carolina Press, 2003), 20–22, 170.

36. Heschel, *Sabbath*, 31, 17–18.

37. Pope John Paul's Apostolic Letter is available at www.vatican.va/holy_father/john_paul_ii/apost_letters (accessed November 1, 2005).

38. Konner, *Unsettled*, 105.

39. On gladiators, see David S. Potter, "Entertainers in the Roman Empire," in D. S. Potter and D. J. Mattingly, eds., *Life, Death, and Entertainment in the Roman Empire* (Ann Arbor: University of Michigan Press, 1999), 307, 315.

40. Brown, *Augustine of Hippo*, 511, 458.

41. James J. O'Donnell, *Augustine: A New Biography* (New York: HarperCollins, 2005), 316. On the popularity of circus games among Christians, see Peter Brown, "The Private Art of Early Christians," *New York Review of Books*, March 20, 2008, 49–51.

42. Augustine quoted in Robert Markus, *The End of Ancient Christianity* (Cambridge: Cambridge University Press, 1997), 93.

43. Augustine quoted in MacMullen, *Christianity and Paganism*, 146.

44. MacMullen, *Christianity and Paganism*, 4, 3...; *Hippo*, 424; Robert Markus, "From Rome to 330–700," in McManners, *Oxford Illustrated H...*

45. MacMullen and Lane, *Paganism and Christiani...*

46. O'Donnell, *Augustine*, 32.

47. Brown, *Augustine of Hippo*, 446.

48. William E. Klingshirn, *Caesarius of Arles: The ...munity in Late Antique Gaul* (Cambridge: C... 1994), 155.

49. Ibid.

50. Weiss, *Day of Gladness*, 21–22.

51. Klingshirn, *Caesarius*, 159, 156.

52. Ibid., 176.

53. Evelyn Waugh, *When the Going Was Good* (B... 239.

54. Klingshirn, *Caesarius*, 184, 101–102.

55. Ibid., 212; Caesarius quoted in Richard Flet... *sion: From Paganism to Christianity* (Berkele... Press, 1997), 51–52.

56. Klingshirn, *Caesarius*, 211.

57. Ibid., 229.

58. Ibid., 163.

59. Bede cited in Julia M. H. Smith, *Europe after ...tory, 500–1000* (Oxford: Oxford University ...

60. Klingshirn, *Caesarius*, 234; Brown, *Rise of W...*

61. Sir Walter Scott, *The Heart of Midlothian,...* Oxford University Press, 1982), 195.

62. Pope Gregory quoted in Fletcher, *Barbarian...* shirn, *Caesarius*, 284.

63. Smith, *Europe after Rome*, 223; Augustine ... Klingshirn, *Caesarius*, 217–218.

64. Smith, *Europe after Rome*, 77. Fletcher, *Barb...*

65. Colin Morris, "Christian Civilization, 1050... *ford History of Christianity*, 223.

66. Markus, "From Rome to the Barbarian Kin... *ford Illustrated History of Christianity*, 73; Kli...

67. Geoffrey Moorhouse, *Sun Dancing* (San Di... 245–246.

68. Richard Janko, "Born of Rhubarb," *Times ...* 22, 2008, 10–11.

69. Crashaw(e) cited in Kenneth L. Parker, *Th...*

16. According to Herold Weiss, "In the extant literature [about the Jews in antiquity] there is no report of the application of capital punishment for Sabbath offenses." See Weiss, *A Day of Gladness: The Sabbath among Jews and Christians in Antiquity* (Columbia: University of South Carolina Press, 2003), 15.

17. Puritan writer quoted in Andrew Gurr, *Playgoing in Shakespeare's London* (Cambridge: Cambridge University Press, 1996), 57.

18. Ibid., 219.

19. Ibid.; Puritan writer quoted in "Introduction," Northbrooke, *A Treatise against Dicing*, xiv; Field quoted in Collinson, *Religion of Protestants*, 204. Brian Vickers, "Thomas Kyd, Secret Sharer," *Times Literary Supplement*, April 18, 2008.

20. Shapiro, *Year in the Life of Shakespeare*, 238.

21. Puritan writer quoted in "Introduction," *Bartholomew Fair*, ed. G. R. Hibbard (New York: Norton, 1977), xxxi.

22. Quoted in Parker, *English Sabbath*, 72, 56.

23. Collinson, *Religion of Protestants*, 207n72.

24. Thomas cited in Collinson, *Religion of Protestants*, 198; ibid., 170–171.

25. Ibid., 204, 200–201.

26. Ibid., ix.

27. James quoted in Leah S. Marcus, *The Politics of Mirth: Jonson, Herrick, Milton, Marvell, and the Defense of Old Holiday Pastimes* (Chicago: University of Chicago Press, 1986), 3.

28. Cited in Parker, *English Sabbath*, 117.

29. Ibid.

30. Marcus, *Politics of Mirth*, 3. The full text of *The Book of Sports*, also known as *The Declaration of Sports*, is available on several websites. The one quoted, which modernizes spelling and punctuation, can be found at www.constitution.org/eng/conpur.htm (accessed May 27, 2008).

31. Marcus, *Politics of Mirth*, 111. See also Parker, *English Sabbath*, 149–151.

32. Collinson, *Religion of Protestants*, 159.

33. Marcus, *Politics of Mirth*, 119, 289n22.

34. Collinson, *Religion of Protestants*, 89, 147, 90.

35. Stephen Foster, *The Long Argument: English Puritanism and the Shaping of New England Culture, 1570–1700* (Chapel Hill: University of North Carolina Press, 1991), 133.

36. MacCulloch, *Reformation*, 516–517.

37. Hugh Trevor-Roper, *Archbishop Laud, 1573–1645*, 2nd ed. (London: Phoenix Press, 1962), 5.

38. Parker, *English Sabbath*, 194.

39. Some biographers argue that Herbert wrote something which angered

one of the king's advisors and this is why he could not obtain a high government post. But all the members of Herbert's family were ignored by the new king.

40. Donne quoted in Marchette Chute, *Two Gentlemen: The Lives of George Herbert and Robert Herrick* (New York: Dutton, 1959), 25.

41. George Herbert, *George Herbert: The Complete English Works*, ed. Ann Pasternak Slater (New York: Everyman's Library, 1995). Subsequent page references to this work will appear in parentheses in the text.

42. Ibid., 430.

43. Peter Burke, *Popular Culture in Early Modern Europe*, rev. reprint (Aldershot, U.K.: Ashgate Publishing, 1999), 208.

44. Delumeau quoted in Richard Fletcher, *The Barbarian Conversion: From Paganism to Christianity* (Berkeley: University of California Press, 1997), 510; Duffy, *Stripping of the Altars*, 283.

45. For an influential discussion of Herbert's religious views, see Richard Strier, *Love Known: Theology and Experience in George Herbert's Poetry* (Chicago: University of Chicago Press, 1983). Auden's remarks are found in Mario A. Di Cesare, ed., *George Herbert and the Seventeenth-Century Religious Poets* (New York: Norton, 1978), 234.

46. Izaak Walton, *The Life of Mr. George Herbert*, in Herbert, *The Complete English Works*, 372, 382. Several modern biographers argue that much of Walton's life of Herbert is unreliable, but there is no question that Herbert loved music.

47. Walton, *Life of George Herbert*, 372.

48. Chute, *Two Gentlemen*, 202.

49. Trevor-Roper, *Archbishop Laud*, 34, 85.

50. Foster, *Long Argument*, 98, 145.

51. Marcus, *Politics of Mirth*, 152; Collinson, *Religion of Protestants*, 283.

52. Marcus, *Politics of Mirth*, 6; Parker, *English Sabbath*, 218.

53. Marcus, *Politics of Mirth*, 16–17.

Four. Sunday in Eighteenth-Century England and Scotland

1. Voltaire, *Letters on England*, trans. Leonard Tancock (London: Penguin, 1980), 37, 41.

2. Julian Hoppit, *A Land of Liberty? England, 1689–1727* (Oxford: Clarendon, 2000), 218.

3. Ibid., 222.

4. See Dana Rabin, "The Jew Bill of 1753: Masculinity, Virility, and the Nation," *Eighteenth-Century Studies*, 39, no. 2 (2006), 157–171.

5. Voltaire, *England*, 41. Voltaire admired the Quakers more than other sects because he thought they were the least dogmatic.

6. Henry Mission de Valbourg quoted in Bonnie Blackburn and Leofranc Holford, eds., *Oxford Companion to the Year* (Oxford: Oxford University Press, 1999), 573.

7. John Wigley, *The Rise and Fall of the Victorian Sunday* (Manchester, U.K.: Manchester University Press, 1980), 205.

8. Hoppit, *Land of Liberty*, 238–239.

9. William Law, *A Serious Call to a Devout and Holy Life*, preface by William Sloane Coffin Jr. (New York: Vintage, 2002). Subsequent page references to this work will appear in parentheses in the text.

10. Edward Gibbon, *Memoirs of My Life*, ed. Betty Radice (Harmondsworth: Penguin, 1984), 55.

11. Keith Thomas, *Man and the Natural World: Changing Attitudes in England, 1500–1800* (Oxford: Oxford University Press, 1996), 248–249.

12. Law, *Serious Call*, 317n16.

13. Marlies K. Danziger and Frank Brady, eds., *Boswell: The Great Biographer, 1789–1795* (New York: McGraw-Hill, 1989), 260.

14. Henry Hitchings, *Defining the World: The Extraordinary Story of Dr. Johnson's Dictionary* (New York: Farrar, Straus and Giroux, 2005), 238.

15. Samuel Johnson, *Diaries, Prayers, and Annals*, ed. E. L. McAdam Jr., with Donald and Mary Hyde (New Haven: Yale University Press, 1958), 269.

16. Frederick A. Pottle, ed., *Boswell's London Journal, 1762–1763* (New York: McGraw-Hill, 1950), 293; Samuel Johnson, *Life of Addison*, in Johnson, *Lives of the Poets*, 2 vols. (London: Oxford University Press, 1973), 1: 427–448.

17. Boswell, *London Journal*, 62, 237.

18. See Joseph Addison, Richard Steele, et al., *The Spectator*, ed. Gregory Smith, 4 vols. (London: Everyman's Library, 1973). Subsequent references to this work will appear in parentheses in the text.

19. Law, *Serious Call*, 41.

20. Johnson, *Lives of the Poets*, 1: 427–428, 425.

21. German visitor quoted in M. Dorothy George, *London Life in the Eighteenth Century* (New York: Capricorn Books, 1965), 289.

22. Goldsmith quoted in Paul Langford, *A Polite and Commercial People: England, 1727–1783* (Oxford: Oxford University Press, 1992), 296.

23. Ibid., 242.

24. Martin C. Battestin, *Henry Fielding: A Life* (London: Routledge, 1989), 570.

25. Thomas, *Man and the Natural World*, 183.

26. James Boswell, *Life of Johnson*, ed. G. B. Hill, rev. L. F. Powell, 6 vols. (Oxford: Oxford University Press, 1934–1950), 5: 69.

27. Ibid., 5: 69n1; Johnson, *Diaries*, 238.

28. Johnson quoted in Hesther Lynch Piozzi, *Anecdotes of Samuel Johnson* (Gloucester, U.K.: Alan Sutton, 1984), 102–103.

29. Ibid., 49.

30. Diarmaid MacCulloch, *Reformation: Europe's House Divided, 1490–1700* (London: Penguin, 2004), 390; Johnson, *Diaries*, 64–65.

31. Boswell, *Life of Johnson* 2: 72; 1: 250; Baretti and Johnson were traveling in France as guests of Mr. and Mrs. Thrale. See Johnson, *Diaries*, 243–244.

32. Boswell, *Life of Johnson* 2: 376.

33. Ibid., 4: 289.

34. Johnson, *Diaries*, 56–57.

35. Ibid., 101, 317.

36. Ibid., 147, 153.

37. Ibid., 225.

38. Ibid., 257–258, 267, 309.

39. Ibid., 80.

40. Ibid., 153; Boswell, *Life of Johnson* 1: 67.

41. Johnson, *Diaries*, 97.

42. Ibid., 153, 129, 277.

43. Ibid., 70, 378.

44. Piozzi, *Anecdotes*, 50; Boswell, *Life of Johnson* 5: 323.

45. Johnson, *Diaries*, 106; Boswell, *Life of Johnson* 2: 423.

46. Johnson, *Diaries*, 105, 414; Boswell, *Life of Johnson* 1: 444.

47. Johnson, *Diaries*, 107, 119.

48. Ibid., 289, 369.

49. Ibid., 383, 414.

50. Ibid., 417–418.

51. Boswell, *Life of Johnson* 2: 440.

Five. Varieties of Sunday Observance

1. James Boswell, *Boswell: The Great Biographer, 1789–1795*, ed. Marlies K. Danziger and Frank Brady (New York: McGraw-Hill, 1989), 107.

2. James Boswell, *Boswell's London Journal, 1762–1763*, ed. Frederick A. Pottle (New York: McGraw-Hill, 1950), 196; James Boswell, *Boswell for the Defence, 1769–1774*, ed. William K. Wimsatt Jr. and Frederick A. Pottle (New York: McGraw-Hill, 1959), 236–237.

3. Boswell quoted in Frank Brady, *James Boswell: The Later Years, 1769–1795* (New York: McGraw-Hill, 1984), 94.

4. Boswell, *London Journal*, 259, 319.

5. Ibid., 165, 249; Boswell, *Great Biographer*, 204.

6. Boswell, *Boswell for the Defence*, 128; Boswell, *Great Biographer*, 53.

7. Boswell, *London Journal*, 107, 331; Boswell, *Boswell for the Defence*, 93; Boswell, *Great Biographer*, 34.

8. Boswell, *Boswell for the Defence*, 216–217.

9. Ibid., 173.

10. Boswell and Boswell's friend are quoted in Peter Martin, *A Life of James Boswell* (New Haven: Yale University Press, 2000), 409, 524.

11. Boswell, *Great Biographer*, 253.

12. Boswell, *London Journal*, 54, 54n6, 107.

13. Brady, *Boswell*, 244.

14. Boswell, *Great Biographer*, 250.

15. Ibid., 115, 286.

16. Brady, *Boswell*, 245.

17. Boswell, *Great Biographer*, 292.

18. Boswell, *London Journal*, 144–145, 211; Boswell, *Great Biographer*, 223.

19. Boswell, *Boswell for the Defence*, 93, 110.

20. James Boswell, *Life of Johnson*, ed. G. B. Hill, rev. L. F. Powell, 6 vols. (Oxford: Oxford University Press, 1934–1950), 4: 414n1; Reynolds' nephew cited in Ian McIntyre, *Joshua Reynolds: The Life and Times of the First President of the Royal Academy* (London: Penguin, 2004), 286, 173.

21. Northcote and Frances Reynolds quoted in Richard Wendorf, *Sir Joshua Reynolds: The Painter in Society* (Cambridge, Mass.: Harvard University Press, 1996), 75.

22. Boswell, *Life of Johnson* 4: 414n1; McIntyre, *Reynolds*, 428n.

23. Joshua Reynolds, *The Letters of Sir Joshua Reynolds*, ed. John Ingamells and John Edgcumbe (New Haven: Yale University Press, 2000), 24; Reynolds quoted in Frederick Hilles, ed., *Portraits of Joshua Reynolds* (New York: McGraw-Hill, 1952), 74.

24. Boswell quoted in Hilles, *Portraits of Joshua Reynolds*, 20n2; Derek Hudson, *Sir Joshua Reynolds: A Personal Study* (London: G. Bles, 1958), 9; McIntyre, *Reynolds*, 182, 143.

25. Northcote quoted in Reynolds, *Letters*, 29; Frances Reynolds quoted in McIntyre, *Reynolds*, 225.

26. Gainsborough quoted in Wendorf, *Reynolds*, 226n63; McIntyre, *Reynolds*, 407.

27. Boswell quoted in McIntyre, *Reynolds*, 526; Boswell, *Life of Johnson* 4: 6; Burke quoted in McIntyre, *Reynolds*, 528.

28. Ricardo Quintana, *Oliver Goldsmith: A Georgian Study* (New York: Macmillan, 1967), 97; Northcote quoted in McIntyre, *Reynolds*, 272.

29. The *OED's* second definition of "decent" is: "Of such appearance and proportions as suits the requirements of good taste."

30. Oliver Goldsmith, *Selected Writings*, ed. John Lucas (New York: Routledge, 2003), 51.

31. Ibid., 52–53.

32. Ibid., 127.

33. Quintana, *Goldsmith*, 43; Goldsmith, *Selected Writings*, 173.

34. Keith Thomas, *Man and the Natural World: Changing Attitudes in England, 1500–1800* (Oxford: Oxford University Press, 1996), 260.

35. Gray quoted in Robert L. Mack, *Thomas Gray: A Life* (New Haven: Yale University Press, 2000), 231.

36. See ibid., 266–268; Gilpin quoted ibid., 675. The translation of Gray's Latin poem is by Robert Mack.

37. Ibid., 144, 391, 542.

38. Ibid., 567. For Gray's description of the Highlands, see Marjorie Hope Nicholson, *Mountain Gloom and Mountain Glory: The Development of the Aesthetics of the Infinite* (Seattle: University of Washington Press, 1997), 358.

39. Mack, *Gray*, 623.

40. Hugh Blair, "A Critical Dissertation on the Poems of Ossian," in James Macpherson, *The Poems of Ossian and Related Works*, ed. Howard Gaskill, intro. Fiona Stafford (Edinburgh: Edinburgh University Press, 1996), 345–399. Many people, including Johnson and Hume, thought Macpherson had composed the poems himself, since Macpherson never produced a genuine Gaelic manuscript. Most critics think Macpherson wrote down fragments of poems that were recited to him in the Scottish Highlands and turned them into his own poetry. Fiona Stafford calls them "the Ossianic poems of James Macpherson."

41. Blair, "Critical Dissertation," 355, 370, 395.

42. Ibid., 395.

43. Herder quoted in Isaiah Berlin, *Vico and Herder: Two Studies in the History of Ideas* (New York: Viking, 1976), 171. See also Landeg White, "In Bonaparte's Backpack," *Times Literary Supplement*, April 14, 2006, 24; Tom Shippey, "So Say the Folk," *Times Literary Supplement*, September 28, 2007, 24–25.

44. Peter Gay, *Weimar Culture: The Outsider as Insider* (New York: Harper and Row, 1970), 77.

Six. The Rise and Decline of the Victorian Sunday

1. Roy Hattersley, *The Life of John Wesley: A Brand from the Burning* (New York: Doubleday, 2003), 148.

2. Mark A. Noll, *The Rise of Evangelicalism: The Age of Edwards, Whitefield and the Wesleys* (Downers Grove, Ill.: InterVarsity Press, 2003), 15, 102.

3. Hattersley, *Wesley*, 225.

4. Ibid., 191; Anne Stott, *Hannah More: The First Victorian* (Oxford: Oxford University Press, 2003), x–xi, 109.

5. Ibid., ix, 12.

6. "The Bas Bleu" appears in More, *The Works of Hannah More, Part One* (New York: Harper and Brothers, 1843; rpt. Whitefish, Mt.: Kessinger Publishing, n.d.), 14–18. The poem originally circulated in manuscript and was published in 1786. Johnson quoted in Stott, *More*, 64.

7. Stott, *More*, 80.

8. More quoted in Ian McIntyre, *Joshua Reynolds: The Life and Times of the First President of the Royal Academy* (London: Penguin, 2004), 298.

9. Stott, *More*, 69, 79.

10. Ibid., 96.

11. Ibid., 86.

12. John Henry Cardinal Newman, *Apologia Pro Vita Sua*, ed. David J. DeLaura (New York: Norton, 1968), 17.

13. Newman quoted in Richard D. Altick, *Victorian People and Ideas* (New York: Norton, 1973), 212.

14. John Wigley, The *Rise and Fall of the Victorian Sunday* (Manchester, U.K.: Manchester University Press, 1980), 59; Craig Harline, *Sunday: A History of the First Day from Babylonia to the Super Bowl* (New York: Doubleday, 2007), 265; Newman, *Apologia*, 27. See also Boyd Hilton, *A Mad, Bad and Dangerous People? England, 1783–1846* (Oxford: Clarendon, 2006), 468–475.

15. Stott, *More*, 95, 83.

16. Ibid., 102, 83, 102.

17. Samuel Johnson, *Diaries, Prayers, and Annals*, ed. E. L. McAdam Jr., with Donald and Mary Hyde (New Haven: Yale University Press, 1958), 94.

18. Horne quoted in B. W. Young, *Religion and Enlightenment in Eighteenth-Century England* (Oxford: Oxford University Press, 1998), 150; Stott, *More*, 54, 136.

19. Stott, *More*, 97.

20. Ibid.

21. Ibid., 98.

22. Hattersley, *Wesley*, 187.

23. Harline, *Sunday*, 245–246.

24. Stott, *More*, 230–231.

25. Ibid., 124.

26. More, *Works*, 176.

27. Ibid., 236.

28. Stott, *More*, 202–203.

29. Ibid., 131–132.
30. The full title is *Village Politics Addressed to All the Mechanics, Journeymen and Day Labourers in Great Britain, by Will Chip, a Country Carpenter*. See Stott, *More*, 139–140.
31. Stott, *More*, 142–143.
32. Ibid., 145.
33. Ibid., 160; Hattersley, *Wesley*, 405.
34. Stott, *More*, 159.
35. Ibid., 169, 172, 174.
36. Ibid., 178–179, 182.
37. Austen quoted ibid., 278.
38. Eliot quoted ibid., 334.
39. Ibid., 273.
40. Ibid., 199, 308.
41. Hannah More, "Publisher's Address," in More, *Works*, v; Stott, *More*, 314.
42. Tim Hilton, *John Ruskin* (New Haven: Yale University Press, 2002), 436.
43. John Ruskin, *Praeterita*, ed. Tim Hilton (New York: Everyman's Library, 2005); subsequent page references to this work will appear in parentheses in the text. Hilton, *Ruskin*, 254.
44. Hilton, *Ruskin*, 254.
45. Ibid., 888n47.
46. Ibid., 831.
47. Ibid., 285–286.
48. Ibid., 629–630.
49. Ibid., 527–528.
50. Ibid., 527–528, 406.
51. Ibid., 13.
52. Ibid., 63.
53. Ibid., 346.
54. John Ruskin, "The Mystery of Life and Its Arts," in Ruskin, *The Genius of John Ruskin: Selections from His Writings*, ed. John D. Rosenberg (Boston: Houghton Mifflin, 1963), 354.
55. Hilton, *Ruskin*, 351, 354.
56. Ibid., 331, 330.
57. Ibid., 406, 408, 553.
58. Ruskin, *Genius*, 286; Hilton, *Ruskin*, 374.
59. Hilton, *Ruskin*, 452.
60. Ruskin, *Genius*, 91.
61. Hilton, *Ruskin*, 452, 226.
62. Ibid., 256.

63. Ibid., 452, 334.
64. George Eliot, "Evangelical Teaching: Dr. Cumming," in George Eliot, *Selected Essays, Poems and Other Writings,* ed. A. S. Byatt and Nicholas Warren (London: Penguin, 1990), 39.
65. Trevelyan quoted in Noel Annan, *Leslie Stephen: The Godless Victorian* (Chicago: University of Chicago Press, 1984), 234; Larkin quoted in David Yezzi, "A Journey from Irony to Mystery," *Wall Street Journal,* June 24–25, 2006, P18.
66. James Hamilton, *Turner* (New York: Random House, 2003), 318–319.
67. Ibid., 380, 272, 371.
68. Edmund Gosse, *Father and Son,* ed. William Irvine (Boston: Houghton Mifflin, 1965); subsequent page references to this work will appear in parentheses in the text. Gosse quoted in Evan Charteris, *The Life and Letters of Sir Edmund Gosse* (London: William Heinemann, 1931), 88.
69. Ann Thwaite, *Edmund Gosse: A Literary Landscape* (Chicago: University of Chicago Press, 1984), 325. On Sunday evenings Gosse presided over dinner parties for a smaller group.
70. Janet Browne, *Charles Darwin: The Power of Place* (Princeton: Princeton University Press, 2002), 387.
71. Gosse quoted in William Irvine, "Introduction," *Father and Son,* viii.
72. Ann Thwaite says that Gosse exaggerates the extent of his isolation. See Thwaite, *Gosse,* 26–29.
73. Ibid., 13.
74. See Stott, *More,* 180.
75. Thwaite, *Gosse,* 132; Charteris, *Gosse,* 32.
76. Thwaite, *Gosse,* 349.
77. Charteris, *Gosse,* 186.
78. Thwaite, *Gosse,* 350, 423.
79. Charteris, *Gosse,* 187.
80. Ibid., 505, 305.
81. Ibid., 61.
82. Wigley, *Victorian Sunday,* 136.
83. Ibid., 34.
84. Harline, *Sunday,* 247.
85. Wigley, *Victorian Sunday,* 68.
86. Ibid., 1.
87. Annan, *Leslie Stephen,* 97–98.
88. Ibid., 93, 91.
89. Wigley, *Victorian Sunday,* 126. On Trollope's antisabbatarianism, see N. John Hall, *Trollope: A Biography* (Oxford: Oxford University Press, 1991), 296–297.

90. J. S. Mill, *On Liberty and Other Writings*, ed. Stefan Collini (Cambridge: Cambridge University Press, 1989), 90–91.

91. Wigley, *Victorian Sunday*, 159.

92. See Harline, *Sunday*, 260–270.

93. Churchill quoted ibid., 269.

94. Russell Baker, *The Good Times* (New York: William Morrow, 1989), 240.

95. Wigley, *Victorian Sunday*, 196.

96. Philip Jenkins, *The Next Christendom: The Coming of Global Christianity*, rev. ed. (Oxford: Oxford University Press, 2007), 109.

Seven. Four American Writers and Sunday

1. David L. Holmes, *The Faiths of the Founding Fathers* (Oxford: Oxford University Press, 2006), 147; Stephen Foster, *The Long Argument: English Puritanism and the Shaping of New England Culture, 1570–1700* (Chapel Hill: University of North Carolina Press, 1991), 275.

2. Samuel Peters quoted in Bonnie Blackburn and Leofranc Holford, eds., *Oxford Companion to the Year* (Oxford: Oxford University Press, 1999), 573.

3. Foster, *Long Argument*, 241.

4. Patricia U. Bonomi, *Under the Cope of Heaven: Religion, Society, and Politics in Colonial America*, updated ed. (Oxford: Oxford University Press, 2003), 102, 61. Massachusetts was the last state to have an established church. In 1833 the legislature voted to disestablish the Congregational church. See also Gordon S. Wood, "American Religion: The Great Retreat," *New York Review of Books*, June 8, 2006, 60–63.

5. Bonomi, *Cope of Heaven*, 6, 102.

6. Edith Wharton, *A Backward Glance* (New York: Simon and Schuster, 1998), 10; Martin E. Marty, *Pilgrims in Their Own Land: 500 Years of Religion in America* (New York: Penguin, 1984), 68–72.

7. Bonomi, *Cope of Heaven*, 90, 16.

8. Ibid., 122, 98.

9. J. H. Elliot, *Empires of the Atlantic World: Britain and Spain in America, 1492–1830* (New Haven: Yale University Press, 2006), 51; Bonomi, *Cope of Heaven*, 5, 97; Holmes, *Founding Fathers*, 61, 97.

10. Bonomi, *Cope of Heaven*, 87; Craig Harline, *Sunday: A History of the First Day from Babylonia to the Super Bowl* (New York: Doubleday, 2007), 285.

11. Bonomi, *Cope of Heaven*, 58, 105, 81; Marty, *Pilgrims*, 127–128.

12. George M. Marsden, *Jonathan Edwards: A Life* (New Haven: Yale University Press, 2003), 84.

13. Holmes, *Founding Fathers*, 55.

14. Marsden, *Edwards*, 122.
15. Ibid., 185.
16. Ibid., 199.
17. Ibid., 204.
18. Bonomi, *Cope of Heaven*, 149; Marsden, *Edwards*, 207, 213.
19. Marsden, *Edwards*, 328.
20. Ibid., 345.
21. Ibid., 369, 349.
22. Ibid., 449, 452.
23. Ibid., 86, 368.
24. Holmes, *Founding Fathers*, 76.
25. Jill Lepore, "Vast Designs," *New Yorker*, October 29, 2007, 88–92.
26. Stevenson quoted in Claire Harman, *Myself and the Other Fellow: A Life of Robert Louis Stevenson* (New York: HarperCollins, 2005), 24.
27. Alexis McCrossen, *Holy Day, Holiday: The American Sunday* (Ithaca, N.Y.: Cornell University Press, 2000), 27.
28. Debby Applegate, *The Most Famous Man in America: The Biography of Henry Ward Beecher* (New York: Doubleday, 2006), 86; McCrossen, *Holy Day*, 43.
29. Stowe and the *Harper's* writer cited in McCrossen, *Holy Day*, 43.
30. Robert D. Richardson Jr., *Emerson: The Mind on Fire* (Berkeley: University of California Press, 1995), 287; Ralph Waldo Emerson, *Essays and Lectures*, ed. Joel Porte (New York: Library of America, 1983), 84.
31. Emerson, *Essays and Lectures*, 87.
32. Ibid., 87, 88, 89.
33. Richardson, *Emerson*, 299; Phillip F. Gura, *American Transcendentalism: A History* (New York: Hill and Wang, 2007), 116.
34. Emerson, *Essays and Lectures*, 1056; Richardson, *Emerson*, 557.
35. Emerson, *Essays and Lectures*, 1076; Richardson, *Emerson*, 97.
36. Richardson, *Emerson*, 185.
37. Gura, *Transcendentalism*, 216; Richardson, *Emerson*, 152, 52; Emerson, *Essays and Lectures*, 414; Richardson, *Emerson*, 557.
38. Richardson, *Emerson*, 9, 291, 384.
39. Ibid., 418, 522; Henry James, *Literary Criticism*, ed. Leon Edel (New York: Library of America, 1984), 264.
40. Orestes Bronson quoted in Gura, *Transcendentalism*, 97.
41. James, *Literary Criticism*, 253. Harold Bloom, *The American Religion: The Emergence of the Post-Christian Nation* (New York: Simon and Schuster, 1992), 16, 32.
42. James, *Literary Criticism*, 256.
43. Gura, *Transcendentalism*, 147–148, 217–218.

44. Ibid., 296, 301.
45. Henry D. Thoreau, *A Week on the Concord and Merrimack Rivers*, ed. Carl F. Hovde, William L. Howarth, and Elizabeth Hall Witherell (Princeton: Princeton University Press, 1980), 76; subsequent page references to this work will appear in parentheses in the text. Robert D. Richardson Jr., *Henry Thoreau: A Life of the Mind* (Berkeley: University of California Press, 1986), 193.
46. Richardson, *Thoreau*, 193, 196.
47. Ibid., 358, 50.
48. Robert D. Richardson Jr., "Thoreau and Concord," in Joel Meyerson, ed., *Cambridge Companion to Thoreau* (Cambridge: Cambridge University Press, 1995), 13.
49. Henry D. Thoreau, *Walden*, ed. Jeffrey S. Cramer (New Haven: Yale University Press, 2006), 94.
50. Lowell quoted in Linck C. Johnson, "A Week on the Concord and Merrimack Rivers," in Meyerson, *Cambridge Companion to Thoreau*, 41.
51. Richardson, *Thoreau*, 222, 354.
52. Ibid., 115.
53. Henry David Thoreau, *Cape Cod*, ed. Joseph J. Moldenhauer (Princeton: Princeton University Press, 1988). Subsequent page references to this work will appear in parentheses in the text.
54. Henry David Thoreau, "Walking," in *The Portable Thoreau*, ed. Carl Bode (New York: Viking, 1964), 592.
55. Ibid., 610, 630.
56. Richardson, *Thoreau*, 196; Denis Donoghue, "Introduction," *Walden*, vii; Lawrence Buell, "Thoreau and the Natural Environment," in Meyerson, *Cambridge Companion to Thoreau*, 171.
57. Walter Harding, "Thoreau's Reputation," in Meyerson, *Cambridge Companion to Thoreau*, 9.
58. Thoreau, *Walden*, 75.
59. Walt Whitman, *Complete Poetry and Collected Prose*, ed. Justin Kaplan (New York: Library of America, 1982), 923; subsequent page references to this work will appear in parentheses in the text. Alcott quoted in Justin Kaplan, *Walt Whitman: A Life* (New York: Simon and Schuster, 1980), 220.
60. Kaplan, *Whitman*, 70.
61. Ibid., 231, 70.
62. Ibid., 232, 254.
63. Ibid., 19.
64. Ibid., 190.
65. Ibid., 275, 296.

66. Ibid., 276, 280–281.
67. Ibid., 253.
68. Applegate, *Beecher*, 275.
69. Ibid., 35–36, 126.
70. Ibid., 275, 299.
71. Kaplan, *Whitman*, 76.
72. Ibid., 232, 280.
73. James Bryce, *The American Commonwealth*, 2 vols. (Indianapolis: Liberty Fund, 1995; orig. pub. 1888), 2: 1390.
74. Kaplan, *Whitman*, 221; Harold Bloom, *The Western Canon: The Books and School of the Ages* (New York: Riverhead Books, 1994), 267.
75. Brenda Wineapple, *Hawthorne: A Life* (New York: Random House, 2004), 231.

Eight. Sunday Nostalgia, Sunday Despair

1. George M. Marsden, *Jonathan Edwards: A Life* (New Haven: Yale University Press, 2003), 501; James Bryce, *The American Commonwealth*, 2 vols. (Indianapolis: Liberty Fund, 1995; orig. pub. 1888), 2: 1387n1.
2. John N. Serio, "Introduction," in Serio, ed., *Cambridge Companion to Wallace Stevens* (Cambridge: Cambridge University Press, 2007), 6n1.
3. Wallace Stevens, *Letters of Wallace Stevens*, ed. Holly Stevens (Berkeley: University of California Press, 1996), 125, 173. Subsequent page references to this work will appear in parentheses in the text.
4. Joan Richardson, *Wallace Stevens: A Biography—The Later Years, 1923–1955* (New York: William Morrow, 1988), 297.
5. Wallace Stevens, *Collected Poetry and Prose*, ed. Frank Kermode and Joan Richardson (New York: Library of America, 1997), 842.
6. Ibid., 841.
7. All citations from Stevens' poetry are from Stevens, *Collected Poetry and Prose*.
8. See Jacqueline Vaught Brogan, "Stevens and the Feminine," in Serio, *Cambridge Companion to Wallace Stevens*, 184.
9. Stevens, *Collected Poetry and Prose*, 841.
10. Ibid., 905.
11. Helen Hennessy Vendler, *On Extended Wings: Wallace Stevens' Longer Poems* (Cambridge, Mass.: Harvard University Press, 1969), 236.
12. Frank Kermode, *Wallace Stevens* (Edinburgh: Oliver and Boyd, 1967), 86; Richardson, *Stevens, The Later Years*, 322, 327; Stevens, *Collected Poetry and Prose*, 901.
13. Stevens, *Collected Poetry and Prose*, 911.
14. Joan Richardson, "Wallace Stevens: A Likeness," in Serio, *Cambridge*

Companion to Wallace Stevens, 13; Stevens, *Collected Poetry and Prose*, 902.

15. Richardson, *Stevens: The Later Years*, 329.
16. Vendler, *On Extended Wings*, 47.
17. Serio, "Introduction," in Serio, *Cambridge Companion to Wallace Stevens*, 4.
18. Stevens, *Collected Poetry and Prose*, 903, 871.
19. Richardson, *Stevens: The Later Years*, 427.
20. Stevens, *Collected Poetry and Prose*, 750.
21. Robert Lowell, *The Letters of Robert Lowell*, ed. Saskia Hamilton (New York: Farrar, Straus and Giroux, 2005), 487. Subsequent page references to this work will appear in parentheses in the text.
22. Robert Lowell, *Collected Poems*, ed. Frank Bidart and David Gewanter (New York: Farrar, Straus and Giroux, 2003), 137–140. All citations from Lowell's poetry are taken from this edition.
23. Ibid., 146.
24. Ibid., 147–148.
25. Ibid., 127.
26. Ibid., 138.
27. Paul Mariani, *Lost Puritan: A Life of Robert Lowell* (New York: Norton, 1994), 93, 100.
28. Ibid., 113–114.
29. Ibid., 93.
30. Ibid., 113.
31. Ibid., 178–179, 182–183.
32. Lowell quoted in note to his poem "For George Santayana," in Lowell, *Collected Poems*, 1036; Santayana quoted in Lowell, *Letters*, 710n192.
33. Mariani, *Lost Puritan*, 236.
34. Ibid., 359, 227.
35. Ibid., 285.
36. See Lowell, *Letters*, 739n348.
37. Frank Bidart, "Introduction," Lowell, *Collected Poems*, xv.
38. Lowell, *Collected Poems*, 1067.
39. Lowell, "After Enjoying Six or Seven Essays on Me," *Collected Poems*, 991.
40. Quoted in Brenda Wineapple, *Hawthorne: A Life* (New York: Random House, 2004), 244.

Nine. Sunday Now

1. Ralph Waldo Emerson, "Spiritual Laws," in Emerson, *Essays and Lectures*, ed. Joel Porte (New York: Library of America, 1983), 305–323; idem, *The*

Spiritual Emerson: Essential Writings by Ralph Waldo Emerson, ed. David Robinson (Boston: Beacon, 2003).

2. James Wood, "God's Dictionary," *New Republic*, December 26, 2005–January 9, 2006, 26; Robert D. Richardson Jr., *Emerson: The Mind on Fire* (Berkeley: University of California Press, 1995), 291; David Martin, "And Then There's Ufology," *Times Literary Supplement*, June 16, 2006, 28; Martin Marty quoted in Leigh E. Schmidt, "Spirit Wars," *Wilson Quarterly*, Summer 2005, 42–48.

3. *Newsweek*, August 29–September 5, 2005, 48.

4. Wharton quoted in R. W. B. Lewis, *Edith Wharton: A Biography* (New York: Harper and Row, 1977), 120, 510–511.

5. Edith Wharton, *A Backward Glance: An Autobiography* (New York: Simon and Schuster, 1998), 54.

6. Robert D. Richardson Jr., *William James: In the Maelstrom of American Modernism* (Boston: Houghton Mifflin, 2006), 433; Lawrence Buell, *Emerson* (Cambridge, Mass.: Harvard University Press, 2004), 181; William James, *The Essential Writings*, ed. Bruce W. Wilshire (Albany: State University of New York Press, 1984), 287–288; Richardson, *James*, 258–261.

7. William James, *The Varieties of Religious Experience: A Study in Human Nature* (New York: Modern Library, 1929), 19, 31–32.

8. Richardson, *James*, 309, 203; James, *Varieties*, 509; Benjamin Paul Blood quoted in Ross Posnock, "The Influence of James on American Culture," in Ruth Anna Putnam, ed., *The Cambridge Companion to William James* (Cambridge: Cambridge University Press, 1997), 323; James, *Varieties*, 509, 513.

9. Richardson, *James*, 203; James, *Varieties*, 513.

10. Richardson, *James*, 365; James, *Varieties*, 8.

11. James, *Varieties*, 8; Richardson, *James*, 251; Erin Leib, "God's Pragmatist," *New Republic*, June 24, 2002, 38–41.

12. Alan Wolfe, *The Transformation of American Religion* (Chicago: University of Chicago Press, 2003), 182–183; *Newsweek*, August 29–September 5, 2005.

13. Charles Taylor, *The Varieties of Religion Today: William James Revisited* (Cambridge, Mass.: Harvard University Press, 2002), 113–114; Lionel Trilling, "The Fate of Pleasure," in Trilling, *Beyond Culture: Essays on Literature and Learning* (New York: Viking, 1965), 83.

14. *Wall Street Journal*, July 20, 2007, W12; David Brooks, "The Catholic Boom," *New York Times*, May 25, 2005, A19.

15. On Paine, see Gordon S. Wood, *Revolutionary Characters: What Made the Founders Different* (New York: Penguin, 2006), 221–222; on the USA To-

day/Gallop Poll and the Barna Group study, see *Washington Post*, September 15, 2007, A14; on the Pew Forum's studies on religion in American life, see pewforum.org.

16. Pew report quoted in *New York Times*, February 26, 2008, A1.

17. William H. Pritchard, *Frost: A Literary Life Reconsidered*, 2nd ed. (Amherst: University of Massachusetts Press, 1984), 224; Jay Parini, *Robert Frost: A Life* (New York: Henry Holt, 1999), 15, 23.

18. On Anthony Kenny, see John Cottingham, "Credit Reports," *Times Literary Supplement*, June 1, 2007, 27.

19. Richardson, *Emerson*, 469; Frances Fitzgerald, "Come One, Come All," *New Yorker*, December 3, 2007, 52.

20. Wolfe, *Transformation*, 3.

21. James B. Twitchell, *Shopping for God: How Christianity Went from in Your Heart to in Your Face* (New York: Simon and Schuster, 2007), 24; Martin Marty, "The Long and Winding Road," *Newsweek*, August 29–September 5, 2005, 68.

22. Peter Berger, "The Challenge to Secularism," address at the New School for Social Research, William Phillips Lecture Series, October 10, 2007. The website is www.religioustolerance.org/us. The word for Sunday in Sanskrit means "day of the sun." In Hinduism Sunday is the day of the sun, the first day, and the day of rest. See Amartya Sen, *The Argumentative Indian: Writings on Indian History, Culture and Identity* (New York: Picador, 2005), 317–333.

23. City University of New York Graduate Center, "American Religious Identification Survey," October 2001, results posted at www.gc.cuny.edu/faculty/research; *Los Angeles Times*, February 27, 2008 (accessed at the newspaper's website February 27, 2008); *Washington Post*, November 3, 2007, B9.

24. Ben McGrath, "The Cloth: Interfaith at Work," *New Yorker*, June 6, 2005, 32; Brenda Wineapple, *Hawthorne: A Life* (New York: Random House, 2003), 4.

25. Stephen Prothero, "The Variety Show of Religious Experience," *New York Times Book Review*, July 2, 2006, 15; *New York Times*, May 28, 2005, A12; *Washington Post*, February 19, 2007, C1.

26. On the Internet and religion, see *Wilson Quarterly*, Spring 2006, 89; *New York Times*, December 30, 2005 (accessed at the newspaper's website December 30, 2005).

27. Pope Benedict XVI quoted in Twitchell, *Shopping for God*, 93.

28. Peter J. Boyer, "The Big Tent," *New Yorker*, August 22, 2005, 47.

29. Philip Kevin Goff, quoted in *Wall Street Journal*, September 15, 2006; W11; Twitchell, *Shopping for God*, 24.

30. Jacqueline Simon, "Latin Makes a Comeback," *Washington Post*, November 24, 2007, B9.

31. *New York Times*, July 24, 2006 (accessed at the newspaper's website July 24, 2006); *Washington Post*, August 4, 2007, B9.

32. *Washington Post*, June 4, 2006, C11.

33. *New York Times*, August 29, 2005 (accessed at the newspaper's website August 29, 2005).

34. *Washington Post*, June 16, 2007, B9.

35. *New York Times*, March 4, 2007 (accessed at the newspaper's website March 4, 2007).

36. *New York Times*, June 13, 2006, A14; *Washington Post*, May 5, 2007, B9.

37. *New York Times*, May 28, 2005, A14; and May 16, 2007, A11. "Paganism" is a loose term. There are differences between Thoreau's paganism and the contemporary pagan movement, but all are grounded in nature worship. On modern paganism, see Ronald Hutton, *The Triumph of the Moon: A History of Modern Pagan Witchcraft* (Oxford: Oxford University Press, 2001).

38. Larissa MacFarquhar, "Two Heads," *New Yorker*, February 12, 2007, 56; Lucretius, *The Way Things Are*, trans. Rolfe Humphries (Bloomington: Indiana University Press, 1968), 56.

39. *Wall Street Journal*, April 27, 2007, W2.

40. Jenine Lee–St. John, "Sunday School for Atheists," *Time*, November 21, 2007 (accessed at the magazine's website November 26, 2007).

41. Mark Twain, *The Portable Mark Twain*, ed. Tom Quirk (New York: Penguin, 2004), 458, 460.

42. Craig Harline, *Sunday: A History of the First Day from Babylonia to the Super Bowl* (New York: Doubleday, 2007), 364.

43. Alexis McCrossen, *Holy Day, Holiday: The American Sunday* (Ithaca, N.Y.: Cornell University Press, 2000), 19.

44. Russell Baker, "Baker's 'World,'" *New York Review of Books*, January 12, 2006, 14.

45. *Christian Science Monitor*, December 5, 2003 (accessed at the newspaper's website April 19, 2005).

46. *The State*, June 23, 2007 (accessed at the newspaper's website June 23, 2007). I thank Barton Swaim for calling this legislation to my attention.

47. Harline, *Sunday*, 360; Jeff MacGregor, *Sunday Money* (New York: HarperCollins, 2005), 231. See also Jonathan Miles, "Nascar Nation," *New York Times Book Review*, May 22, 2005, 1.

48. *Washington Post*, December 4, 2004, A3; *New York Times*, July 8, 2006 (accessed at the newspaper's website July 8, 2006).

49. The petition can be found at www.petitiononline.com.

50. McCrossen, *Holy Day,* 137; Noah Feldman, *Divided by God: America's Church-State Problem and What We Should Do about It* (New York: Farrar, Straus and Giroux, 2005), 56.

51. Twain, *The Portable Mark Twain,* 463.

52. Christopher D. Ringwald, *A Day Apart: How Jews, Christians, and Muslims Find Faith, Freedom, and Joy on the Sabbath* (New York: Oxford University Press, 2007); the quotations from Taking Back Sunday and from BlueLaws can be found on their websites.

53. *Custom Retailer,* September 12, 2007 (accessed on the magazine's website September 25, 2007); Dale Buss, "Restlessness," *Wall Street Journal,* January 16, 2004 (accessed at the newspaper's website September 26, 2007).

54. Buss, "Restlessness."

55. Mark Bittman, "I Need a Virtual Break. No, Really." *New York Times,* March 2, 2008 (accessed at the newspaper's website March 5, 2008).

56. *Wall Street Journal,* September 16–17, 2006, B3.

57. *Washington Post,* June 24, 2007, A12.

58. Wendell Berry, *A Timbered Choir: The Sabbath Poems, 1979–1997* (New York: Counterpoint, 1998).

Index